Advance Praise

Voices in Verses takes us into the markets and palaces, brothels and salons of nineteenth-century India to hear women speak of their lives and feelings through poetry. Rare biographical compendia, known as *tazkira*s, are treated to a wonderfully sensitive analysis that reveals women's compositions to be at once exemplary and defiant of their literary and social worlds. An inspired and inspiring book that is a joy to read.

Siobhan Lambert-Hurley, University of Sheffield

Farhat Hasan must be commended for his evocative, nuanced, and multifaceted explorations of women's Urdu and Persian verses – women from public, secluded, royal, and ordinary walks of life – as compiled in a couple of nineteenth-century compendia, the *tazkirat-i zanāna*. These compositions come mediated through male authors and prefaced with biographical sketches that direct and constrict meaning-making. Hasan displays his masterly historian's skills in unpacking layered striations of words, performances, textures, and gestures – the sensoria through which we may grasp their variegated fields of significations. By facilitating access to this as yet 'veiled' literary archive, Hasan opens up 'subjugated knowledge' to assert its insistent and salient presence in shaping literary and cultural praxis in the richly varied world of Persianate Hindustan. *Voices in Verses* tells of the deep and diverse histories of cultural inheritances embedded in South Asian ethos before the complicities and complexities of colonial and national confinements. This volume is a triumph of gendered reading that enriches the discipline of South Asian history.

Anshu Malhotra, University of California

In *Voices in Verses*, Farhat Hasan reads the *tazkira* archive along and against the grain to recover and interpret for us the verses and biographies of Urdu women poets. A wide and rich corpus comes into view that plays with codes of veiling and unveiling and nuances emotions of joy and loss.

Francesca Orsini, SOAS University of London

Voices in Verses

This book opens up an archive of women's verses found in the extant, but overlooked, women's biographical compendia (*tazkira-i zanāna*) written in the nineteenth century. As commemorative texts, these compendia written in Urdu draw our attention to their memories – celebrated and contested – in cultural spaces. In drawing connections between memory and literature, this study contests the commonplace assumption that the literary public sphere was markedly homosocial and gender exclusive, and argues instead that the women poets, coming from a wide variety of social groups, actively participated in shaping the norms of aesthetics and literary expression; they introduced fresh signifiers and signifying practices to apprehend their emotions, experiences, and world views. Women's poetry was a kind of 'subjugated'/'erudite' knowledge that enriched the literary culture, even as it evoked considerable anxieties, and stood in a paradoxical relationship with the dominant episteme, both reinforcing and challenging its cultural assumptions and truth-claims. Their lyrics were forms of self-narratives or an act of 'unveiling', but in order to appreciate their meanings we need to be sensitive to the multi-medial mode of meaning-apprehension. This work suggests that the women's *tazkiras* performed an act of 'epistemic disobedience' contesting not only the British imperial representations of India, but also the Indo-Muslim modern reformers on issues of domesticity, conjugal companionship, and love and desire.

Farhat Hasan is a professor of history at the University of Delhi (New Delhi). His articles on the literary culture, gender relations, state formation, and public sphere in early modern South Asia have been published in reputed journals and edited works. He is the author of *State and Locality in Mughal India: Power Relations in Western India, c. 1572–1730* (Cambridge University Press, 2004) and *Paper, Performance, and the State: Social Change and Political Culture in Mughal India* (Cambridge University Press, 2021).

Voices in Verses

Women's Poetry and Cultural Memory in Nineteenth-Century India

Farhat Hasan

CAMBRIDGE
UNIVERSITY PRESS

Shaftesbury Road, Cambridge CB2 8EA, United Kingdom

One Liberty Plaza, 20th Floor, New York, NY 10006, USA

477 Williamstown Road, Port Melbourne, VIC 3207, Australia

314–321, 3rd Floor, Plot 3, Splendor Forum, Jasola District Centre, New Delhi – 110025, India

103 Penang Road, #05–06/07, Visioncrest Commercial, Singapore 238467

Cambridge University Press is part of Cambridge University Press & Assessment, a department of the University of Cambridge.

We share the University's mission to contribute to society through the pursuit of education, learning and research at the highest international levels of excellence.

www.cambridge.org
Information on this title: www.cambridge.org/9781009453035

© Farhat Hasan 2024

First published 2024

Printed in India by Avantika Printers Pvt. Ltd.

A catalogue record for this publication is available from the British Library

ISBN 978-1-009-45303-5 Hardback

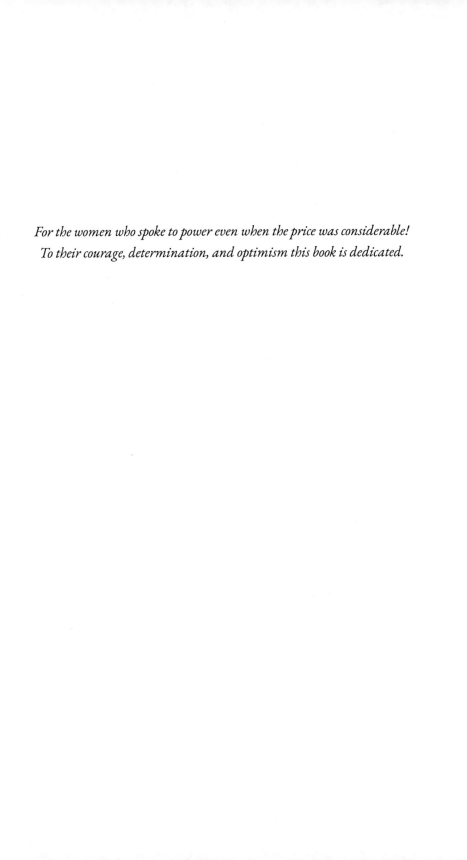

For the women who spoke to power even when the price was considerable!
To their courage, determination, and optimism this book is dedicated.

Contents

Acknowledgements

Urdu is a language on the ventilator today, and even as people in northern India converse in the language, the number of those who can read and write the script is fast dwindling. It is not taught in most schools, colleges, and universities these days, and there are very few job openings for those who, against all odds, still make an effort to learn the language. I should, therefore, begin by acknowledging my parent's love for the language, and the efforts they made to ensure that their children not only know but also appreciate its nuances and niceties. My interest in Urdu literature comes from my parents, but it was continually nourished by the cultural life at Aligarh where I came in contact, as I was growing up, with some of its leading scholars and poets: Ale Ahmad Suroor, Waheed Akhtar, Khalil-ur-Rahman Azmi, Qazi Abdus Sattar, and Akhlaq Shahryar. My brother, Rahat Hasan, is an accomplished Urdu poet, and I have learnt a lot about the fine distinctions in Urdu poetry from my long association with him.

While I was a student at Aligarh, and later Cambridge, History did not gel well with Literature; focused on the 'big issues' in History, historians neglected literary writings and rarely, if ever, made an effort to construct bridges of conversations across the two fields. My own work on the Mughal period was also firmly ensconced within that fold, but while I was doing my Ph.D. at Cambridge, my supervisor, Gordon Johnson, did occasionally prod me to look into the literary sources of the Mughal period, a suggestion that I acted on very late in the day. The drift to cultural history among Mughal historians took a long time to arrive, and in this context, the work of Muzaffar Alam, Sanjay Subrahmanyam, and Sunil Sharma have been my source of inspiration.

Reading poetry to do History was still a tall order, but my efforts in the direction were facilitated by the development of emotions history, and I found the work of Margrit Pernau, Katherine Butler Schofield, and Imke Rajamani particularly useful. I did have the opportunity of clarifying my confusions with Margrit during one of her visits to India, and I remain ever so grateful to her for that. Of course, the 'cultural turn' has complicated the relations between language and history, and amid issues of shifting and multiple meanings, it has become far more complicated to read poetry within a historicist frame of reference. In that context, the writings of Francesca Orsini and Anshu Malhotra are particularly instructive indeed. Anshu Malhotra's work on the *kafi*s of Piro, a Muslim prostitute-turned-Sikh-saint, has certainly helped me develop a better understanding of the devotional verses in my sources. I have had long and repeated discussions with her on these issues, and I have benefitted from her immense knowledge in the field.

In introducing the world of Urdu literature to western academia, the contribution of Ralph Russell, Khurshidul Islam, C. M. Naim, and Naimur Rahman Faruqui, among others, cannot be overemphasized. Even so, we should recognize the services of Urdu scholars teaching in different capacities in the universities in India and Pakistan as well; writing as they do in Urdu, their work scarcely gets noticed in more global centres of scholarship and excellence. One of the two sources that I study here, *Bahāristān-i Nāz*, was actually brought to my notice by an Urdu scholar based in Aligarh, Rahat Abrar. His own work was on its author, Hakim Fasihuddin Ranj, in which he studied his poetry, religious compositions, and prose writings. I am very grateful to him for our discussions and his generosity in sharing his knowledge and expertise with me. As I read the Urdu texts for this book, I was not infrequently confronted with difficulties in comprehension and translation. I am grateful to Muhammad Sajjad's prompt assistance in the matter. In situations where I went wrong, my colleagues and friends at Aligarh – in particular, Jabir Raza and S. A. Nadeem Rezavi – were there to promptly correct me.

It took a long time for historians to notice women's work in Urdu, and we are ever so grateful to Gail Minault, Barbara Metcalf, and Carla Petievich for their pioneering efforts. Their efforts have received a huge fillip in the last several years in the work of Siobhan Lambert-Hurley and Asiya Alam, among others. Lambert-Hurley began with studying the lives and work of the Begums of Bhopal, but has recently moved on to Muslim women's autobiographies, culminating in the publication of the fascinating book, *Elusive Lives*. I have closely followed her work and remain ever so grateful to her for her interest in my academic ventures.

In writing this book, I was also assisted by my young friends whose interest in the subject gives me hope and reassurance. Shivangini Tandon has helped me locate a couple of references, and, more importantly, her own study on the literary culture in Mughal India has helped me reformulate some of my arguments here. I would also like to thank Mukhtar Ahmad and Heena Goswami for locating books, articles, and manuscripts for this study. They have also been no less helpful in resolving many of my confusions while I was writing this book.

I would like to thank the staff of the Cambridge University Press, in particular Qudsiya Ahmed, Anwesha Rana, and Koyena Roy, for handling the publication of this book with due competence. Qudsiya was, as always, very welcoming and immediately got into action when I approached her with my proposal. Anwesha and Koyena have impressed me with their efficiency and diligence, and the interest they have had in the publication of this book.

I would like to thank the staff of the following libraries and archives for giving me access to their collections, and for their support and cooperation: Maulana Azad Library (Aligarh Muslim University, Aligarh), British Library (London), University of Delhi Library (New Delhi), Center for Advanced Study in History Library (Aligarh Muslim University, Aligarh), National Archives (New Delhi), Raza Library (Rampur), and Khuda Baksh Library (Patna).

In the end, I would like to thank my family – Fauzia, Sana, Hamza, and Mariam – for their patience and cooperation. Without their support, this book would most certainly have not seen the light of day. In my academic ventures, I have always been encouraged and supported by Anwar Jahan Zuberi. When research and writing became exhausting, the much needed digression came from the welcoming home of Nighat and Nurul Abidin, and besides them I would also like to thank Farah, Maryam, and Hira for their kind hospitality.

A Note on Transliteration

For transliteration, I have largely depended on Steingass' *Persian–English Dictionary*. I have kept the use of diacritical marks to the bare minimum. I have used the stress mark/macron to indicate a long vowel. The *hamza* in Persian and Urdu is indicated with an inward apostrophe ('), and the alphabet *ain* is indicated with an outward apostrophe ('). I have avoided using diacritics in names of people and places.

Abbreviations

BN   Hakim Fasihuddin Ranj, *Bahāristān-i Nāz* (Lahore, Pakistan: Majlis-i Taraqqi-i Adab, 1965 [reprint]).

TN   Durga Prashad Nadir, *Tazkirat-un*-Nisā (Lahore, Sang-i Mil Publishers, 2016 [reprint]).

1

Introduction

This work is an exploratory study of the commemoration of women in cultural spaces during the early colonial period in South Asia. Based on a reading of the rather neglected compendia of women writers composing verses in Urdu and Persian in the varied and multiple pasts of Hindustan,[1] it looks at memories of women's active participation in the literary spaces. Written in the nineteenth century, these compendia (*tazkiras*) written in Urdu were texts of memorialization, and reproduced memories of the freshness and depth that women poets brought to the literary culture. I read these texts as, following Pierre Nora, 'sites of memory' (*lieu de memoire*),[2] and the life stories and poetic compositions found therein indeed serve to remind us of women's participation

---

[1] This is how the Indian subcontinent is described in our *tazkiras*. In pre-colonial literature, the subcontinent is mentioned as Hindustan, and even as the colonial period saw its displacement with 'India', the idea of Hindustan persists in Persian and Urdu literary practices. Even as 'Hindustan' and 'India' are today understood as synonyms, they represented distinctly different social imaginaries. Hindustan represented a sociocultural space that was markedly diverse and polyvalent, and was shaped by the multiple conversations between the Indic and Persianate practices, belief systems, and arts and letters. 'India' was, on the other hand, a product of what Manan Ahmed describes as the 'colonial episteme', and represented a perception of South Asia as an exclusive, homogenous, and antagonistic cultural space. He describes the change as 'the loss of Hindustan and the invention of India'. Manan Ahmed Asif, *The Loss of Hindustan: The Invention of India* (Cambridge, MA: Harvard University Press, 2020).

[2] Pierre Nora and Lawrence D. Kritzman (eds.), *Realms of Memory: The Construction of the French Past, vol. 1: Conflicts and Divisions*, trans. Arthur Goldhammer (New York: Columbia University Press, 1996).

in the 'literary public sphere'.[3] These texts are not acts of recollection, but exercises in construction crucially motivated by significant sociopolitical considerations, one of which was to push for women's literacy within an indigenous frame of reference and to dispel the picture of the culture in Hindustan, found in British imperial writings and policy initiatives, as marked by inertia and stasis, particularly in matters relating to the lives of women.

This study then contests the commonplace assumption that the literary public sphere in the colonial period was markedly homosocial and gender exclusive, and argues instead that female scholars actively participated in shaping the norms of aesthetics and literary expression, and introduced fresh signifiers and linguistic practices to apprehend their emotions, experiences, and world views. Based on a reading of the largely ignored *tazkiras* of women poets, I suggest here that their compositions could be seen as a form of, in the language of Foucault, 'erudite' knowledge in that they enriched the literary space, even as they evoked considerable anxieties, and stood in a paradoxical relationship with the dominant episteme, both reinforcing and challenging its cultural assumptions and truth-claims.[4] Women's poetry was neither antithetical nor excluded from the prevailing episteme and was in circulation in dispersed cultural spaces, such as

---

[3]   By the 'literary public sphere', I mean the cultural spaces of inter-subjective communication in which social actors came together to institute literary norms and practices, and shared their emotions and experiences to reproduce their interior selves, and communicative subjectivities. Even as the literary public sphere was certainly facilitated by the development of print, the sphere was also enriched by the oral and performative traditions as well. Jurgen Habermas, *The Structural Transformation of the Public Sphere: An Enquiry into a Category of Bourgeois Society*, trans. Thomas Burger and Fredrick Lawrence (Cambridge, MA: MIT Press, 1989); Geoff Boucher, *Habermas and Literature: The Public Sphere and the Social Imaginary* (London: Bloomsbury Academic, 2021). For an understanding of the South Asian literary public sphere, see Megan Eaton Robb, *Print and the Urdu Public: Muslims, Newspapers, and Urban Life in Colonial India* (Oxford: Oxford University Press, 2021); Francesca Orsini, *The Hindi Public Sphere, 1920–1940: Language and Literature in the Age of Nationalism* (New Delhi: Oxford University Press, 2000).

[4]   In his study of the power/knowledge ensemble, Foucault refers to the contestations with the dominant episteme by 'subjugated' knowledges, and sees these knowledges as divided into 'erudite' and 'disqualified' forms of knowledges. 'Erudite' knowledges are a part of the dominant cultural relations, but are 'masked' by these relations. They reproduce the dominant knowledge forms, paradoxically by contesting and reinforcing the prevailing episteme. The 'disqualified' knowledges are positioned outside the epistemic field, and are excluded and disqualified from participation. Michel Foucault, *Power/Knowledge: Selected Interviews and Other Writings, 1972–1977*, ed. Colin Gordon (Brighton: Harvester Press, 1980); Michel Foucault, *The Archeology of Knowledge* (London: Routledge, 1989).

the salons of the courtesans, the marketplace, household assemblies, and literary meetings. Indeed, in memorializing their voices from such dispersed locations, the authors of women's *tazkira*s were undertaking a genealogical exercise of recovering the 'subjugated' and suppressed voices in literary culture. At the same time, we should be careful, and remain attentive, when reading their work, to their own elisions, exclusions, and silences as well.

Reading the Women's Biographical Compendia: Gender in the Literary Public Sphere

The *tazkira*s that we study here are written in Urdu and deal primarily with Urdu poets, but they include in their collection women poets writing in Persian as well. As it is, historians, literary critics, and specialists have largely chosen to ignore the literary biographical compendia, but when it comes to the *tazkira*s of women poets (*tazkira-i zanāna*), the indifference is even more conspicuous. This, of course, serves to facilitate the construction of the literary space as gender specific, marked by the near, if not total, exclusion of women, at least up until the early decades of the twentieth century, if not later. In ignoring women poets, modern literary critics are actually following an entrenched tradition, for the well-known literary *tazkira*s written in the eighteenth to nineteenth centuries either fail to mention them or mention a bare handful among them in order to represent the literary space as gender exclusive, where the agency of women was of little significance.

Interestingly, in the contemporary literary tradition of compiling the life stories and poetic compositions of scholars, women – when not conspicuously absent – only make incidental presences; they are mentioned as a reluctant digression, and when compared with the other literary figures mentioned therein, they are a needle in the haystack. Let us take a couple of instances here. In the mid-eighteenth century, the famous Rekhta[5] poet Mir Taqi Mir wrote a *tazkira* of Rekhta poets, *Nikāt-ush-Shu'arā* (The Exquisiteness of Poets), and this was followed by Saiyad Fateh Ali Husaini Gardezi writing another compendium of poets, *Tazkira-i Rekhta Goyān* (Life Stories of Rekhta Conversationists). As early initiatives in compiling verses of poets writing in Urdu, these were indeed commendable efforts, and even as they differed in terms of narrative details, they were alike in excluding women and denying any space in their texts to the life stories and compositions

---

[5]   Rekhta was the name given to the early form of the Urdu (and Hindi) language. A mixed dialect, Rekhta combined elements of Persian with Hindavi, and came to be known as Urdu later in the nineteenth century.

of women poets.[6] In the early decades of the nineteenth century, Ghulam
Hamadani Mushafi authored another literary compendium of 'Hindi speaking
poets' (*hindi-goyān*), *Tazkira-i Hindī*;[7] he does not mention any female poet in the
main body of his text but felt constrained to add an appendix (*khātima*) to provide
space to just five women poets: Dulhan Begum, Jina Begum, Guna Begum, Zeenat
(nom de plume: Nazuk), and Moti.[8]

The biographical compendia of women poets that we study here challenge
these representations, and in the process open up an archive of women's speech
that has been ignored and largely forgotten in modern South Asian scholarship.
While the women's *tazkiras* are certainly not without their own elisions and
silences, they are crucial in drawing attention to the voices of literate women,
and the force with which these voices were silenced from historical registers
and social memories. The *tazkiras* that we study here awaken us to a deliberate
act of historical silencing and provide a basis for the construction of a counter-
memory, one in which women indeed had a remarkable presence in the literary
culture. As texts of memorialization, the *tazkiras* of women poets resist the erasure
of their voices and recover their speech, as it were, from the dark dungeons of
damning silence.

It is argued here that women's poems should be read as a kind of life story,
involving an effort at self-articulation, and an act of unveiling in a society that
insisted on veiling them – their bodies and speech. The unveiled self was itself
a construction, but its articulation in the language of poetry enabled women
to represent their selfhood in polysemous terms and their gender within an
intersectional framework. The women poets discussed in the nineteenth-century
tazkira-i zanāna come from diverse social locations and did not experience
or represent their gender in any uniform and undifferentiated terms. Gender
was clearly entangled with class, caste and ritual status, and levels of privilege
and marginalization, but the important point is that gender was articulated in

---

[6]   Mir Taqi Mir, *Nikāt-ush-Shu'arā* (1751–52), ed. Mahmud Ilahi (Lucknow: Uttar Pradesh
      Urdu Academy, 1984); Saiyad Fateh Ali Husaini Gardezi, *Tazkira-i Rekhta Goyān* (1752–
      53), (New Delhi: Anjuman Taraqqi Urdu (Hind), 1933).

[7]   Ghulam Hamadani Mushafi, *Tazkira-i Hindī* (1816–17), ed. Maulvi Abdul Haq (Delhi:
      Jamia Barqi Press, 1933).

[8]   Mushafi, *Tazkira-i Hindī*, 279–82. Mushafi informs us that Moti was initially a courtesan,
      but an aristocrat, Mirza Ibrhim Beg, fell in love with her, and took her in his care, and she
      renounced her vocation to live with him in his household (Mushafi, *Tazkira-i Hindī*,
      281–82).

ambiguous terms, within a frame of reference that transcended its entrapment within the male–female binaries. Gender was certainly 'a useful category'[9] but not the 'primary' experience through which these women wrote about their experiences, emotions, and aesthetic sensibilities.

Reading the poems found in the women's *tazkiras*, one realizes that their compositions enriched, but also contested the dominant literary norms and aesthetics. Of course, women's poetry functioned within the Persianate literary allusions, allegories, and figures of speech, but we find them experimenting with new forms of expression and aesthetics as well. Even as their literary forms were constrained by the standard conventions, they did engage in innovative methods of linguistic expression and succeeded in articulating new emotions, experiences, and sensibilities. Clearly, then, despite the constraints of language, women did speak![10] Of course, a speech-act is contingent on its reception – the act of listening – and if their speech was not heard, it would naturally be annihilated or pushed to the 'silenced margins'. Even as the dominant literary culture was largely dismissive of women's presence, there were, as we learn from our texts, alternate sites, inclusive and diverse, where their compositions were read and appreciated, recited and remembered. It is within these 'counter-spaces' that women poets adopted heterogeneous subject positions to relate their emotions and experiences, and enriched the dominant literary culture with their literary experiments and innovations.

Within these counter-spaces, literary connoisseurs and critics waxed eloquent on women's lyrical compositions and the efforts of the authors of women's *tazkiras*.

---

[9] Joan Wallach Scott, 'Gender: A Useful Category of Historical Analysis', *American Historical Review* 91, no. 5 (December 1986): 1053–75; Joan Wallach Scott, *Gender and the Politics of History* (New York: Columbia University Press, 2018 [revised edition]). For a critical assessment of her formulations, see Afsaneh Najmabadi, 'Beyond the Americas: Are Gender and Sexuality Useful Categories of Historical Analysis?' *Journal of Women's History* 18, no. 1 (Spring 2006): 11–21; and Jeanne Boydston, 'Gender as a Question of Historical Analysis', *Gender and History* 20, no. 3 (November 2008): 558–83. Also see Afsaneh Najmabadi, *Women with Mustaches and Men without Beards: Gender and Sexual Anxieties of Iranian Modernity* (Berkeley: University of California Press, 2005).

[10] The debate on the issue was initiated by Gayatri Chakravorty Spivak in her influential piece: 'Can the Subaltern Speak?', in *Colonial Discourse and Post-Colonial Theory: A Reader*, ed. Patrick Williams and Laura Chrisman, 66–111 (New York: Columbia University Press, 1994). Also see Rosalind C. Morris (ed.), *Can the Subaltern Speak? Reflections on the History of an Idea* (New York: Columbia University Press, 2010).

Reviewing the *tazkira-i zanāna* of Durga Prashad Nadir[11] (discussed later), Shah
Bahauddin Bashir described women's verses therein as 'the songs of the sweet-
sounding parakeets' (*naghma-i tūtiyān-i khwush al-hān*).[12] Another scholar
described the women's lyrics found in his *tazkira* as 'sweet mangoes':

Look at the effects of mellifluous speech
Each and every verse (in the compendia) is like a sweet mango.

Dekhnā shīrīn kalāmī ka asr
Us kā har fuqrah hai goyā mīthā ām[13]

For this study, I have focused on two contemporary *tazkira*s written in the
second half of the nineteenth century. The first one is *Bahāristān-i Nāz* (The
Blandishments of Spring; hereafter *BN*) written by a physician of local repute,
Hakim Fasihuddin Ranj (1836–85); written in 1864, it is usually considered
the first *tazkira* of women poets in South Asia.[14] Our second biographical
compendium, briefly mentioned earlier, was authored by a petty scribe of the
kāyasth community, Durga Prashad Nadir, and is entitled *Tazkirat-un Nisā*
(Women's Life-Stories; hereafter *TN*); written in 1884, it is more detailed and
includes several interesting entries that had evaded Ranj.[15] Writing in the same
period, both authors borrowed from each other's work. Nadir had consulted *BN*
before he set out to write his book, and Ranj, similarly, had taken notes from the
other *tazkira*s that Nadir had written earlier and which were now incorporated
in his much larger and more detailed *TN*. We will be discussing these texts
later in the next chapter, but it needs to be mentioned here that these *tazkira*s
were in conversation with each other, and that is my excuse for taking them
together here. Their significance also comes from the fact that they were some of
the earliest women's *tazkira*s to be written in Hindustan; they were clearly the

---

[11] Durga Prashad Nadir, *Tazkirat-un Nisā* (1884), ed. Rifaqat Ali Shahid (Lahore: Sang-i
Mil Publications, 2016), p. 250 (hereafter *TN*). I have compared it with the 1884 edition,
but, unless mentioned otherwise, the references are to the former. Durga Prashad Nadir,
Tazkirat-un Nisā (Delhi: Akmal-ul Mutabi', 1884).
[12] Nadir, *TN*, 250.
[13] Nadir, *TN*, 252.
[14] Hakim Fasihuddin Ranj, *Bahāristān-i Nāz* (1882: third edition) (Lahore: Majlis-i Taraqqi-i
Adab, 1965 [reprint]) (hereafter *BN*).
[15] Nadir, *TN*.

guiding posts and inspiration for other women's *tazkira*s that were written later in the period.[16]

The *tazkira*s are commemorative texts and seek to memorialize bodies, words, and spaces, and the interactions among them. In drawing connections between bodies and words, and their co-constitutive relations, most of them actually primarily focus on men; women are, as mentioned earlier, rarely ever mentioned in the large number of poetic compendia and works of literary criticism. Our *tazkira*s are perhaps the only clues we have for recovering the memorialization of women scholars in cultural spaces, but there is a bewildering diversity of such women in our texts. Ranj and Nadir broadly divide women poets into 'public women' (*bāzārī 'aurat*) and 'secluded women' (*pardah-nashīn 'aurat*), and these categories are further split into numerous others. Women poets come from a wide range of social positions, community and caste affiliations, and styles of living and experiences of lives. In fact, in these *tazkira*s there is a range of terms that serve to define and elaborate the 'public women': 'the pleasure-providing beloved' (*mahbuba-i farhat bakhsh*), 'the vendor of beauty in the marketplace' (*husn farosh-i bāzārī*),[17] and 'the alluring attractions of the market' (*hasīnān-i bāzārī*).[18] Among those described as 'public women' were the courtesans (*tawā'if*) who usually had their own salons (*kotha*s) or entertained the affluent urban elites with their dance and songs at the salons of their owners. Known as the authentic purveyors of cultural norms and values, they enjoyed a social respectability unavailable to those lower down the scale. These *tazkira*s refer to several among them whose connections with affluent and resourceful men enabled them to lead a lavish and extravagant lifestyle. One such courtesan, discussed in some detail by both Ranj and Nadir, was Mahlaqa Chanda, who had about 500 soldiers in her employ, and patronized a large number of poets. She was presumably the first woman to have a poetic compilation (*diwān*) of her own, but along with literary pursuits, she was equally invested in bodily exercises and wrestling (*warzish aur pahlwānī*), horse riding, and archery.[19]

---

[16] See, for example, Abdul Hai's *tazkira* of women poets written in 1882: Maulvi Abdul Hai, *Tazkira-i Shamīm Sukhan* (Lucknow: Nawal Kishore, 1891 [reprint]). Also see Nasiruddin Hashmi, *Khwatīn-i Dakkan ki Urdu Khidmāt* (Hyderabad: Razzaqi Press, 1940).

[17] Nadir describes Farhat, a public performer, particularly skilled in vocal recitals, as a 'pleasure-providing beloved'; Ranj describes her as 'the vendor of beauty in the *bāzār*' (*TN*, 181; *BN*, 180).

[18] This is how Ranj describes Pari, a courtesan based in Calcutta; praising her literary skills, he says: 'There was no one like her when it came to the creative application of words (*chusti-e alfāz*) and binding the themes (*bandish-i muzāmīn*)'. (*BN*, 116–17).

[19] *TN*, 139–41; *BN*, 127–28.

Of course, not all 'public women' were quite as fortunate, and we come
across a large number of poets who were prostitutes (*randī/kasbī/khāngī*), slave
girls (*kanīz*) and concubines (*gharistān*), and singers and dancers performing
on the streets, marketplaces, and at houses for families on special occasions,
such as childbirth, circumcision, and marriage. While their 'origins' were banal,
their life stories were not always unexceptional. Banno, to take an instance, was
the concubine of Gulab Singh Ashufta, a *khatrī*[20] merchant based in Delhi,
and such was his love for Banno that he could not bear her separation and killed
himself; Banno followed him and died a mere six months after his death.[21]
Some among them were particularly talented and were widely appreciated for
their singing and dancing skills. About Sharfan, a public dancer (*raqāsa*) in
Lucknow, it was said: 'The rattle of her *pānzeb*[22] bring the dead back to life.'[23]
The range and diversity of poets who were termed as 'public women' was
immense and reached down to some of the most deprived and marginalized
sections of society. It included Kamman, a 'dark complexioned' (*sabzah rang*)
poet who was found in the markets in Bharatpur selling *bhāng*[24] and composing
and reciting verses while doing so; untrained in the subtleties of language,
expectedly, Nadir thus describes her linguistic skills: 'She shocked most people
with the crookedness of her language (*zila'-jugat*) and vulgar choice of words
(*phadakpan*).'[25] With these strong reservations, interestingly, she still finds a
place in cultural memory, and her verses are memorialized in the work of both
Nadir and Ranj. The latter interestingly extends his approval for this poet by
insistently pointing out that 'she had a pleasant disposition (*taba'-i mauzun*)
and creative mind (*zahn rasāi*)'.[26]

Among the poets described as 'secluded women', there is again immense
diversity; seclusion was a crucial marker of difference, and women described
thus usually came from elite social backgrounds, and included in this list were
several imperial women as well. Among them were rulers such as Sultan Raziya,

[20] *Khatri* is a caste in northern India predominantly associated with mercantile activities.
[21] *TN*, 129–31.
[22] *Pānzeb* is a string of small bells that women wear around their ankles when dancing or as
decorative ornament.
[23] *TN*, 166.
[24] *Bhāng* is a paste prepared from the leaves of marijuana, and served with milk (or water) as an
intoxicating drink. It is also mixed with sweets and snacks which are served as delicacies on
festive occasions.
[25] *TN*, 183.
[26] *BN*, 186.

who composed poems under the poetic name Shireen in the thirteenth century,[27] and queen consorts like Nur Jahan, who co-shared the perquisites of sovereignty with her spouse, emperor Jahangir (1605–27).[28] Women in the Mughal harem were quite well educated, and in both *BN* and *TN* their compositions are remembered to serve as inspiring examples for contemporary women; besides Nur Jahan, these *tazkiras* have entries on the daughter of Babur, Gulbadan Begum (c. 1523–1603),[29] Shahjahan's favourite daughter, Jahanara Begum (1614–81),[30] and Aurangzeb's daughter, Zebun Nisa (1638–1702), who composed poems under the pen name Makhfi.[31] Interestingly, while the Mughal imperial women

---

[27] *TN*, 79–80; *BN*, 157–58. Sultan Raziya (r. 1236–40) was the only female ruler in the Delhi Sultanate. She captured the throne by virtue of her political astuteness and military skills. In the sources of the period, her close association with an African Siddi slave, Yaqut, is presented as the chief reason for her downfall. The story is reiterated by Nadir, but is not mentioned in Ranj's *tazkira*. For details concerning her accession and tragic death, see Peter Jackson, 'Sultan Radiyya bint Iltutmish', in *Women in the Medieval Islamic World: Power, Patronage, Piety*, ed. Gavin R. G. Hambly, 81–97 (New York: Palgrave, 1998); Peter Jackson, *The Delhi Sultanate: A Political and Military History* (Cambridge: Cambridge University Press, 1999); and Alyssa Gabbay, 'In Reality a Man: Sultan Iltutmish, His Daughter, Raziya, and Gender Ambiguity in Thirteenth Century Northern India', *Journal of Persianate Studies* 4, no. 1 (January 2011), 45–63.

[28] *BN*, 223–26; *TN*, 92–96. For details about her life and administrative acumen, see Ruby Lal, *Empress: The Astonishing Reign of Nur Jahan* (Gurgaon: Penguin Random House, 2018); and Ellison Banks Findly, *Nur Jahan: Empress of Mughal India* (Oxford: Oxford University Press, 1993).

[29] Gulbadan Begum was quite a well-educated princess, and wrote an important historical account of the early phase of Mughal expansion in Hindustan, *Ahvāl-i Humāyunī*; authored by a woman, the account is exceptional in drawing attention to the political agency of imperial women, and the interconnections between the harem and the imperial court. See Ruby Lal, 'Historicizing the Harem: The Challenge of a Princess's Memoir', *Feminist Studies* 30, no. 3 (October 2004): 590–616; Ruby Lal, *Domesticity and Power in the Early Mughal World* (Cambridge: Cambridge University Press, 2005).

[30] *BN*, 126; *TN*, 75–76. Jahanara was an exceptionally talented scholar, and wrote several books and tracts on religious themes. For details about her life and work, see Afshan Bokhari, 'Gendered Landscapes: Jahan Ara Begum's (1614–1681) Patronage, Piety, and Self-Representation in Seventeenth Century Mughal India' (PhD dissertation, Universität Wien, 2009); Afshan Bokhari, 'Imperial Transgressions and Spiritual Investitures: A Begum's "Ascension" in Seventeenth Century Mughal India', *Journal of Persianate Studies* 4, no. 1 (January 2011): 86–108.

[31] *BN*, 199–200, 83–87. Also see her poetic compendium: *Diwān-i Makhfi* (Lucknow: Nawal Kishore, 1876).

are discussed in these *tazkiras*, so are their slaves, and the witty, poetic exchanges they had with them. One such poet was Amani, who was the 'specially chosen slave' (*kanīz-i khās bā-ikhtisās*) of Zebun Nisa, and both were, it seems, fond of testing each other's wit and sense of humour.[32]

Except for someone like Amani, these women associated with the Mughal imperial harem were quite well known, and, as we know from several European travellers' accounts, they were often discussed and 'constructed' (and 'reconstructed') in public spaces by ordinary subjects. That they were all poets is also well attested by Mughal sources of the period, and their verses, some genuine, others apocryphal, were recited in literary spaces, as a memorializing practice. Indeed, it is probable that the larger bulk of their verses mentioned in these *tazkiras* were latter-day constructions. The search for authentic verses or the effort to sift through and separate the 'genuine' from the 'apocryphal' compositions is actually a futile one. The important thing for us is to see how these women were remembered in literary spaces and, from the verses that were attributed to them, make a sense, however vague and imprecise, of popular perceptions of their subjectivity and agency. Memorializing Mughal women poets, as also those in the Sultanate period, in the nineteenth century, of course, had a political purpose and, as suggested earlier, was linked with the need to engage with – imbibe and repudiate – British imperial representations of India, and, more specifically, relocate the British project of women's reforms within an indigenous and broadly inclusive Persianate cultural world.

Among the contemporary poets discussed in the *tazkiras*, the pride of place belongs to the house of the deposed Awadh dynasty. They mention the last ruler of Awadh Wajid Ali Shah's wife-consort, Alam, who accompanied him to Calcutta in exile. She was a prolific poet and had her own *diwan*. In addition, she was also an accomplished sitar player.[33] Also mentioned in these women's *tazkiras* is one of his earlier wives, Mahbub, and the finely educated wives of Nawab Asaf-ud-Daula (1748–97), in particular, Begum Jan Jani and Begum Dulhan Begum, who used her name, Dulhan, in her poetry.[34] The Awadh kingdom had been annexed by the British imperial powers in 1856, and in remembering their women poets and their generous patronage to men of arts and letters, there is a quiet sense of hurt and

---

[32]   *TN*, 72–73; *BN*, 104.

[33]   *BN*, 174; *TN*, 177–78.

[34]   For the entries on Mahbub, see: *BN*, 206–07; *TN*, 191; for Begum Jan Jani, see *BN*, 121; *TN*, 137; and for details on Dulhan Begum, see *BN*, 141; *TN*, 149–50.

anguish at the loss of the dynasty, and the violence with which the ruling house was deposed and exiled away to Calcutta.

The list, of course, does not end there, and also includes the women rulers of the Bhopal dynasty, in particular, Shahjahan Begum (r. 1868–1901) – who composed poems under the pen name Shireen – and Sultan Jahan Begum Makhfi (r. 1901–26). They are not only described as particularly gifted poets but as generous patrons of arts and literature as well.[35] To add to the diversity, among the secluded poets we also come across the names of educated daughters of talented poets and scholars. The daughter of one of the finest poets of Urdu literature, Mir Taqi Mir, was also a poet of some repute writing under the nom de plume Begum.[36] Adding to the heterogeneity, we come across women poets born of mixed parentage, having a British father and an Indian mother, and there were some among them who were also married to British officials; expectedly, the *tazkiras* make it a point to emphasize their expertise in English, but even as they knew the western culture, they still composed poems in Urdu and seemed well versed in the subtleties of Indian dance and music. One such woman was a Christian lady (*'isai' 'aurat*), Jamiat. She was an Indian from her maternal side, but her father was an English gentleman who got her married to another Englishman serving as a major in the British army. Jamiat was quite knowledgeable in 'the art of music' (*'ilm-i mosaqi*), and her songs were popular with the 'singing communities' (*gawaiyon*) in the city of Agra.[37]

These are the kinds of poets and their compositions that we discuss here, but we need to be clear that these women coming from diverse classes, caste groups, regions, and professions did not experience or represent their gender in any uniform and undifferentiated terms. Gender was, as mentioned earlier, clearly

---

[35] For details concerning Shahjahan Begum, see *TN*, 109–10, 171–72; *BN*, 123–24. For Sultan Jahan Begum, see *TN*, 191–92; *BN*, 207. For an understanding of the work and contribution of the Bhopal *begums*, see Siobhan Lambert-Hurley, *Muslim Women, Reform and Princely Patronage: Nawab Sultan Jahan Begum of Bhopal* (London: Routledge, 2007); Siobhan Lambert-Hurley, 'Historicising Debates over Women's Status in Islam: The Case of Nawab Sultan Jahan of Bhopal', in *India's Princely States: People, Princes and Colonialism*, ed. Waltraud Ernst and Biswamoy Pati, 139–56 (London: Routledge, 2007); and Siobhan Lambert-Hurley, 'Princes, Paramountcy and the Politics of Muslim Identity: The Begums of Bhopal on the Indian National Stage, 1901–1926', *Journal of South Asian Studies* 26, no. 2 (2003): 169–95.

[36] *TN*, 131–32.

[37] *TN*, 138.

entangled with their social location and levels of privilege and marginalization, and was articulated in polysemic and ambiguous terms. Even so, let us not forget that their voices have reached us through the *tazkira*s of women poets, a genre that is not without its own sifting filters and norms of appropriate speech. There are for sure elisions and silences, and there are instances where the authors of our *tazkira*s fail to mention verses they found unpalatable. Nadir, for instance, dismisses Shahi Gilani in a single sentence and expresses his inability to cite her verses because they were 'obscene' (*fuhsh kalām*).[38] Furthermore, while prostitutes and dancing girls figure in their compilations – and are appreciated for their literary skills – in these *tazkira*s we notice, not infrequently, indications about the social anxieties that these groups evoked as well. Ranj, for example, thus describes Amir Jan, a prostitute: 'Just like a locust (*tedhi*) [that destroys crops], she has devoured many decent gentlemen.'[39] Or, about another prostitute (*randī*), Achpal, based in Saharanpur, he says: 'It is her job to fleece the ignoramus and affluent people'; approvingly citing the Urdu satirical magazine, *Oudh Punch*, he further adds that 'she is the alley (*pagdandī*) that takes you to the city of destruction (*shahr-i barbādī*)'.[40]

Women's voices, particularly the ones we study here, come to us through multiple mediations. Certainly, our *tazkira*s record the compositions of women poets but feel free to omit the ones they find commonplace, dull, or socially unacceptable. The selection of works is an important device through which the authors control their voices and the semiotics of their compositions. All poetic compositions are preceded with a bio-note that serves to guide the reader into predetermined patterns of meanings. Across these constraints we can still hear the faint resonance of women's speech, and that is precisely what we aim to do here – to listen to women speaking, and, hopefully, relish and learn about their experiences, emotions, and literary aesthetics.

Memorialization, Language, and Translation: Remembering Lives and Transmitting the Arts

It is important to ask how these texts, as exercises in memorialization, remember the contribution of women in literary spaces. In seeking to uncover the entanglement

---

[38] *TN*, 110.
[39] *BN*, 105.
[40] *BN*, 106.

of memory with literature[41] in women's *tazkiras*, we need to move beyond the dominant frameworks in memory studies that are largely derived from western historical experience and, in the case of the colonial world, are additionally inflected by the experience of colonialism and/or nationalism.[42] First, our texts, as argued earlier, dispense with gender binaries, so central to western apprehension of sociocultural experience. However, it is not just this but several other binaries too that they prompt us to question and reflect on more critically – the binaries of history and memory, mimesis and inventiveness, and high literature and popular culture. Indeed, our *tazkiras* see history (*tārikh*) as a resource for memory building, and memories as enriching history. The tendency in memory studies to posit cultural remembrance in opposition to state-imposed and elite-centred constructions of the past, that is, history, does not quite apply to the historical experience in South Asia (or, for that matter, the Persianate cultural world). History and memory were entangled categories, together shaping shared, and contested, imaginations of the past and constructions of identities in the present.

Indeed, the distinction between conformity and creativity in the modern knowledge system does not quite hold true for the literary culture in South Asia.

---

[41] For an understanding of the relations between literary theory and memory studies, see Astrid Erll, *Memory in Culture*, trans. Sara B. Young (London, UK: Palgrave Macmillan, 2011); Astrid Erll and Ansgar Nunning (eds.), *Cultural Memory Studies: An International and Interdisciplinary Handbook* (Berlin and New York: De Gruyter, 2010); Michael Rothberg, *Multidirectional Memory: Remembering the Holocaust in the Age of Decolonization* (Stanford: Stanford University Press, 2010); and Marianne Hirsch, *The Generation of Postmemory: Writing and Visual Culture after the Holocaust* (New York: Columbia University Press, 2012). Also see the special issue on *Memory and Literature* guest edited by Urania Milevski and Lena Wetenkamp, *Journal of Literary Theory* 16, no. 2 (2020): see, in particular, the following essays: Urania Mlievski and Lena Wetenkamp, 'Introduction: Relations Between Literary Theory and Memory Studies', 197–212; Michael Basseler and Dorothee Birke, 'Mimesis of Remembering', 213–38; and Manuel Muhlbacher, 'Plotting Memory: What Are We Made to Remember When We Read Narrative Texts', 239–63.

[42] Jeffrey K. Olick, Vered Vinitzky-Seroussi, and Daniel Levy (eds.), *The Collective Memory Reader* (New York: Oxford University Press, 2011). A lot of work has come out in the last several decades on the dominance of western regimes of knowledge, and the need to decolonize and 'provincialize' all fields of knowledge, including, of course, memory studies. See, for example, Dipesh Chakrabarty, *Provincializing Europe: Postcolonial Thought and Historical Difference* (Princeton: Princeton University Press, 2000); Nelson Maldonado-Terres, *Against War: Views from the Underside of Modernity* (Durham and London: Duke University Press, 2008); Sylvia Wynter, *We Must Learn to Sit Together and Talk about a Little Culture: Decolonizing Essays, 1967–1984* (Leeds, UK: Peepal Tree Press Ltd., 2022); and Katherine McKittick (ed.), *Sylvia Wynter: On Being Human as Praxis* (Durham and London: Duke University Press, 2014).

The women poets that are discussed in these *tazkira*s hardly ever drift away from the established literary conventions, but still bring to the table a range of fresh feelings, emotions, experiences, and literary tropes and analogies; mimicry and inventiveness go together in their constitution of the aesthetic field. Entrenched in Persianate forms of literary expression, their poems might appear to a careless reader as reflecting an attitude of indifference towards the changing times. In fact, beneath the pretence of conformity and continuity, we are not infrequently confronted with verses that apprehend a changed, different world. Take note, for example, of the following couplet of a female poet, Wazir:

> Every hiccup (*hichki*) reminds me of my beloved,[43]
> On the station of my heart (*dil ke isteshan*) rests the train of my sorrows (*gham ki rel*).
> *Khabar detī hai' hichkī mujhe dilbar ke āne ki*
> *Hamārē dil ke isteshan pe gham kī rēl jārī hai'*[44]

These lines bring out the changing times, and are remarkable in suggesting how the newly emergent modern world came to be represented in women's poetry in South Asia. The poet creatively intermeshes the icons of modernity – the train and the railway station – with Persianate metaphors and analogies. Indeed, even as these poets worked within the prevailing literary norms and practices, they were not averse to experimenting with new metaphors and analogies, and introducing innovations in the forms of linguistic expression.

One of the important things to note here is that these *tazkira*s were drawing attention to a long history of women's participation in literary activities, and in doing so they were contesting the British imperial characterization of Hindustani civilization as marked by perennial depravity and decadence symbolized in their treatment of women. As against the 'orientalist' representation of Indian women as mere chattels of their male masters, deprived since antiquity of the social respectability that comes with education, these texts present women as active social agents, intelligent, suave, and well educated, continually shaping the norms of aesthetics and literary expression. Even as the decline in women's education in contemporary times is a matter of concern for both Ranj and Nadir, they still reject European teleology, and in drawing attention to the presence of women poets in literary spaces in the multiple pasts of Hindustan, they plead for a return to the roots of Hindustani culture, and not to modern Europe for inspiration. Interestingly, while looking at the global endeavours in women's education, *TN* sidesteps Europe

---

[43] In the popular beliefs in Hindustan, a hiccup was seen as linked to the remembrance of a loved one.

[44] *TN*, 227.

and mentions several Asian countries, including, interestingly, China, as providing the right direction towards the educational uplift of women.[45]

It could be argued that the women's biographical compendia written in the colonial period, in particular the ones we are discussing here, were performing an act of 'epistemic disobedience' in that they were resisting the dominant epistemologies and Eurocentric systems of thought. Walter Mignolo describes 'epistemic disobedience' as an act of resistance against the western hegemonic thought and its assumptions and frames of imagination.[46] What we notice here is an act of resistance that is registered in several registers. These *tazkiras* contest 'orientalist' essentialism and the Anglicist and utilitarian characterization of India as a decadent civilization insensitive to the concerns of women and historically marked by their segregation and exclusion from socio-economic and literary-cultural activities. They were also resisting the Indian reformers when they linked their project for women's reforms, in particular the agenda for their education, with Victorian notions of domesticity and family values. Even as these concerns remain important for Ranj and Nadir, they see women's education as imparting to women not just the skills to efficiently manage their households but also the ability to develop a taste – *zauq* – for the arts and the resources to actively participate in the literary sphere and reshape it by bringing in their emotions, experiences, and linguistic innovations. The emphasis on domesticity in the movement for women's education in the colonial period was never absolute, and, as has been shown by Asiya Alam in her interesting study of the variegated discourses on family (and the position of women therein), there were all along voices of disapproval and discord. In her study of familial intimacies in the Urdu press, her work reveals what she terms as 'Muslim feminism' challenging the patriarchal assumptions of didactic social reform by raising issues of women's freedom and rights.[47]

Written in the genre of the *tazkira*s, how do our texts translate women's lyrical compositions? It is important to remind ourselves that a large number of their verses were etched in cultural memory and circulated in multiple sites of sociability within a dynamic and ever-creative performative and oral tradition.

---

[45]   *TN*, 119–20.

[46]   For an elaboration of the concept of 'epistemic disobedience', see Walter D. Mignolo, 'Epistemic Disobedience, Independent Thought and De-Colonial Freedom', *Theory, Culture and Society* 26, nos. 7–8 (December 2009): 159–81; Walter D. Mignolo, 'Decolonizing Western Epistemology/Building De-Colonial Epistemologies', in *Decolonizing Epistemologies: Latina/o Theology and Philosophy*, ed. Ada Maria Isasi-Diaz and Eduardo Mendieta, 19–43 (New York: Fordham University Press, 2011); and Walter D. Mignolo and Catherine E. Walsh, *On Decoloniality: Concepts, Analytics, Praxis* (Durham and London: Duke University Press, 2018).

[47]   Asiya Alam, *Women, Islam and Familial Intimacy in Colonial South Asia* (Leiden: Brill, 2021).

Reconfigured as texts and reproduced in print in a biographical compendium, they lost their linkages with the performance cultures and stood as isolates, de-contextualized from their sociocultural world. Indeed, their 'inscription' in print served to suppress the inter-medial means of meaning apprehension; centred on the primacy of the printed word, women's poems now lost the conversations they prompted between the text and the auditory and tactile modes of experience and meaning-making. One of my efforts here is to see them in terms of their entangled relations with the performance-oriented forms of meaning and, to the extent possible, be attentive to the sensorial modes of readings that served to inflect and constantly diversify their significations. Indeed, we need to be wary of and find ways of circumventing the text-centred paradigms when reading women's poetry found in the *tazkira*s written in the nineteenth century.[48]

There are deeper problems in my translation of women's compositions, and it is appropriate to own them right away. It would be naïve to believe that any interlingual translation can ever establish equivalences, and it is reasonable to assume that the translated poem is more an act of composition than reproduction, trying to reach out to, with varying degrees of success, the reading community in the host language. At the same time, my work, like the *tazkira*s it studies here, is also a commemorative exercise, seeking to memorialize the contribution of women in the shaping of the modern literary sphere and complicate our understanding of the South Asian literary heritage. Even so, I am conscious of the disparities in power here, for, while the language of their compositions is local or vernacular, that of their host bears considerable privilege and prestige; it is, after all, a language of global interactions and exchange. Translation is certainly not just about communication, an effort to establish bridges across cultural divides, but also equally about finding resources to challenge western translation categories and concepts, and resist the marginalization of local cultures and linguistic practices.[49]

---

[48] For a discussion on the interstitial spaces between performance cultures and translation practices, see the special issue on 'Translation and Performance Cultures', guest edited by Christina Marinetti and Enza De Francisci, *Translation Studies* 15, no. 3 (2022); see in particular Christina Marinetti and Enza De Franisci, 'Introduction: Translation and Performance Cultures', 247–57. Also see Monica Boria, Angeles Carreres, Maria Noriega-Sanchez, and Marcus Tomalin (eds.), *Translation and Multimodality: Beyond Words* (London: Routledge, 2020); and the special issue on 'Translation in India', guest edited by Hephzibah Israel, *Translation Studies* 14, no. 2 (2021).

[49] For an understanding of the issues in poetry translation, see the special issue on 'Poetry and Translation', *Translation Studies* 4, no. 2 (2011); see in particular Lawrence Venuti, 'Introduction: Poetry and Translation', 127–32. For a discussion on the issues concerning inter-lingual translation, see Sarah Maitland, *What Is Cultural Translation?* (London and New York: Bloomsbury Publishing, 2017).

Women's Voices in Colonial India:
A Historiographical Overview

One of the objectives of this study is to open up an archive and disclose the voices of women in nineteenth-century South Asia. In doing so, it draws attention to the evidence of an impressive presence of women in the literary sphere, rubbing shoulders with men in shaping and remoulding norms of aesthetics and literary expression. Historians interested in women's lives have recovered exceptional stories of women learning to read and write against huge odds, and those among them who took the pen in their hands to tell their life stories and shared their experiences and contestations with the forces of patriarchy. The autobiography of a Bengali upper-caste housewife, Rashundari Debi, entitled *Amar Jiban* (My Life, 1868) is exceptional in that respect and reveals the trials and tribulations a woman faced in acquiring an education.[50] She was, of course, not alone, and studies on women's autobiographical writings reveal that educated women from heterogeneous sociocultural backgrounds felt a compelling desire to narrate their life stories during the early modern period. Their self-narratives were, as has been argued by Anshu Malhotra and Siobhan Lambert-Hurley, strongly marked by performance and were – unlike western autobiographies, which presented the self in autonomous terms – exercises in the construction of selfhood in gendered and relational terms.[51] Indeed, the last several decades have seen an impressive expansion of interest in women's self-narratives, and scholars have brought to light several life stories written by women in South Asia.[52]

In my study of women's poetic compositions, I look at their verses as a form of self-narrative and, borrowing from Margot Badron, an act of

---

[50] Tanika Sarkar, *Words to Win: The Making of Amar Jiban – A Modern Autobiography* (New Delhi: Zuban Books, 2013).

[51] Anshu Malhotra and Siobhan Lambert-Hurley (eds.), *Speaking of the Self: Gender, Performance, and Autobiography in South Asia* (Durham and London: Duke University Press, 2015).

[52] See, for example, Siobhan Lambert-Hurley, *Elusive Lives: Gender, Autobiography, and the Self in Muslim South Asia* (Stanford, CA: Stanford University Press, 2018); Anshu Malhotra, *Piro and the Gulabdasis: Gender, Sect, and Society in Punjab* (New Delhi: Oxford University Press, 2017); Malavika Karlekar, *Voices from Within: Early Personal Narratives of Bengali Women* (New Delhi: Oxford University Press, 1993); and Aparna Basu and Malavika Karlekar (eds.), *In So Many Words: Women's Life Experiences from Western and Eastern India* (New Delhi: Routledge, 2008).

'final unveiling'.[53] Actually, as explained by Farzaneh Milani, in a 'veiled society', it is not just the female bodies, but even 'the words and feelings are veiled'. It is for this reason, she argues, that women's life stories in Iran should be understood as the 'ultimate form of unveiling'.[54] The same could perhaps be said of women's poetry in Hindustan insofar as it enabled them to express their emotions, feelings, and 'interior' selves. At the same time, 'unveiling' to me is an act of construction, and the use of language in women's poems enabled them to construct – not 'recover' – a selfhood that was articulated in multiple, often aporetic, contexts.

In the context of South Asian history, Muslim women's voices have been relatively less researched, but historians such as Barbara Metcalf and Gail Minault, among others, have for decades explored and discussed writings by and for women. Thanks to their efforts and those who followed in their footsteps, a large archive of Muslim women's writings has been uncovered, and this includes their contributions to journals and magazines, travelogues, and works of fiction.[55] More recently, Siobhan Lambert-Hurley has studied Muslim women's autobiographies in India written during the twentieth century. Appropriately entitled *Elusive Lives*, her work is an exceptionally brilliant effort to explore modern Muslim women's self-narratives and the constitution of their selfhood in terms of community identities,

---

[53] This is how she describes the memoirs of the Egyptian nationalist Huda Shaarawi (1879–1947) but the term seems quite appropriate to describe women's poetry in Hindustan as well. Margot Badran, 'Expressing Feminism and Nationalism in Autobiography: The Memoirs of an Egyptian Educator', in *De/Colonizing the Subject: The Politics of Gender in Women's Autobiography*, ed. Sidonie Smith and Julia Watson, 270–93 (Minneapolis: University of Minnesota Press, 1992).

[54] Farzaneh Milani, 'Iranian Women's Life Narratives', *Journal of Women's History* 25, no. 2 (Summer 2013): 130–52. Also see Roberta Micallef, 'Identities in Motion: Reading Two Ottoman Travel Narratives as Life Writing', *Journal of Women's History* 25, no. 2 (Summer 2013): 85–110; and Marilyn Booth, 'Locating Women's Autobiographical Writing in Colonial Egypt', *Journal of Women's History* 25, no. 2 (Summer 2013): 35–60.

[55] Gail Minault, *Gender, Language and Learning: Essays in Indo-Muslim Cultural History* (Delhi: Permanent Black, 2009); Gail Minault, *Secluded Scholars: Women's Education and Muslim Social Reform in Colonial India* (New Delhi: Oxford University Press, 1998); Barbara D. Metcalf, *Perfecting Women: Maulana Ashraf Ali Thanawi's Bihishti Zewar* (Berkeley and Los Angeles: University of California Press, 1990); Sylvia Vatuk, '*Hamara Daur-i Hayat*: An Indian Muslim Woman Writes Her Life', in *Telling Lives in India: Biography, Autobiography, and Life History*, ed. David Arnold and Stuart Blackburn, 144–74 (Bloomington and Indianapolis: Indiana University Press, 2004); Haris Qadeer and P. K. Yasser Arafath (eds.), *Sultana Sisters: Genre, Gender, and Genealogy in South Asian Muslim Women's Fiction* (New Delhi: Routledge, 2022).

nationalism and nationalist ideologies, and modern education.[56] Of course, the biographical compendia we study here are indifferent to these concerns, and the life stories of women poets and selection of verses therein are unconcerned with forms of modern identities. Written in the nineteenth century, these texts were surely aware of the changes wrought by colonial modernity, but in their efforts to memorialize women poets, their frame of reference was the Persianate cultural world, where women cherished and questioned both their inherited and acquired norms and values.

How do we read the biographical compendia or *tazkira*s written before the modern nation states and the emergence of nationalism as the dominant ideological force, defining, almost exclusively, a person's sense of selfhood and belonging? There have been several interesting studies on the *tazkira*s in the early modern Persianate world, and they point to their significance as life narratives that constitute identity and selfhood by reproducing entangled interconnections between texts and spaces.[57] Even so, as has been persuasively argued by Mana Kia, the 'the Persianate selves' were constituted in varied and multiple contexts, defined by shifting identifications with place, origin, and lineage. The crucial point here is that these texts were aporetic and imbibed heterogeneous, often contradictory, perspectives and identifications.[58] Women's literary *tazkira*s are aporetic, for sure, and they are apparently more complicated to read than the ones that are devoted to rulers, nobles, bureaucrats, and Sufi saints. They certainly open up an archive of women's voices, but it is quite a challenge to locate the freshness of thought and expression that they brought to bear on the literary culture and, more importantly, discover, through the thicket of rhetoric and analogies, their gendered experiences and articulations. As it is, gender was intermeshed with other markers of difference, and their literary exercises were just as much about their class, caste, and community identities as

---

[56] Lambert-Hurley, *Elusive Lives.*

[57] Marcia K. Hermansen and Bruce B. Lawrence, 'Indo-Persian Tazkiras as Memorative Communication', in *Beyond Turk and Hindu: Religious Identities in Islamicate South Asia*, ed. David Gilmartin and Bruce Lawrence (New Delhi: India Research Papers, 2002); Nile Green, 'The Uses of Books in a Late Mughal Takiyya: Persianate Knowledge Between Person and Paper', *Modern Asian Studies* 44, no. 2 (March 2010): 241–65; Nile Green, *Making Space: Sufis and Settlers in Early Modern India* (New Delhi: Oxford University Press, 2012). Also see Louise Marlow, *The Rhetoric of Biography: Narrating Lives in Persianate Societies* (Boston, MA: Ilex Foundation; distributed by Harvard University Press, 2011).

[58] Mana Kia, *Persianate Selves: Memories of Place and Origin Before Nationalism* (Stanford, CA: Stanford University Press, 2020).

about gender. Furthermore, women's voice was mediated in these texts through a multiplicity of devices and strategies. One such strategy was the biographical notes that preceded the verses of the poets; these strategic insertions were clearly intended to discipline their voice and guide the reader into patterns of predetermined semantics. We seek to apprehend both their biographical sketches and literary compositions to listen to the voices of women through centuries of silence.

2

Unravelling the Texts

Memory, Reforms, and Literary *Sulh-i Kul*

This study has two related ambitions: one is to recover women's poetic compositions, and the other is to see how their participation in the literary sphere was remembered and represented by connoisseurs, critics, and the common folk in the early modern period. In order to do so, it focuses, as discussed earlier, on two biographical compendia (*tazkiras*) of female poets, both written in the nineteenth century, and this poses several problems before us. For one, we need to understand the implications of recovering women's lyrics from the *tazkiras* since our access is mediated by the selection, observations, and biographical notes that their authors provide before citing their poetic compositions. In line with the standard format of literary *tazkiras* followed across the Persianate world, in almost all entries there is a selection of verses, but these are preceded by biographical clips of varying lengths. The question then is: how are these life stories to be read and interpreted, particularly when they purportedly intend to highlight and preserve the contribution of women to the shaping of the literate tradition? Related to this, we need to be attentive to the disciplining thrust in the life stories and the inbuilt exclusions and silences that were integral to the discursive incorporation of women's poems within the early modern literary culture.

Raising the issue of 'authenticity' in texts of memorialization only fetches diminishing returns, and it is important to realize that our *tazkiras* not only carry verses that were 'authentic' but also the ones whose genuineness was suspect, but they were still in circulation in commemorative spaces. Not an inconsiderable number of women poets had poetic compilations or *diwāns* of their own, and when their work is mentioned in the *tazkiras*, one could be fairly certain about their genuineness. It also happened not infrequently that married men provided to the authors poems composed by their wives; or the tutors, impressed by some of their female students, shared their couplets with them. Even so, our authors also picked up a large amount of their material from gossip and discussions in the markets (*bāzār*), coffee houses (*qahwa-khāne*), courtesan's quarters (*kotha*), and poetic assemblies (*mushā 'ira*). While we have every reason to suspect their authenticity, they are invaluable in providing clues to the memories of women littérateurs in sociocultural spaces. As commemorative texts, the *tazkiras* were concerned with the memorialization of women's active participation in cultural spaces, and their objective was not to sift through and differentiate the genuine from the apocryphal verses, but to retrieve women's lyrics circulating in the diffused and heterogeneous literary spaces.

The story we unfold here is, therefore, not just about what women said and wrote; it is equally about what the aesthetically informed audience, elites and the ordinary people alike, represented as the voice of women in the cultural domain. While the authors of women's *tazkiras* were interested in preserving their voices, they did certainly seek to control and regulate them through motivated selection – choosing some verses while omitting others. All poetic specimens, as mentioned earlier, are preceded in their works with brief biographical sketches, and one of their objectives indeed is to influence the reader and shape her or his reception of the verses. While reading these *tazkiras*, we need to be attentive to the complex techniques and devices through which their authors sought to control the narrative, shape perception, and discipline the semantic field in the process of their commemoration of female poets.

Hakim Fasihuddin Ranj and His Social and Intellectual Circle

The author of our first text is Hakim Fasihuddin Ranj (1836–85), and while we are concerned here with his *tazkira*, it is important to bear in mind that he was himself a poet of some repute. His *diwān* was published posthumously in 1891 by his son, Hakim Fakhruddin,[1] who was persuaded into doing so by an interesting French orientalist scholar, George Puech Shor (1823–94).[2] His reasons for prodding Fakhruddin were obvious; himself an accomplished Rekhta poet, Shor was quite

---

[1]   Fasihuddin Ranj, *Kulliyāt-i Ranj*, ed. Hakim Muhammad Fakhruddin (Meerut: Matba' Hashmi, 1891).

[2]   George Puech Shor was an Urdu littérateur and was the author of several poetic compilations (*diwāns*). He also wrote a diary in Urdu during the 1857 uprising which provides an interesting eyewitness account of the events in Meerut where he was based at the time; the diary is called '*Waqā 'i Hairat Afzā*'. For his diary and poetic compositions, see Rahat Abrar, *1857 Ke Inqilāb Ka 'Aini Shahid: George Puech Shor* (Delhi: Educational Book House, 2010), 63–132, 133–96.

impressed with the literary abilities of Ranj and saw him as embodying 'the soul of eloquence' (*jān-i sukhan*); his verses, he believed, were simply 'magical' (*jādu kalām*).[3] Ranj's close association with French orientalists and British officials and statesmen should have had some influence over his writings, more so when these men were a source of patronage for the cash-strapped poets. When his *tazkira* was first published in 1864, it was found to be carrying far too many mistakes and needed to be republished, but this entailed expenses that our poor author could not afford to bear. It was the timely assistance of George Ernst, the collector and magistrate of Meerut, and William Smutt, the commissioner in Aligarh, that made this possible, and Ranj brought out the second edition of his *tazkira* in 1869.[4] Clearly, his literary circle was quite wide and included British statesmen and high officials who had relations with and provided patronage to Hindustani scholars.

From the sketchy details available to us, it seems that Ranj was for much of his professional life based in Meerut, a town in present-day Uttar Pradesh, where he was a successful physician (*hakim*), having taken over the clinic (*matab*) of his father-in-law after the latter's death. His was a family of scholars, and the intellectual environment in his home rubbed on him as well. It is with some pride that he refers to his diverse skills, and if we are to trust him, he was educated in a variety of subjects: accountancy, arithmetic, literature, rhetoric, astronomy, and theology, among others. In his own words:

In the company of littérateurs, I have excelled myself in a wide range of literary forms. At times, it was poetry (*nazm*) that enamoured me, while other times it was prose writing (*nasr*) that kept me preoccupied. For a while, I learned medicine (*hikmat*), and ran a clinic (*matab*) to treat patients. I also tried my hand at astronomy (*'ilm-i hi'at*) and architecture (*hindasi*), but my impatience (*iztirāb-i qalb*: 'the restlessness in my heart') got the better of me. I got interested in theology, and then found myself in the thick of discussions on philology (*sarf-o-nahw*). I drifted to the study of rhetoric (*muntiq*), and began to enjoy studying the art of eloquence and elaboration (*ma'ani'-wa-biyān ki balāghat*). For a while, I became adept in numbers and their multiplication (*'ilm-i taksīr*), but all this while I kept away from feelings of jealousy and resentment. So it is that my disposition revealed before me so many colours (or attractions), but my

---

3 Abrar, *1857 Ke Inqilāb*, 60–61.
4 For details about the life and work of Hakim Fasihuddin Ranj, see Rahat Abrar, *Urdu Shā'irat Ka Auwalin Tazkira Nigār: Hakim Fasihuddin Ranj Meruthi* (Delhi: Bharat Offset Press, 1999), and Khalilur Rahman Daudi's introduction in *BN*. For his connections with British officials and their support towards the publication of his work, see *BN*, 83–84.

heart was hard to persuade [and ultimately found solace in literary pursuits, one of the results of which is this *tazkira*].[5]

The objective of this autobiographical interlude within the *tazkira* was not just a narcissistic claim to comprehensive knowledge but was also intended to remind the reader that the author's literary practices came from his heart, and his work was the fruit of his passion.[6] At the same time, of course, the effort here is to convince the reader of the seriousness of his effort, which should not be trivialized only because it was about women. In order to drive home the point, he describes in some detail the struggles of his life, and even as they left him vexed and dejected, he did not and could not give up writing. Describing those moments of his life, he says:

> Misfortune raised its head and the wind of adversity (*hawā-i kulfat*) threw me around, turning me into a ball (*gola*) that was pushed around all over the place. It is me and my heart alone that knows the extent of my sorrows. My body ached bearing the burden of the mound of hardships (*koh-i musībat*). In that moment of loneliness (*tanhā'ī*), pain was my only friend (*yār*).[7]

There were hardships, issues of livelihood, and dejected loneliness, and still, like a warrior, driven and focused, he wrote this biographical compendium on women poets; it was indeed too significant an undertaking to be given up amidst the uncertainties of existence. The larger point behind this autobiographical interlude is to suggest that his project was not an exercise in trivia; after all, he seems to imply, a *tazkira* devoted to women was just as significant as the one devoted to men. Of course, as a littérateur, he wrote other stuff as well, but the pride of place belongs to his *tazkira*, and, as the first of its kind, it was noticed, appreciated, and critiqued in literary circles, but, more importantly, inspired other biographical compendia of women poets during the nineteenth and twentieth centuries.

As mentioned, he was a poet as well, and the spark in his poetry came not insignificantly from his association with one of the finest Urdu poets, Mirza Asadullah Ghalib (1797–1869). Ranj was his student and imbibed from him the skills of exquisite imagination, eloquence, and rhetoric.[8] His language is chaste

---

[5] *BN*, 81.

[6] Explaining his objectives in writing the *tazkira*, he says: 'In this effort, my intention is not to accumulate fame (*nāmwarī*), but to serve talent and knowledge' (*BN*, 84).

[7] *BN*, 81.

[8] Scholars of Urdu working on Ghalib mention Ranj as belonging to his charmed circle of students. See, for instance, Malik Ram, *Talāmiz-i Ghālib* (Delhi: Maktaba Jamia Limited, 1984); and Imtiaz Ali Arshi, *Makātib-i Ghālib* (Rampur: Matba Sarkari Riyasat, Rampur, 1943).

and simple, but he still succeeds in expressing the most intimate emotions with subtlety and grace. He was particularly popular in literary circles for his poems in praise of Prophet Muhammad, known as *na't-goi'*. His collection of *na'ts*, called *Gulshan-i Na't*, was first published in 1860 but soon ran out of print and had to be printed a second time in 1889.[9] His poetic inclinations should have prompted an interest in women's poetry, but the brief biographical details that accompany their poems indicate an interest in their lives as well.

We are concerned here not with his poems but his biographical compendia (*tazkira*). Entitled *Bahāristān-i-Nāz*, or 'the blandishments of spring', the work was perhaps the first of its kind in that, unlike the other *tazkira*s written in Hindustan, this one was exclusively devoted to women poets, writing in Urdu and Persian, and was written with the objective of memorializing their lives and literary compositions. First published in 1864 at Meerut by one Wajahat Ali, it had unfortunately far too many errors, some the doing of the author, and the others, the scribe (*kātib*). It was therefore republished in 1869 and, as mentioned earlier, largely at the insistence of and financial assistance from appreciative British officials.[10]

A few years thereafter, in 1876 to be precise, another women's *tazkira* was published; entitled *Chaman Andāz* (The Shape of the Garden); its author was a scribe (*munshi*), Durga Prashad Nadir. Unlike Ranj's *tazkira*, this one was exclusively devoted to female poets writing in Persian. Nadir followed this up with another *tazkira* in 1878, *Tazkirat-un-Nisā* (Women's Life Stories), which was about women's poetry in Urdu. It is obvious that Ranj must have been one of his sources of inspiration, and in his enthusiasm he copied information about several poets from Ranj's work. Ranj accused him of stealing details from his work, and in what looks like a tit-for-tat spat, Nadir charged him of doing the same, copying information from his work without even bothering to verify it. When Ranj published the third edition of his *tazkira* in 1882, the number of entries had increased from 70 to 174; this was certainly an impressive jump, but the increase in the entries was, among other factors, facilitated by the availability of Nadir's *tazkira*s, and Ranj borrowed details from them to make his *tazkira* look more detailed and comprehensive.

Durga Prashad Nadir and His Work

Durga Prashad Nadir Dehlawi (1833–1903) is our second author, who combined his two smaller *tazkira*s, one on women composing Persian poetry

---

[9] Fasihuddin Ranj, *Gulshan-i Na't* (Meerut: Fakhrul Mutaba, 1889).

[10] Hakim Fasihuddin Ranj, *Bahāristān-i Nāz* (second edition) (Meerut: Matba' Darul 'Ulum Meerut, 1869).

(*Chaman Andāz*) and the other on Rekhta poetesses (*Tazkirat-un-Nisā*; also called *Mir'āt-i Khyālī*), into a much enlarged and substantially modified *tazkira* of Persian and Rekhta women poets, called *Tazkirat-un-Nisā* (*TN*). Published in 1884, *TN* was actually an enlarged and substantially revised version of these two separate books which he wrote earlier, both devoted to women poets. In the process of conjoining the two books together, of course, the author undertook extensive revisions and substantially enlarged the number of entries; considering the range and extent of these revisions, it is reasonable to see *TN* as a distinct work, separate from the other two *tazkira*s authored by him. *TN* contains a total of 54 women poets writing in Persian and 143 who composed verses in Urdu. In addition, the text has sections on quatrains composed by women, and the appendix has verses by women who could not be accommodated in the main body of the text. The text has a couple of appendices, and one such appendix is a note in response to Ranj's charges against his work.

About the life of Nadir, not much is known, and what he chooses to reveal about himself through his writings helps us catch glimpses of his life in an obviously piecemeal manner. The *tazkira*s of poets written in the period or later do not usually provide any details about his life, and the one that does so, *Tazkira-i Asārush Shu'ara-i Hunūd* (Biographies of Leading Hindu Poets), wrote about him from the notes provided by Nadir himself. He describes himself as a Dehlawi, an identity rooted in the city, but also identifies himself as a Khatri-Jhunjhuni, thereby highlighting the significance of his sub-caste or *jāti* affiliation in shaping his identity. His patrilineal ancestors were associated with state service, and in adherence to the family tradition, his father, Munshi Mansaram Natwan, served as a petty clerk (*ahlkār*) in the establishment of the charismatic female ruler of Sardana, Begum Samru,[11] recording documents and maintaining accounts. Later, he fulfilled the same administrative responsibilities in the employ of the Oudh kingdom before joining the service of the English Company, where he was employed in multiple capacities. He was, like any well-trained clerk (*munshi*) in that period, well versed in Persian, Urdu, and Braj and could read and write in all three languages. His son, Nadir, was a product of the famous Delhi College, wherefrom he studied Persian, Arabic, English, Braj, and Mathematics.[12] After acquiring the requisite training in geometry, he was appointed as an instructor for

---

[11] For details about Begum Samru, see Julia Keay, *Farzana: The Woman Who Saved an Empire* (London: I. B. Tauris, 2014).

[12] For details about the Delhi College, see Margrit Pernau (ed.), *The Delhi College: Traditional Elites, the Colonial State, and Education Before 1857* (New Delhi: Oxford University Press, 2006).

the training of the record keepers (*patwāri*s) in Rohtak. After shuttling between Delhi and Lahore for several years, teaching Mathematics and Persian in schools and colleges, he ultimately settled down in Delhi, where he opened a bookshop called Delhi Book Society.

Women in Cultural Memory: Commemorative Texts and Female Scholars

The change that authors such as Ranj and Nadir represented can be appreciated from the fact that in the literary *tazkira*s written during the period, women were usually conspicuously absent, and where this was not the case, women still made only fleeting and exceptional appearances. The literary culture was presented as gender exclusive, and only rarely were women recognized as contributing to the enrichment of culture. *Tazkira*s are commemorative texts, and in choosing to ignore women's compositions, these texts denied their interventions in the literary sphere, and helped shape a cultural memory in which women probably had no more than a marginal role in shaping the norms of arts and aesthetics. Earlier in the introduction, we mentioned Shaikh Ghulam Hamdani Mushafi's *Tazkira-i Hindi* (1794), a biographical compendium of Urdu poets that has just five entries on women poets.[13] In his literary *tazkira* titled *Farah Baksh* (Transmitting Bliss, 1871), Yar Muhammad Khan Shaukat cared to mention just one woman, and presumably only because of her political influence; that solitary woman was Shahjahan Begum, the ruler of Bhopal.[14] Similarly, the number of women mentioned in Mohsin's biographical compendia, *Sarāpā Sukhan* (Pure Eloquence, 1861), stands at three.[15] Further, to take yet another example, the *tazkira* of Nawab Mustafa Khan Shefta, *Tazkira-i Gulshan Be-Khār* (A Garden without Thorns, 1835), has just four entries on women.[16]

Our *tazkira*s – BN and TN – are a powerful testament of literate women's agency and, more importantly, demonstrate with particular vigour the gender-based elisions and erasures in the commemoration of cultural heritage. At the same time, it is important to bear in mind that the verses they record and life stories they tell were in circulation in the cultural spaces, and even as the highbrow literati

---

[13] Ghulam Hamdani Mushafi, *Tazkira-i Hindī*, ed. Maulvi Abdul Haq (Delhi: Jamia Barqi Press, 1816–17 [reprint 1933]).

[14] Yar Muhammad Kahn Shaukat, *Farah Baksh* (Kanpur: Matbaʻ Nizami, 1871).

[15] Mir Mohsin Ali, *Sarāpā Sukhan* (Lucknow: Nawal Kishore, 1861).

[16] Nawab Mustafa Khan Shefta, *Tazkira-i Gulshan Be-Khār* (1835) (Lahore, Pakistan: Majlis Taraqqi-e Abdab, 1973).

ignored them, they were nonetheless ingrained in social memory. The authors of the *tazkira*s recovered women's versified compositions from dispersed sites of cultural reproduction, such as the marketplace, courtesan's *kotha*s, street corners, coffee houses, and tea stalls. It is indeed true that there were quite many women poets who had left behind compilations of their poems, and Ranj and Nadir found details about several poets from the incidental notices in literary texts as well. However, there were a great number of poets about whose lives and lyrics they learnt from conversations with friends at the coffee houses, interactions with scholars in poetic assemblies, nocturnal visits to the *kotha* of the courtesan, and functions and festivities in affluent households to which were invited professional singers and dancers. Quite like Foucault's 'erudite knowledge', women's literary compositions participated in but were still suppressed by the dominant literary culture; women scholars both reinforced and contested its aesthetic and sociocultural assumptions and paradigms.

Women's Reforms and Commemorative Texts: Representation of Female Education in the *Tazkiras*

Interestingly, following the publication of these *tazkira*s, we find several other literary critics writing biographical compendia of female poets, and in this respect, our authors could well be considered worthy trendsetters. In 1882, Maulvi Abdul Hai wrote a biographical compendium on women poets, entitled *Tazkira-i Shamīm Sukhan* (Biographies of Fragrant Voices), and a comparison with *BN* and *TN* reveals interesting similarities and differences in approach.[17] He was concerned with women's education and placed his efforts in composing the *tazkira* as resulting from his concern with their educational backwardness, which he thought was related to the social assumption that literacy was a male prerogative, redundant and irrelevant for women.[18] In this he was actually scarcely different from Ranj and Nadir, both of whom found the decline in women's education disconcerting and a matter of concern. Sharing his concerns, Adbul Hai says:

> In our country, Hindustan, women's education (*t'alīm-i masturāt*) is not heeded even though it is absolutely necessary. The benefits of education are known to everybody. It is a wealth that never diminishes (once acquired); a burglar cannot

---

[17] Maulvi Abdul Hai, *Tazkira-i Shamīm Sukhan* (Lucknow: Nawal Kishore, 1882 [1891 reprint]).

[18] Hai, *Tazkira-i Shamīm Sukhan*, 2–6.

steal it, and a tyrant cannot snatch it. The more you expend this wealth, the wealthier you become.[19]

Abdul Hai is quite condemnatory of gender exclusion in education and describes any such thought as 'a vulgar and unjust idea' (*behūda wa nā-wājib khyāl*).[20] Women's literacy is just as important as literacy among men because 'men have to attend to the outside affairs (*berūn*), and women are responsible for the management of the inner affairs (*andrūn*) of the household'.[21] 'The uneducated woman', says Hai, 'is a source of disorder and destruction in the household' (*fasād wa barbādi khāndān*).[22] Probably, this was the general tenor in women's *tazkira*s, but where Abdul Hai differs from the authors of *BN* and *TN* is in the treatment of the women poets.

In describing the poets, Ranj and Nadir have a distinct sense of the differences between the elite, respectable women, whom they describe as 'secluded women' (*pardah nashīn*), and the public performers, courtesans, and prostitutes, termed by both our authors as 'public women' (*bāzārī 'aurat*). These categories, it seems, were in currency in literary circles, but where Abdul Hai differs from these authors is in treating the latter as a polluting category; they were literate and skilled for sure, but they were, for him, still a threat to the moral order. Taking a dig at Ranj and Nadir (without mentioning them by name), he says: 'I have divided this work into two separate sections. In the first section, I discuss [the life and poetry of] the public women ('*aurat-i bāzārī*) and in the second, the secluded women ('*aurat-i pardah nashīn*). I thought it was shameful to remember the public women and the chaste women together at the same place without distinction, as the other *tazkira* writers had done.'[23]

His distaste for 'public women' is particularly strong, and it is with considerable reluctance that he acknowledges their influence in the literary field: 'When I was writing this *tazkira*, I found, despite my best efforts, very few respectable and chaste women knowledgeable in poetry, and it was the *bāzārī* women who dominated the field.'[24] He does not want respectable women (*pardah nashīn 'aurat*) to emulate them, nor does he want them to compose love poetry like they do: 'It is not our

---

[19] Hai, *Tazkira-i Shamīm Sukhan*, 2.

[20] Hai, *Tazkira-i Shamīm Sukhan*, 2.

[21] Hai, *Tazkira-i Shamīm Sukhan*, 2–3.

[22] Hai, *Tazkira-i Shamīm Sukhan*, 3.

[23] Hai, *Tazkira-i Shamīm Sukhan*, 5.

[24] Hai, *Tazkira-i Shamīm Sukhan*, 5.

intention that respectable women should be drawn towards poetry; and we do not want them to entertain thoughts of love (*'ishqiya khyālāt*).'[25]

We do not find a similar disdain for 'the woman of the *bāzār*' in *BN* and *TN*, and while their authors draw a distinction between them and the woman in the household, their biographical notes and snippets concerning 'public women' have elements of jest and banter, but not disdain. In describing their lives, they do not rest content with biographical details, but often go on to eloquently describe their looks, face, personalities, skin colour, and visible marks. Let us take a couple of examples here. Introducing a courtesan from Lucknow, Amir, the author of *BN*, describes her in the following words: 'She lives in Lucknow, and is as beautiful as a rose (*gulfām*). Among the peddlers of beauty in the market (*husn faroshān bāzārī*), she is a source of envy. She is a friend of infidelity (*be-wafāī*), and a foe of faithfulness (*wafādāri*).'[26] Noticing the dark colour of another talented courtesan, Naz, Ranj says: 'She comes from the market of enchantresses in Azimabad, and this is her ancestral homeland. She has an innocent face (*bholī surat*), delicate lips (*ghuncha dahn*), and is dark coloured (*sānwlā rang*); she is twenty-five years of age.'[27] Unimpressed by the appearance of a well-known courtesan of Agra, Basti, Ranj thus describes her: 'Even though her looks were ordinary, she had an endearing disposition.'[28] Our second *tazkira* writer, Nadir, is no different in this respect. This is how he describes a poetess, Dhab, whose untimely death reminded him of their mutual affection: 'She had a delicate body (*nāzuk badan*), pleasing form (*khush andām*), was beautiful (*khūbsūrat*), and had a virtuous temperament (*nek sīrat*). She was involved in pious activities (*neku afaʿāl*), and was seventeen or eighteen years of age.'[29] Appreciating her looks without much inhibition, he further adds: 'Her beauty was breathtaking; it was as if she had been specially created by God with his own hands (*kis qayāmat ka husn payā thā*; *aap Allah ne banāya thā*).'[30] Referring to their mutual liking for each other, he says: 'I had feelings of pure love (*dilī pāk*) for her. This chaste lady would also look at me with feelings of affection (*ulfat*).'[31] Or to take another instance from Naidr's *tazkira*, discussing the poetry of Umrao Jan, a famous courtesan in Delhi, the short

---

[25] Hai, *Tazkira-i Shamīm Sukhan*, 5.

[26] *BN*, 100.

[27] *BN*, 215.

[28] *BN*, 111.

[29] *TN*, 150.

[30] *TN*, 150.

[31] *TN*, 150.

biographical snippet has the following details about her: 'An adolescent, she is the spring of the bloom of youth (*nai' joban ki bahār*).'[32]

In the Persianate literary culture, the person and his poetry constituted each other, and in most literary *takiras*, discussions about an author's work or reproductions from his compositions were accompanied by details about his life. Our *tazkiras* about women poets – *BN* and *TN* – were following an entrenched practice where they prefaced their selection of verses with biographical snippets, usually terse and succinct. Of course, the mind–body distinction does not apply to this world, and it was unthinkable to separate the body of the artist from her reflexive mind. This explains the persistence of the body in these biographical notices; its charms and pleasures, and excess and limitations are described with the objective of enabling the reader to understand the poets' literary compositions. However, the world was changing, and Abdul Hai's *tazkira* captures the tensions therein. With a new moral universe on the horizon now, one that was informed by colonial modernity, these narrative forms were contested by the literati as immoral and tasteless. Abdul Hai finds the bodily descriptions in biographical compendia offensive, and expresses his distance from these *tazkiras* in the following words: 'In this work [his *tazkira*] I have not described, to the extent possible, the form and appearance (*khat-o-khāl*) of women, nor have I praised any of them for their beauty and physical charms.'[33]

Both Ranj and Nadir preface their work with a fairly detailed rumination on the lack of literacy among women and how this reflects the cultural backwardness among the people in Hindustan. Speaking the language of the modern social reformers, they see women's education as crucial to social development and, like them again, take their indifference to literacy as a reflection of the deep stasis and degeneration that marked the cultural practices of both the 'Hindus' and 'Muslims' here. Making a strong case for the necessity of education, Ranj argues that without knowledge that comes with education, a person is bound to remain uncivil and uncouth, and her or his life without worth; indeed, it is knowledge that distinguishes a human being from an animal. As he says: 'The only thing that differentiates a human being from an animal is knowledge. Knowledge releases her/him from ignorance (*jahālat*), and makes a person rational (*nātiq*).'[34] His reformist stance is nonetheless rooted in Indo-Persian culture, and one of the

---

[32] *TN*, 128.

[33] *TN*, 5.

[34] *BN*, 84–85. For the discussion on women's education in *BN*, see Appendix 2A.2 at the end of this chapter.

persons he cites to buttress his arguments in favour of education is the thirteenth-century Persian poet and scholar Shaikh Sadi.[35]

Given the overwhelming necessity of education for the development of appropriate norms of civility, right religious beliefs and practice, and for removing 'the darkness of ignorance', Ranj finds the lack of interest in education among Hindustani women particularly disconcerting. He accuses them of holding an attitude of contempt (*nafrat*) towards education and believes that they suffer an ignominious existence because of the lack of education.[36] Since they were 'deficient in reason' (*nāqis-ul-ʿaql*), they led miserable lives, and their miseries would not end with the end of their mortal lives either; ignorance leads them to profess and pursue sinful rituals and practices, and leads them into eternal damnation. 'Hindustan (*wilāyat-i Hind*)', he says, 'is accursed in that women here hold education in absolute contempt (*kulliyāt-o-nafrat*); and this is the reason for the ignominy and indignities (*zillat-o-khwārī*) they suffer here.'[37] He adds further: 'Leave everything else aside, this is also the reason why they are ignorant of the appropriate form of worship. Deficient in reason (*nāqis-ul-ʿaql*), they lose both this world and the world thereafter (*ākhirat*). These [Hindustani] women are so naive (*nādān*) that they don't even realize that ignorance (*jahl*) conceals truth (*maʿrifat*); an uneducated (*be-ʿilm*) person imbibes more darkness than the burnt-out lamp in the house.'[38]

Admittedly, there is a noticeable influence of colonial modernity in the way Ranj compares Hindustani women with British women. In England, he says, it is an established tradition – 'custom' (*riwāj*) – for both women and men to acquire education 'to fulfil their worldly and spiritual obligations'. Since the women there are well educated, 'they are never dependant (*muhtāj*) on men for reading or writing anything'.[39] To lend credence to his point, he further adds:

---

[35] *BN*, 85. Shaikh Sadi (1210–1291) was an influential Persian scholar who conveyed social truths and moral lessons through short stories written in the classical literary tradition. He is best known for *Bostān* (The Orchard) and *Gulistān* (The Rose Garden). For the reception of Sadi's work in early modern Hindustan, see Mana Kia, '*Adab* as Literary Form and Social Conduct: Reading the *Gulistan* in Late Mughal India,' in *No Tapping Around Philology: A Festschrift in Celebration and Honor of Wheeler McIntosh Thackston Jr.'s 70th Birthday*, ed. Alireza Korangy and Daniel J. Sheffield, 281–308 (Wiesbaden, Germany: Harrassowitz Verlag, 2014).

[36] *BN*, 85.

[37] *BN*, 85.

[38] *BN*, 85.

[39] *BN*, 85.

'One marvels at the quality of female scholars (*'allāma-i 'asr*) and intellectuals (*fahām-i daurān*) there; and you cannot but wonder at the dedication with which women [in England] keep themselves busy in taking lessons and imparting education.'[40] Invoking the modern progressivist notion of time and discipline, he accuses the Hindustani women of wasting time in frivolous pursuits, gossiping around, spending long hours in decorating their bodies, and so on. As against 'the British women (*mastūrāt-i wilāyat-i inglisia*) who are deeply immersed in learning and acquiring knowledge', the women here 'idle away their time in gossip and sleep. Their only concern is to adorn their bodies (*tan parwarī*) and decorate (*tazai'n*) themselves'.[41] The Eurocentric implications of the modernist teleology in his formulations here are discursively set aside in the repeated invocation of Persian scholars, in particular Sadi, suggesting to the readers that his reformist position is well within their own cultural world.[42] This is actually obvious from the choice of his subject – the women poets in the Persianate world, in particular Hindustan – who are presented in the *tazkira* as inspiring examples, models of emulation for contemporary women. Furthermore, while he admits to the better position of British women, he realizes that this is historically contingent and is not located in the hierarchically inferior 'essence' of the culture in Hindustan. It is distressing, he says, that Hindustani women are not drawn to education even as 'they possess sound intellect and refined temperament (*fazā'il aur sharā'if*)';[43] there was, and that is the point he is drawing home here, no difference in terms of mental make-up and aptitude that explains the relative educational backwardness of Hindustani women when compared to the European 'ladies' (*mai'm*).[44]

Like Ranj, our other *tazkira* writer, Nadir, sees his work as related to his reformist inclinations, and he hopes to see the women scholars mentioned in his biographical compendia inspire women to welcome education, and reject their present condition marked by indifference, even hostility towards literacy. He views education as the real jewel that educated women give to their children, while the illiterate women are constrained to content with handing over to their children ornaments that portend strife and ruination:

---

40 *BN*, 85.
41 *BN*, 86.
42 *BN*, 85.
43 *BN*, 85–86.
44 *BN*, 86.

If a woman is educated (*khwāndah*) she would adorn her child with the ornaments of knowledge (*'ilm ke zewar*). If that's not the case, she would, like any other illiterate woman, adorn her daughter with material ornaments (*zewar-i zahiri*), and deck her with gold and silver jewellery, which is a source of the ruination of many children, as is routinely reported in the news-reports (*akhbār*).[45]

In an important departure from the aristocratic *nawabi* culture, he argues that social respectability or *sharf* comes not from birth, family, or descent but from education and learning (*t'alīm aur ta'allum*); and yet 'it is often noticed that men these days keep their women uneducated (*be-'ilm*), under the mistaken belief that this would enhance their respectability'.[46] In her work on the Indo-Muslim reformist literature, Gail Minault notices a shift in the meaning of *sharīf* (plural *ashrāf*) in the nineteenth century from 'nobility' derived from birth and lineage to one obtained through cultured behaviour, knowledge, and discipline. As she puts it: 'A *sharif* gentleman [in the nineteenth century] was pious without being wasteful, educated without being pedantic, and restrained in his expression of emotion.'[47] This semantic shift is evident in Nadir when he places the *sharf* of a *sharīf* to her/his knowledge and education.

Nadir rejects the progressivist notion of time, and in presenting his case in favour of women's education he does not hold modern Europe as a paradigmatic model, but instead exhorts Hindustani women to return to their own past, and derive inspiration and find worthy models for emulation from within their own histories. Among the Hindus, he believes, there is a long history of creative women writing in Sanskrit, and, as instances of the same, he mentions Parvati (the consort of Lord Shiva) and Sita (the spouse of Lord Ram). There were, he asserts, women in the ancient period who could read and write in vernacular languages and dialects, in particular Prakrit and Bhasa.[48] In the pre-British period, he believes, in most localities there were schools for women's education (*zanāne madrase*) and educational associations (*'ilm-i majlis*); in an obvious rejection of the teleology of colonial modernity, he sees the modern educational institutions as

---

[45] *TN*, 46. For Nadir's views on women's education, see Appendix 2A.1, at the end of this chapter.

[46] *TN*, 45.

[47] Gail Minault, *Secluded Scholars: Women's Education and Muslim Social Reform in Colonial India* (New Delhi: Oxford University Press, 1998), 4–5.

[48] *TN*, 45.

their imitations: 'The educational institutions (*anjumans*) and societies that have sprung up today are modelled on these earlier associations'.[49]

Referring to the Muslims, he says that the lack of literacy among their women is particularly disheartening since they are enjoined by their faith to acquire knowledge.[50] Like the Hindus, they have also had a distinguished history of women's participation in literary activities, and in that context he particularly mentions Aisha, Prophet Muhammad's wife, Bibi Fatima, his daughter, and Zubaida Khatun, the wife of the famous Abbasid ruler Harun Rashid. In addition, he mentions several biographical compendia that refer to women as poets and scholars in the Islamic world.[51] For both Hindus and Muslims, it was imperative to provide education to their women, and like the reformers, he relates their education to the need to reform the domestic spaces; educated women would make better companions for their spouses and teachers to their children. 'It is actually incumbent (*wājib*) on god-fearing spouses,' he says, 'to acquire education so that they learn their rights of service (*khidmat guzārī ke haq*) toward their spouse, and know the virtues of preserving one's chastity and keep away from sins knowing the punishments that accrue in following them.'[52]

It is interesting that Nadir does not see this malaise of the lack of education among women as uniformly applicable to all the communities and caste groups in Hindustan. Instead, he cites his own caste group, the *kāyastha*, as an exception and presents them as leading the movement for the education for women:

> You still find *kāyasth* women who can converse in Persian, and they are certainly the shining stars of the community; in fact, women in this community (*qaum*) are embracing English, as well, and why should it be otherwise. It was one of the first communities [in Hindustan] to have learned Persian and has similarly been the earliest community to have taken a fancy for English as well. Surely, if they don't take the initiative in women's education (*tā'līm-i niswān*), no one else would.[53]

If caste is one axis around which he ruptures the unity of his narrative, religion is another. Toeing the line of the British imperial scholars and statesmen, he accuses the 'Muslim invasion' for the decline in women's education, and lauds the British for changing things and for taking definite steps to improve their condition. As he says:

---

[49]   *TN*, 45.

[50]   *TN*, 47.

[51]   *TN*, 47–49.

[52]   *TN*, 46.

[53]   *TN*, 46–47.

Look here! When the Hindus were in power, women were getting educated, and there was considerable progress [in this matter].... The Muslim invasion destroyed (*m'adum*) the pace of the movement. Later, supported by the British government, we had the rule of the English Company ('Company Bahadur'), and the push for education received a new lease of life. After the revolt of 1857, Queen Victoria took control over the affairs of Hindustan, and since then the department [of education] has received a lot more consideration [than ever before].[54]

Historians have extensively written on women's reforms, and, working on different regions and communities, their work reveals the extent to which the movement for women's education was tied to the anxieties relating to the perceived threats to cultural values and religion. For men, in addition, these anxieties were also linked to new norms of manliness centred on notions of companionate marriage and familial intimacies.[55] In an important intervention in the debate, Partha Chatterjee has argued that the late nineteenth century saw the 'resolution of the women's question' with the construction of the 'inner' domain – the domain of marriage, family, and conjugal bonds – and its separation from the 'outer' domain, which was the space where men worked, earned their wages, and served the state.[56] While men were indeed sovereign masters within the inner spaces, the responsibility for their management fell on women, who were then expected to earn their spouses' affections, educate and discipline their children, and manage their homes within their modest resources, all of which required women to acquire education. The loss of power in the public domain was compensated by the construction of a

---

[54] *TN*, 121.

[55] The literature on women's reforms in the colonial period is considerable, and ever-growing, but for a good overview, see Sumit Sarkar and Tanika Sarkar (eds.), *Women and Social Reform in Modern India: A Reader* (Bloomington: Indiana University Press, 2008); Geraldine Forbes, *Women in Modern India* (New Delhi: Cambridge University Press, 2015 [reprint]); Minault, *Secluded Scholars*. Also see Indrani Chatterjee (ed.), *Unfamiliar Relations: Family and History in South Asia* (New Brunswick, NJ: Rutgers University Press, 2004); Rochona Majumdar, *Marriage and Modernity: Family Values in Colonial Bengal* (Durham, NC: Duke University Press, 2009); and Mytheli Sreenivas, *Wives, Widows, and Concubines: The Conjugal Family Ideal in Colonial India* (Bloomington and Indianapolis: Indiana University Press, 2008).

[56] Partha Chatterjee, 'The Nationalist Resolution of the Women's Question', in *Recasting Women: Essays in Indian Colonial History*, ed. Kumkum Sangari and Sudesh Vaid, 233–53 (New Brunswick, NJ: Rutgers University Press, 1990). This influential essay is reprinted in the collection of his essays entitled *Empire and Nation: Selected Essays* (New York: Columbia University Press, 2010), 116–35.

sovereign and insulated inner space that was led and controlled by men but required educated and disciplined women for its effective management. In a significant critique of Chatterjee, Tanika Sarkar points out that his arguments do not take into account the agency and subjectivity of women, and impose a picture of homogeneity when, in fact, the domestic arrangements in the period displayed considerable diversity, tenuousness, and change. He has also been criticized for imposing a dichotomy between the 'inner' and the 'outer' domains, when in historical reality they were inter-penetrative spaces that could hardly be conceptually distinguished from each other.[57] In her study of the discourses on family and familial intimacies in Urdu journals and newspapers, Asiya Alam's study draws our attention to the voices of contestations, and how 'feminist' scholars challenged the emphasis on domesticity in the women's reform movements in the nineteenth century.[58]

These are important points of critique, and warn us against constructing determinist models of social change. They also force us to reflect on the contestations within the reformist movement, particularly in matters of women's reforms and their educational uplift. While the reformers seemed to agree that women's education was necessary for the reorganization of domestic spaces, they were less sure about the pedagogy and curriculum of instruction. The spread of literacy among the Muslim service gentry and elites was accompanied by anxieties about the impact of books on the organization of social life. The apprehensions that reading provoked were particularly marked in the case of women, and there are interesting discussions in reformist texts on books that they should read and those that they should stay away from. In the Indo-Muslim reformist literature, the list of 'suitable literature' included household manuals, religious texts, didactic novels, works on Islamic law, and school textbooks.[59] They are instructed to shun

---

[57] Tanika Sarkar, *Hindu Wife, Hindu Nation: Community, Religion and Cultural Nationalism* (New Delhi: Permanent Black, 2001); also see Minault, *Secluded Scholars*, 6–7; and Charu Gupta (ed.), *Gendering Colonial India: Reforms, Print and Communalism* (New Delhi: Orient Blackswan, 2012).

[58] Asiya Alam, *Women, Islam and Familial Intimacy in Colonial South Asia* (Leiden: Brill, 2021).

[59] In his work for the instruction of women, Ashraf Ali Thanawi, a reformist scholar, shares his anxieties about books, and the need to control and supervise women's reading habits. In his reformist text, *Bihishti Zewar* ('The Ornament of Paradise'), he provides a fairly detailed list of books that women should and another list of books that they should not read. Barbara Daly Metcalf, *Perfecting Women: Maulana Ashraf Ali Thanawi's Bihishti Zewar – A Partial Translation with Commentary* (Berkeley and Los Angeles: University of California Press, 1992).

love poetry, mythical tales, erotic literature, and texts that promote superstitions.[60] It was, of course, not expected of them to read women's poetry, least of all the poems of courtesans, prostitutes, dancing girls, and street performers. This is where our *tazkira*s differ from the modern reformers, even as their authors share their concern for women's education.

Both Ranj and Nadir claim to have brought out their compendia on women poets only because they hoped that their example would serve to inspire women and remind them of the contribution of their gender in shaping the literary culture in Hindustan. In their compilations, there are verses of the elite courtesans, ordinary prostitutes, dancers, and singers performing in the marketplaces, and street performers trying their hand with lyrical compositions. Not only do they want respectable (*ashraf*) men and women to read them but also follow them in their acquisition of education, skills in language, and aesthetic and literary acumen. Our *tazkira*s represent an important strain in the Persianate culture in Hindustan, one which recognized the courtesan, and even the prostitute, as imbibing and enriching the literary *adāb*, or the norms and postulates of aesthetics and literary expression. Under the mid-Victorian ideology of companionate marriage and closed family, this particular facet in the literary culture was under stress during the colonial period, but it never quite died down.

It has been argued by Durba Mitra that modern knowledge about India, a joint project of European scholars and their Indian counterparts, was centrally shaped by perceptions of deviant female sexuality. In the nineteenth century, the emergent knowledge tradition had found in the figure of the prostitute a somatic representation of the ever-present deviant female sexuality; and the need to control and discipline the prostitute informed the understanding of social life in India. Clearly, the prostitute was not a person anymore, but an idea that represented deviant female sexuality. Focusing on her eroticized and deviant body, modern knowledge about social life sought to control and discipline female sexuality.[61] While her thesis is interesting, there is an attribution of insularity that

---

[60] For a discussion on the 'suitable literature', see Minault, *Secluded Scholars*, 58–104.

[61] Durba Mitra, *Indian Sex Life: Sexuality and the Colonial Origins of Modern Social Thought* (Princeton: Princeton University Press, 2020). For a discussion on perceptions of prostitution and female sexual deviance in nineteenth-century Europe, see Judith R. Walkowitz, *Prostitution and Victorian Society: Women, Class, and the State* (Cambridge: Cambridge University Press, 1982); Judith R. Walkowitz, *City of Dreadful Delight: Narratives of Sexual Danger in Late-Victorian London* (Chicago: University of Chicago Press, 1992); and Alain Corbin, *Women for Hire: Prostitution and Sexuality in France after 1850*, trans. Alan Sheridan (Cambridge, MA: Harvard University Press, 1990).

is problematic; there were contestations and interesting alternative formulations within the knowledge tradition over issues of women's agency that her model fails to encapsulate. In the texts that we are studying here, women are represented as creative and aesthetically informed human beings, and while the physical attributes of the 'public women' are not infrequently mentioned in sensorial terms, these descriptions are not allowed to overwhelm the dominant narrative centred on their mental skills, linguistic expertise, aesthetic sensitivities, and creative attributes. They are appreciated for these talents and skills, and all women are exhorted to derive inspiration from their examples.

Sources of Information: Written Texts, Oral Performances, and Bazaar Gossips

How did the authors of our *tazkira*s collect their information? How did they find details about their lives, including their physical appearances, behavioural qualities, particular skills and talents, and the names and backgrounds of their parents, tutors, patrons, and spouses? Wherefrom did they discover the verses of the female poets mentioned in their *tazkira*s? It is often not known and recognized that women wrote not just a couple of poems, but the more enterprising among them even left behind their *diwān*s[62] as well. Ranj found some of these *diwān*s in the libraries (*maktab*), and several others in the collections of patrons, connoisseurs, and poets; but there were still a good number of them that were destroyed in the ravages of time. In their biographical entries, both Ranj and Nadir take care to mention if the poetess under discussion had a *diwān* or *diwān*s to her credit, and it is quite striking that the number of such women was quite substantial. It is a reflection of an important erasure in the history of literary culture that these *diwān*s are scarcely ever mentioned in the literary *tazkira*s, nor are they recognized by their modern commentators. Nadir refers to Umrao Begum, bearing the pen name Abid, as 'the second Makhfi' (the pen name of Zebun Nisa, the daughter of the Mughal ruler Aurangzeb) and the author of two poetic compilations or *diwān*s, one in Persian and the other in Urdu.[63] An accomplished scholar (*fāzīla*), Mah also wrote two *diwān*s, one a collection of her Persian and the other her Urdu poems.[64] Alim, the chief consort (*khās mahal*) of the ruler of Awadh, Nawab Wajid Ali Shah, was a woman of multiple talents; she was an accomplished musician and

---

[62] A *diwān* is a compilation of a poet's compositions.
[63] *TN*, 177.
[64] *BN*, 198; *TN*, 189–90.

enjoyed playing the sitar. She was also a talented poet and had a *diwān* to her credit.[65] Of course, it was not unusual for courtesans and prostitutes to have their own collection of poems as well. Nadir mentions one courtesan, Ali, as the author of a *diwān*.[66] Sadr Mahal, a poetess of Lucknow, wrote two *diwān*s: *Bādshāhnāma* (The Book of Kings) and *Guldasta* (A Bouquet of Flowers).[67]

This is by no means an exhaustive list, and there are many more women poets with *diwān*s of their own that are mentioned in our *tazkira*s. And yet the nineteenth-century critic scarcely, if ever, mentioned them, and nor did their latter-day commentators. In the literary *tazkira*s, exceptions apart, these women and their collection of *ghazal*s fail to find mention, let alone an appreciation of their efforts. There were a few exceptions indeed, and one such exception was Chanda, a courtesan based in Hyderabad, whom our *tazkira* writers describe as 'the first woman to have written a *diwān* in Urdu'.[68] An exceptional woman who patronized poets, soldiers, wrestlers, and archers with the same enthusiasm, her skills with words won the approval of British officials as well.[69] We will be discussing her in greater detail in the following chapter, but suffice it here to mention that she was one of the female poets who received a better press than the other courtesans mentioned in our *tazkira*s.

Of course, not all the women's *diwān*s were accessible to Ranj and Nadir, and they also admit to receiving relevant information from incidental references to women poets and their verses in several biographical compendia available to them. Nadir admits to reproducing the *ghazal* of Mahbub Mahal from another *tazkira*, *Sarāpā Sukhan* (Eloquence Incarnate).[70] He also mentions that the verses of Tanvir, the 'radiant like rose' (*gul andām*), were taken from Hakim Qutbuddin Batin's *Gulshan-i Be-Khizān* (An Ever-Enthralling Garden).[71] While these textual sources certainly helped in the compilation of these *tazkira*s, the more important life stories and verses came from aural sources – through personal interactions

---

[65] *TN*, 177–78.

[66] *TN*, 179.

[67] *TN*, 174.

[68] *BN*, 127–28; *TN*, 139–41.

[69] *BN*, 127–28; *TN*, 139–41. For details about this extraordinary woman, see Shweta Sachdeva Jha, 'Tawa'if as a Poet: Rethinking Women's Self-Representation,' in *Speaking of the Self*, ed. Anshu Malhotra and Sibhan Lambert-Hurley, 141–64 (Durham and London: Duke University Press); and Scott Kugle, 'Mah Laqa Bai and Gender: The Language, Poetry and Performance of a Courtesan in Hyderabad', *Comparative Studies of South Asia, Africa and the Middle East* 30, no. 3 (2020): 365–85.

[70] *TN*, 191.

[71] *TN*, 134.

with women poets or a letter from a friend or acquaintance wherein he mentions his visit to the salon of the courtesan, a tutor sharing a verse of his student, or a husband of his spouse. Nadir, for instance, was provided with the verses of Gunna, a poetess in Lucknow, from one of his well-wishers (*mahrbān*); and it was again one of his friends who provided him with information about Yad, a Mughal princess who used to take lessons in poetry from him.[72] The *ghazals* of the courtesans Lalan and Khairan were recited to Nadir by their vocalist who accompanied them in their dancing performances.[73] Similarly, the biographical details and the poem by Amir Khan Shararat, a courtesan settled in Chawri Bazaar in Delhi, were provided to Ranj by his friend (*dost*), Amir Khan Munir, with whom she shared her lyrical compositions.[74]

Both Ranj and Nadir received poems by post from their 'friends and well-wishers' and picked couplets from conversations in the marketplaces, coffee houses, and feasts and dinners as well.[75] They also happened to know some of the courtesans mentioned in their biographical compendia and refer to their interactions with them. In one instance, Ranj mentions meeting a courtesan, Basti, at a British government function: 'This writer (*rāqim*) had to go to Agra to attend a government function. She [Basti] had come to visit me. She was not particularly charming, but carried herself well. She has disappeared (*mafqūd-ul khabar*) now.'[76] Awestruck by the charms of Muhran Dhab, a young 'chaste Hindu' (*Hindunī pardah-nashīn*) poet, about seventeen–eighteen years in age, Nadir says: 'Her beauty was intoxicating, and yet she was unconcerned with the worldly delights.' Mourning her sudden death, he refers to his deep love for her, and how she reciprocated his affections with coy and timid glances: 'I was in love (*muhabbat*) with this chaste woman. She used to reciprocate by throwing a glance of affection (*nazr-i 'ulfat*) toward me.'[77] Indeed, personal relations with talented courtesans were an important means for the collection of life stories and verses of poets mentioned in these biographical compendia.

The point to note here is that in the Persianate literary culture, literacy and orality worked together, and it would be erroneous to see one as replacing the other. The extent to which orality and literacy reinforced each other is highlighted by Ranj when he discusses the sources for his information, and how his evidence

---

[72] *TN*, 186–87, 206.

[73] *TN*, 189.

[74] *BN*, 161–62.

[75] *TN*, 178–79, 192, 143–44.

[76] *BN*, 111–12.

[77] *TN*, 150–51.

came from both the books he found in libraries and the conversations he had with his friends and well-wishers: 'To the extent possible, I rummaged around and collected [the extant material] and produced the present work. There are some in this volume whose poems were recovered from long-standing libraries (*kutub-i qadīm*), and there are others whose compositions came to me through friends and reputable men (*ahbāb-o-arbāb*).'[78] It was within this space of communication where orality co-existed with literacy that, as I argued in one of my earlier works, the early modern period saw the development of the performative public sphere in South Asia.[79]

Norms of Criticism: *Sulh-i Kul* in Literary Spaces

There is a lively, if bitter, exchange of words between Ranj and Nadir in which both express their reservations about the work of the other.[80] The barbs between them reveal important dimensions of the literary culture, in particular, the literary *adāb*, or the norms that governed writing and criticism. Reflecting an important shift in *adāb*, it was now unacceptable to provide information without due verification, and it is for this reason that the charge of fabrication – of weaving unverified stories – stings the most for both Ranj and Nadir. They also accused each other of copying details from the work of the other without due acknowledgement.[81] In a language that was clearly hurtful, Ranj described Nadir's *tazkira* as based on 'imaginary and bogus women poets' (*farzī aur khyālī shā'ira*),[82] and given the fabricated life stories and unverified verses that abound in his work, it was no more than 'a collection of trash (*raddiyāt*)'.[83] Respect for the masters in the field and humility (*firotnī*) are the other norms of literary *adāb* that Ranj reminded Nadir and his other critics:

> The illiterate (*jāhil*) people enhance their respectability by berating their masters (*ustād*). It is of course true that in the presence of blind people, the one with both eyes would be called a king (*rāja*), but such people are ultimately exposed and put to shame. The primary quality (*nishān-i khās*) of a cultured person

[78] *BN*, 81–83.
[79] Farhat Hasan, *Paper, Performance, and the State: Social Change and Political Culture in Mughal India* (New Delhi: Cambridge University Press, 2021).
[80] *BN*, 90–91; *TN*, 273–80.
[81] *BN*, 90; *TN*, 274–75.
[82] *BN*, 90.
[83] *TN*, 274.

(*sharīf*) is humility (*firotnī*), and without that quality, a person is all conceit and shallow – a castaway chip of a diamond stone.[84]

Nadir, of course, not only rejected these insinuations but turned them around, accusing Ranj of copying from his work and, in the choice of his words, abandoning the *adāb* of literature. He found the tenor of his critique and Ranj's harsh language particularly hurtful. His critique did go against the *adāb* of literary criticism, for it was expected of critics to express their disagreements within an inclusive space that tolerated difference and in a language that was polite and civil. Interestingly, responding to Ranj, Nadir raises the issue of the need to practise *sulh-i kul* or absolute tolerance in the literary space. *Sulh-i kul* was, as we know, a concept that stood for an inclusive political culture in Mughal India, and among the ruling elites it was invoked to promote tolerance (and even appreciation) of difference. When Nadir invokes it in his response to Ranj, he is drawing attention to the need to practise civility and tolerance in literary spaces. In their own ways, despite their mutual differences, both Ranj and Nadir were, insofar as they brought to light women's poetic compositions, pushing for a literary *sulh-i kul*, in which literate voices were not silenced because of gender or the choice of profession (as in the case of the courtesans and prostitutes).

Appendix 2A.1

Durga Prashad Nadir on Women's Education and Their Literary Pasts[85]

Look at how God's authority has made the human species the most noble of His creations (*ashraf-ul-makhluqāt*), and education and learning (*ta'līm aur ta'allum*) the means to acquire social respectability (*sharf*). Even so, it is often noticed that men these days, even as they know that this would enhance their respectability, keep their women uneducated (*be-'ilm*). In the past, there were, among the Hindus, such illustrious scholars of Sanskrit as Sri Parvati, Sitaji, and so on; during that time, there were also women who composed poems (*kabitā*), and they would be discussed in a separate volume. From the time that Prakrit and Bhasa became languages, women had been learning the skills of writing and reading. It is stated in *Bhoj Parbandh* that during the reign of the Raja, there were madrasas for women (*zanāne madrase*), and in every district subdivision

---

[84]   *BN*, 91.
[85]   *TN*, 45–49.

(*parganā*), there were educational associations (*'ilm-i majlis*) as well. The *anjuman*s and societies that have sprung up today are modelled on these earlier associations.

The Hindus of respectable families these days familiarize the child widows (*bāl bidhwā*) and young barren women (*naujawān rānd 'aurat*) with *nāgrī* or *gurmukhī*; and teach them lessons in scriptures, such as Gita, *Ānuk Sikh Mani*, and so on. They are constrained to do so because it is obligatory (*farz*) for a widow to devote herself to the worship of God. For a married woman [that is not required, because] devotion to her spouse is considered as the real form of worship. It is of course absolutely true that 'an illiterate person cannot recognize God', and so it is that widows are provided knowledge so that they can understand God better. It is actually incumbent (*wajib*) on god-fearing wives as well to acquire education so that they learn their rights of service (*khidmat guzārī ke haq*) towards their spouses, and know the virtues of preserving one's chastity and keep away from sins knowing the punishments that accrue from following them. This is what is emphasized by Munshi Makhan Lal in his tract (*risala*) 'On the Rights of the Wife and the Husband' (*Ba huqūq-i zan wa shauhar*), through the sayings of the seers (*rishi*s) that he cites in translation.

Indeed, if a woman is educated (*khwāndah*), she would adorn her child with the ornaments of knowledge (*'ilm ke zewar*). If that's not the case, she would, like any other illiterate woman, adorn her daughter with material ornaments (*zewar-i zāhiri*), and deck her with gold and silver jewellery, which is a source of the ruination of many children, as is routinely reported in the news reports (*akhbār*). The sad thing is that the people of my community are not concerned about these issues, and, unfortunately, if a Hindustani, in particular, a Hindu brethren, raises these issues, his audience gets upset, and either fall silent (in disapproval) or respond with such inappropriate retorts as: 'You should, sir, initiate this [women's education] in your household, and then others would draw inspiration and develop interest (*shauq*).'

This is what I say: 'Those whose hearts are imbued with desire (*shauq*) need nobody to instruct them' (*Shauq dar har dil ki bāshad, rahbarī darkār nest*). If you don't trust the wisdom that comes with experience, then here is a small detail that you could consider investigating: In *qasba* Kol (Aligarh), before the revolt, there resided a *khatri* woman of respectable lineage and genuine nobility. Married to a resident of Benaras, she was so well accomplished in Persian, mathematics, and accountancy that she could write her own letters and keep a record of her household budget. Nobody within her community threw taunts at her! Why have these commendable ways of doing things ceased to continue in our times?

Listen, look around, and you will come across *khatri*s and Brahmin women who know *nāgrī* and *gurmukhī*. You still find *kāyasth* women who can converse in Persian, and they are certainly the shining stars of the community; in fact, women in this community (*qaum*) are embracing English as well, and why should that not be so! It was one of the first communities [in Hindustan] to have learned Persian, and have similarly been the earliest community to have taken a fancy for English as well. Surely, if they don't take the initiative in women's education (*taʿlīm-i niswān*), no one would.

What should I say about the Muslims on this issue [women's education]? They have been instructed by their faith to provide education to their women, and women in respectable families are indeed educated. At the most basic level, once a child reaches the age of four years, four months, and four days, she or he begins taking lessons from the Koran, and this is in obedience to the instruction of the Prophet [Muhammad] that 'the search for knowledge is obligatory for all the Muslim men and women'.

Muslim women have actually taken Arabic, Persian, and Urdu poetry to great heights of perfection, and so it is that Persian biographical compendia – such as *Mirʾāt-ul Khyāl* (The Mirror of Imagination) (the concluding portion), *Jawāhir-ul Hijāb* (The Veiled Jewels), *Kalimātush Shuʿara* (The Eloquent Poets), *Muntkhab-ul Latīf* (A Compendium of Refined Persons), *Gulistān-i Musarrat* (Garden of Joy), *Malahāt-ul Haqqān* (Truthful Stories), *Kharita-i Jawāhir* (A Bag of Jewels), *Riyāz-ul Firdaus* (Training for the Heaven), and so on – include women's poetic compositions. In Urdu, the concluding portion of Hakim Qasim's *tazkira*, *Guldasta-i Nāzniyan* (Bouquet of the Alluring Beloveds) mentions women poets, and sporadic references to women are found in the following *tazkira*s: *Gulshan-i Bekhār* (A Rose Garden Without Thorns), *Makhzan-i Shuʿara* (Storehouse of Poetry), *Tabaqāt-i Shuʿara* (A Compendium of Poets), and *Nādir-ul Azkār* (Priceless Utterances). The concluding part of *Bahāristān-i Gul*, which is written in Urdu but includes Arabic poetry, is similarly adorned with the verses of women poets. Even so, if you go through them, you will not find a Hindustani woman (*Hindnī*) in any of these books. Indeed, in rare cases, you would come across the stray name of some prostitute (*ramjanī*) or a dancing girl/performer (*pātra*), but you cannot trust these names for the information about them comes from unreliable evidence....

One of the important problems, deserving of investigation, is whether women, among the Muslims, are permitted to compose and recite poems. On this issue, we know from Abul Lais' *Jawāhir-ul ʿAjāʾib*, or The Priceless Jewels (citing the work of the second Abu Hanifa, *Bostān*) that once Prophet Muhammad asked his

spouse Hazrat Aisha, when she returned home after visiting her relations, if she
had brought him a gift. Aisha recited a verse and asked it to be counted as a gift....
Similarly, Fatima (the Prophet's daughter) composed an elegy (*marsiya*) for the
Prophet, and one of its verses, taken from *Jawāhir*, is reproduced here:

> The afflictions I have suffered are of such intensity
> They can convert any bright day into the darkness of despair.

We are furthermore informed from *Insha-i Mufīdun Nisā* (Letters of Mufidun
Nisa) that Hazrat Khadija (wife of Prophet Muhammad) and Zubaida Khatun,
spouse of Harun Rashid, the Abbasid caliph, were accomplished poets as well.

What better evidence is required to prove the permissibility of women
reciting poems [in Islam]? The wives of the Prophet recited verses, and he gave
suggestions to improve them. The wives of his successors were poets [and were
free to compose poems]. Certainly, the only condition [among Muslims] is that
the poetic compositions should be about God, the Prophet Muhammad, and his
companions; they could be supplications before God (*munājāt*), reiterations of the
unity of God (*tauhidi*), verses composed in remembrance of Prophet Muhammad
(*na't*), or those written in honour of the Prophet or his companions (*manqabat*).
In no case should their poetry be about profane love (*'ishqiya*).

Appendix 2A.2

Hakim Fasihuddin Ranj on Women's Education: English Women and the Inadequacies of Women in Hindustan[86]

It is incumbent (*lāzim*) on human beings to seek knowledge and learn new skills.
As humans, we should do things in our lives for which we are remembered after
death. Life is a priceless possession and should not be wasted. Nobody should
surround oneself with the darkness of ignorance and rue one's fate. Talent and
knowledge enhance the status of a person, and our ancestors have rightly said,
'Civility comes with knowledge.' The only thing that differentiates a human
being from an animal is knowledge. Knowledge releases one from ignorance
(*jahālat*), and makes a person rational (*nātiq*). [Shaikh] Sadi has said, 'Ignorance
comes from the lack of education.' The difference between worship and pretence
is only known to those who have the essence of humanness (*insāniyat*) in them.

---

[86] *BN*, 84–89.

An illiterate person (*jāhil*) is a living embodiment of shameless faithlessness; after all, 'an illiterate person cannot recognize God'.

We should reflect on the efforts that were undertaken in the kingdoms of the past for the acquisition of knowledge and see how educated people gained wide recognition. In several places of the world (*wilāyat*), it is still a custom (*dastūr*) that women and men deem it obligatory to acquire education and learn enough to fulfil their worldly and spiritual obligations. In England, it is a long continuing tradition (*riwāj*) that all women – elites and ordinary – acquire education and are never dependent (*muhtāj*) on men for reading or writing anything. One marvels at the quality of female scholars ('*allāma-i 'asr*) and intellectuals (*fahām-i daurān*) there; and you cannot but wonder at the dedication with which women [in England] keep themselves busy in taking lessons and imparting education. Hindustan (*wilāyat-i Hind*), on the other hand, is accursed in that women here hold education in absolute contempt (*kulliyāt-o-nafrat*); and this is the reason for the ignominy and indignities (*zillat-o-khwārī*) they suffer. Leave everything else aside, this is also the reason why they are ignorant of the appropriate form of worship. Deficient in reason (*nāqis-ul-'aql*), they lose both this world and the world thereafter (*ākhirat*). These [Hindustani] women are so naive (*nādān*) that they don't even realize that ignorance (*jahl*) conceals truth (*m 'ārifat*); an uneducated (*be-'ilm*) person imbibes more darkness than the burnt-out lamp in the house. As [Shaikh] Sadi puts it, 'even the arrow (changes its course) and runs away from an illiterate person (*jāhil*)'.

It is weird ('*ajab*) and distressing, and shameful for sure, that women in Hindustan (*masturāt-i Hind*) are averse to education, even as they possess sound intellect and refined temperament (*fazā'il aur sharā'if*). Compare them with the British women (*mastūrāt-i wilāyat-i inglisia*) who are deeply immersed in learning and acquiring knowledge; a British lady (*maim*) – an elite or an ordinary woman – is accomplished in the knowledge of craft and literature. She is without equal in education (*t'alīm*) and knowledge of language (*zubān dānī*). British women acquire education and instruction from the best government schools (*sarkāri school*), and they are all, without exception, well trained to reap the benefits of knowledge. When an illiterate woman (*jāhila*) comes into their contact, she is immediately impressed and develops a strong urge to attain education. The only preoccupations they have concern the perfection of skills; and the conversations they have are all about knowledge. In contrast, women in Hindustan idle away their time in gossip and sleep. Their only concern is to adorn their bodies (*tan parwarī*) and decorate (*tazai'n*) themselves. If only they could devote just one period in the eight periods (*pahr*) of a day for the acquisition of education, they would gradually but surely lose their state of ignorance and overcome their inadequacies.

They would then develop a new awareness in their worship (*'ibādat*), and would refrain from unwittingly engaging in despicable activities that make them sinners (*gunehgār*).

Appendix 2A.3

Durga Prashad Nadir on Women's Reforms in China[87]

Let God be praised! I had said in the previous section that we do not have a book in Urdu that informs us about the situation of women in China; if there were one, I would have discussed their condition as well. During the period of the publication of this book, an article appeared in *Oudh Akhbar* (issue no. 6, September 1874) that was certainly useful for our purpose here. The objective of the piece was to draw attention to a book, entitled *Tushan*, or 'Guiding Women' (*hidāyat-i niswān*), that was much in circulation, and people there moulded their lives according to its injunctions. A translated version of some of its instructions, which are so very useful for people in every region and city, belonging to any community and service group (*har qaum-o millat-i rozgār*), are presented below:

- It is obligatory (*lāzim*) for girls to consider their elder brothers and sisters as equivalent to their parents.
- They should greet the elders in the household once in the morning, and then again late in the evening.
- They should always remain keen and desirous of their approval.
- If they lose their temper and yell at them, they [the girls] should bow down their heads and utter not a word; instead, they should refrain from repeating the things that upset them.
- They should strive to acquire education and learn to read and write.
- They should read the books of scholars who lived before them but should strictly keep away from books with erotic themes (*'ishqiya mazāmīn*).
- It is absolutely necessary (*amr-i zarūrī*) for them to learn arithmetic (*hisāb*), for if they don't do so, they would remain ignorant of the records of household expenditure (*masārif-i khāngī*).
- They should reinvent themselves as a luminous jewel (*jauhar-i zātī*), and should embrace: polite conversation (*narm goī*), modest conversation (*kam goī*), pious company (*nek khalqī*), move around gracefully (*āhista rawī*), and should render obedience to the dictates of the respectable elders (*buzurgān*).

---

[87] *TN*, 119–20.

- They should deem it absolutely necessary to renounce the following habits: hurtful conversation (*sakht kalāmī*), mean temperament (*tursh rui'*), dressing up immodestly (*be-hijābī*), shameless behaviour (*be-sharmī*), defiance of authority (*'adul-i hukmī*), and standing up to those in authority over them (*jawāb dahi ba hukm-i wāliyān*).

[Instructions for] Women who are married:

- They should not erase the memory of their parents, but should, with the consent of the husband, regularly go and visit and look after them.
- They should treat their parents-in-law as no different from their real parents.
- They should inculcate the quality of humility (*firotnī*) within them.
- They should deem it obligatory (*farz*) on their part to comply with the instructions of the elders (*buzurgon*).
- They should keep away from fickle-mindedness (*talauwun mizājī*).
- While walking on the road, they should not let their eyes wander.
- When a man visits their house, they should ensure that women in the house are shifted to a separate enclosure in the house [inaccessible to men].
- They should not look at men [besides, of course, their husbands] with envy and desire (*hasrat wa hai'rat*); in fact, a sensible wife (*lugai'*) is the one who does not lift her eyes to see a man.
- It is incumbent upon women to not visit temples.
- They should not laugh loudly.
- They should wear modest clothes, and not covet expensive ornaments.

[Instructions for widows]:

- They should remould their existence and embrace absolute abjectness (*bilkul khāksār*); an abjectness so complete that people are repulsed looking at them.

[Instructions for old women]:

- Just as it is obligatory for girls to be obedient to their parents and brothers, and for married women to be subservient to their spouses, so it is likewise necessary for old women to obey their sons.

[Lessons for Indian men and women]:

Observe how the state in China has framed such wonderful rules for women. If they are followed with consistency, the results would be simply amazing. If only our local brethren (*desi bhāi*) follow these instructions and push for women's education, how good would that be!

Look here! When the Hindus were in power, women were getting educated, and there was considerable progress [in this matter].... The Muslim invasion destroyed (*m'adum*) the pace of the movement. Later, supported by the British government, we had the rule of the English Company ('Company Bahadur'), and the push for education received a new lease of life. After the revolt of 1857, Queen Victoria took control over the affairs of Hindustan, and since then, this department [of education] has received a lot more consideration [than ever before].

Appendix 2A.4

Durga Prashad Nadir's Response to Hakim Fasihuddin Ranj's Critique[88]

Submission (*'ariza'*) before Hakim Ranj, the author of *Baharistan-i Naz*:

This is the submission of Durga Prashad, the author of *Tazkirat-un Nisa-i Nadiri* (also called *Mir'at-i Khyali*), which was published in two separate volumes: *Gulshan-i Naz* and *Chaman Andaz* in 1292 A.H. by Munshi Ambi Prashad, a merchant running a publishing house in Delhi; the two volumes have now been joined together here, along with the conclusion and appendices.

It is addressed to Hakim Fasihuddin, an aristocrat (*ra'is*) of Meerut [in present-day western Uttar Pradesh], the author of a unique (*yakta-i zamana*) biographical compendia (*tazkira*) of women poets. You have done me an honour by remembering me [in your work]. In the third edition of your work, *Baharistan-Naz*, published in 1299 A.H. (1881–1882 CE), you have repeatedly mentioned *Chaman Andaz*, referring to it as 'a collection of trash (*raddiyat*) called *Chaman Andaz*'. Perhaps, you did not have access to the complete text, nor did you go through *Gulshan-i Naz*. But then, as someone has said, 'if you gain notoriety, you also gain fame'. I don't want to take issue with you, for my faith (*mazhab*) is *sulh-i kul* [tolerance of difference]. I have not uttered an uncivil word against you in my work, and I merely pointed out the errors in your work. You have uttered indignities without inhibitions against me.... You say on page 10, line 11 that, 'prompted by jealousy, he [Nadir] has written this work by stealing information from this *tazkira* [*Baharistan-i Naz*] and adding fictitious compositions of women poets who were imaginary and bogus (*farzi aur khyali sha'ira'*)'.

Bearing the need for justice in mind, will you admit how much you have stolen from *Chaman Andaz*? You are a compiler, and cannot claim to be the author; the work of compilation (*talif*) is like building a house with an assortment

---

[88] *TN*, 273–80.

of bricks and gravel (*kahīn ki īnth kahīn ka roda, bhān mati ne kunba jodā*)....
In my work there is a discussion on the compositions (*kalām*) of two hundred and
fifty women. Even in the third enlarged edition of your *tazkira*, *Bahāristān-i Nāz*,
it is the compositions of merely one hundred and seventy-four poetesses that are
listed, and if you actually count them, they are one short.... Now when my *tazkira*
is published again, I have added fifty more women poets in the appendix of the
first volume, *Gulshan-i Nāz*, and another fifty in the second volume, *Chaman
Andāz*; in all, the complete *tazkira* now has above three hundred women poets in
the collection. Now tell me! Who is copying from whom?

As far as the charge of fabrication is concerned, let me remind you that I have
in most cases mentioned my source (*manqūl 'anah*), but, as they say: 'A person
cannot think beyond his capabilities' (*fikr-i har kas ba-qadr-i himmat-i ūst*).
Or, as is often said: 'Each one of us is possessed by our thoughts.' Probably, you
may have yourself practised it, and thought others do the same.

You state on page 5, line 11: 'I read through hundreds of *tazkira*s, searched
them out from almost everywhere, but there was none that concerned women.'
You failed to provide a list of these *tazkira*s; nobody can find more than a handful
of *tazkira*s in the libraries (*kutub khāna*) in Hindustan. How could you then
consult hundreds of them? You may have looked at the multiple copies of a [single]
published *tazkira*. And you failed to see *Jawāhar-ul 'Ajā'ib*, published by Nawal
Kishore [Lucknow]. It does seem surprising that you also failed to notice the list
of fourteen *tazkira*s carrying the poetic compositions of women on page four of
my *Gulshan-i Nāz*. How would you have read it when you dismissed it as trash
(*raddī*)? Now when you reprint your book the fourth time, you can make the
necessary modifications. I will present the complete text to you. And if you accept
it, I would be honoured (*gar qabūl uftad zahe 'izz-o sharf*).

And, to borrow a verse of [the poet] Qazi Akhtar: 'If I am forgiven, can
I submit [that]/I don't deserve to be cursed (*'itāb*) by you (*taqsīr ho mu'āf to ek 'arz
karūn/mujhke na kījīye jo morid 'itāb kā*).

In writing your *tazkira*, you have copied from several other *tazkira*s; how then
could you claim to be the author (*maujid*)? When you assert that this is the first
work of its kind [by virtue of being a *tazkira* of women poets], I would draw your
attention to *Jawāhir-ul 'Ajai'b*, which was written in Akbar's time. Since you are
not the author [and, at best, an editor], how can I be accused of copying from
you? You wrote your book by copying (*taqlīd*) from the works of past scholars,
and I have done the same here. What is so wrong in this? By honouring my work,
Chaman Andāz with the epithet of junk (*raddī*), you have unnecessarily disfigured
the beauty of your work.

[The author then goes on to provide specific instances from Ranj's *tazkira* where he has copied from his work, invented a poetess, and erred in attributing verses to the wrong person. The gist of his observations is presented below:]

Asir: She was not there in Ranj's original work, and he came to know about her from his *tazkira*. In the following edition of his work, Ranj mentions her, borrowing details from Nadir's *Chaman Andāz*.

Ashk: 'All that you mention about her is simply an assertion without evidence (*d'awā-i be-dalīl*); you should have provided evidence of the truth of your claims'.

Bismillah: The details are incorrect, and the author cites Ranj's description of Munshi Inamullah Beg Sahib in the section on Bismillah as full of inaccuracies.

Hijab: The details have been lifted from Nadir's work, and Ranj has not bothered to verify them: 'The demands of research (*muqtaza-i tahqīq*) expected you to make your own investigations (*tahqīq*), remove your doubts in the matter, and point out the errors in my account (if any).'

Manjhu Khanam, the female servant (*kaniz*): 'The quatrain (*ruba'i*) that you attribute to her is actually written by Mir Ali Rashk.' He asks Ranj to look at Mir Ali's *diwān, Nazm-i Mubarak*, and, with a tinge of mockery, suggests to him to remove the mistake when he republishes his book the fourth time.

Faridan: Note the element of restrained derision in how the author comments on Ranj's note on Faridan: 'Your observations about her are absolutely right, and expectedly so, because you are an aristocrat (*ra'is*) who regularly visits her residence [Meerut]. From the time that the city became habitable, I am sure you would have the complete list of the prostitutes (*randi*) living in Meerut.'

Kaniz: Nadir believes that the poet was the slave (*laundi*) of Fatima Begum and not someone by the name of Fatima Begum Kaniz. Ranj had asserted in his work that the name of the poet was Fatima Begum, and her nom de plume was Kaniz.

Mahlaqa: Durga Prashad Nadir accuses Ranj of lifting the lone verse by Mahlaqa for his *tazkira* from *Chaman Andāz*, adding: 'I had come across just a single verse by her, and I reproduced it in *Chaman Andāz*. You copied it from my work, even as you describe it as trash (*raddi*); this is like a wrongdoer unabashedly announcing his innocence (*chori aur sina zori*), is it not?'

Zeenat Khan Nazuk: Nadir accuses him of copying her couplets from *Chaman Andāz*, and prods him to admit doing so, for, he says, if you had acknowledged taking her compositions from my work, 'no *qāzi* would have complained'.

Waftan Jan Nazuk: Nadir accuses Ranj of misrepresenting facts about her life, and one place where he is definitely in error is when he says that Nazuk was a frequent visitor to the establishment (*dera*) of the prostitute (*randi*) Munna Jan. She had actually moved in and had become a resident member of

Munna Jan's establishment. She was responsible for arranging for the funeral of Munna Jan when she died.

Nadir pokes fun at Ranj's claim that the verses he cites in his work were recited to him by Nazuk and were, therefore, reliable, having come to him straight from the horse's mouth. This is, according to Nadir, an absolute lie: 'During the time that you were collecting her verses (for your work), it was impossible for anyone unrelated to her to see her, let alone talk with her.'

[The note ends with Nadir listing the spelling mistakes and other errors in the text.]

> Date: 20 November 1882
>
> Written by: Durga Prashad Nadir

Appendix 2A.5

Hakim Fasihuddin Ranj on His Objectives in Writing the Tazkira[89]

I was in this state of agitation and restlessness (*iztirāb wa intishār*) when my interest in writing gripped me, and I came to realize that intense reflection served to enhance my creativity. I was now inclined towards the *tazkira*s of poets, and the inclination in no time turned into an obsession (*dillagī*). Even so, my heart fell for the new literary trends (*tarz-i nau*'), and the taste for the contemporary style (*jadīd lazīz*) became an obsession. All day long, I was engrossed in reading these *tazkira*s, oblivious to the world around me. One day it so happened that I chanced upon the poetic compositions of Makhfi; the effect her verses had on me is beyond description. I was left wondering: why do we know so little about other women poets, besides Makhfi? Are there other women too in this assembly (*bazm*) of littérateurs, or is Makhfi the only woman holding the fort? In finding an answer to this problem, I looked at hundreds of *tazkira*s and recovered some among them from odd places. When I perused them, I found incidental notices about exceptional women, but there was not a single *tazkira* that was exclusively devoted to women poets. Thereupon, the thought came to my mind that I should, to the extent possible, take an initiative in the matter, and should make known the compositions of the poetesses (*masturāt kā bhī zāhir nām kījiyē*). My friends, genuine and well intentioned, kept up the pressure on me, and my close relations showed an unrelenting interest in this project. This was the only topic that my

---

[89] *BN*, 81–83.

companions thought of talking about when I was in their company. Whenever a couple of my acquaintances hung out together, they would recite [women's] verses and force me to jot them down. When the insistence of friends became unrelenting, I decided to go ahead with this project. To the extent possible, I rummaged around and collected [the extant material] and produced the present work. There are some in this volume whose poems were recovered from long-standing libraries (*kutub-i qadīm*), and there are others whose compositions came to me through friends and reputable men (*ahbāb-o-arbāb*). Once this was done, I prepared a list of the poetesses in alphabetical order, and completed the task of compilation. With the assemblage and compilation satisfactorily completed, the present *tazkira* took a completed shape, and was given the title of *Bahāristān-i Nāz*.

3

Representing an Inclusive Literary Culture

Women Poets in the Bazaars and *Kothas*

Studying the women poets in *BN* and *TN*, the reader is quickly confronted with two important components in the narrative structure. The first is the biographical prelude that precedes their literary compositions; in both the *tazkira*s, there is a clipping from their life stories that sets the context for delving into their poems. This is a standard writing technique in poetic *tazkira*s, but it is not without some significance here; one of its objectives is to guide the reader into the poet's work. It is as if a woman poet's life story or clippings therefrom provide the framework for the appreciation of her work. There is a thick enmeshment of the art with the person, and the life (and the body) of a poet with her poetic compositions. The second important element of the narrative structure is an overwhelming, but still permeable, distinction between 'the secluded women' (*pardah nashīn*) and 'the public women' (*bāzārī 'aurat*); interestingly, the latter are further divided by the fluid and often overlapping categories of the courtesan (*tawā'if*), the prostitute (*randī*), the slave girl (*kanīz*), the skilled dancer-cum-harlot (*khāngī*), the lower caste prostitute (*kanchanī*), and professional entertainers (*domnī*s).[1]

'Women of the Bazaar': Internal Hierarchies and the Representation of Difference

There were many more distinctions that divided the *bāzārī* women, but the shifting boundaries among them always made it difficult to define any of these categories

---

[1] *Domnī*s were professional female entertainers who performed only before women, in gender segregated spaces.

with any sense of precision.[2] In an interesting interlude, Nadir informs us that the *kanchanīs* were called *kanjar*s in Punjab, and in some places in Hindustan, they were also called the 'children of Lord Ram' or *rām-janiyān*. At several other places, he says, they were called *pātar*, *gāyinān*, and *abchar*; while they all came from lower caste groups, the distinctions in nomenclature referred not only to the regional specificities but also their sub-caste affiliations.[3] In his ethno-historical aside on 'public women', he points out that owing to the lower social status of the *kanchanīs*, the *khāngīs* refrained from associating with them, even as they were both engaged in prostitution. He further informs us that the *khāngī* community was a close-knit group, with strict rules of inclusion. As he says:

> When a woman of loose character (*chināl*) leaves her home, and adopts this degrading profession, she is called a *khāngī*. The *khāngī*s consider others in their profession base and lowly, except for those prostitutes who are, after a ritual feast, brought into their fold, and become one of them. They deem it demeaning to associate themselves with the community of the *kanchan*s, even as the two communities work close together in dance performances, and are joined with each other by the strings of the *ghungru*[4] [on their ankles].[5]

This ethno-historical aside in Nadir's work is instructive in sensitizing us to the immense diversity among women entertainers and prostitutes. The internal hierarchies and the allusions to caste and community linkages reveal their socially entrenched existence, and prompt us to consider the extent to which they were entangled with the sociocultural arrangements and institutions. It is within and through their linkages with the social set-up that an impressive number among them took up literature and the arts, and ended up becoming accomplished poets participating in poetic gatherings, writing their own compendia of poems or *diwāns*, composing lyrics for musical evenings, and sharing their poems with friends and scholars. It is obvious that the representation of these public entertainers is not insular, but is nuanced along lines of class, community, and

---

[2] For a discussion on the range and variety of female performers, see Katherine Butler Schofield, 'The Courtesan Tale: Female Musicians and Dancers in Mughal Historical Chronicles, c. 1556–1748', *Gender and History* 24, no. 1 (April 2012): 150–71; and Sumanta Banerjee, *Dangerous Outcast: The Prostitute in Nineteenth Century Bengal* (Kolkata: Seagull Books, 1998).

[3] *TN*, 163–64.

[4] An ornament that women, particularly dancers, wore around their ankles, consisting of multiple metallic bells strung together.

[5] *TN*, 164.

caste affiliations. However, for both Ranj and Nadir, it was equally important to retain the position of the critic and assess them by virtue of their work: their linguistic skills, aesthetic sensibilities, and, above all else, conformity to the social and literary etiquette, or *adāb*.

While the biographical descriptions of courtesans and prostitutes have variety and detail, in the case of women defined as 'secluded' – a metonym for 'chaste' – or *pardah nashīn*, the description is usually more restrained and respectful, rarely if ever going beyond details about their families, tutors, and education. Apparently, the division between 'public' and 'chaste' women in these biographical compendia reflected the distance between them, which was reinforced and exacerbated by the newly emergent notions of companionate marriage and the social investment in familial relations. While some of these developments in the reorganization of domestic spaces were influenced by Victorian ideology, the role of the newly emergent social classes, in particular the gentry and the middle classes, should also be borne in mind.[6] Historians have explained how these developments contributed to the shifts in the perception of prostitutes and entertainers, and led to their aggressive social marginalization and exclusion from the household spaces.[7] In a couple of other studies, the ones that explore their agency and subjectivity, it is their resistance, control over social and economic resources, and rejection of familial norms that are emphasized.[8] These studies, varied and diverse, nonetheless share the assumption of the separation of the household space from the space of the salon, of the courtesan giving exquisite dance and music performances from

---

[6] The readings on this theme are pretty extensive, but see, in particular, Majumdar, *Family Values in Colonial Bengal;* Mytheli Sreenivas, *Wives, Widows, and Concubines;* Indrani Chatterjee (ed.), *Unfamiliar Relations;* Kenneth W. Jones, *Socio-Religious Reform Movements in British India* (Cambridge: Cambridge University Press, 1989 [reprint]); Minault, *Secluded Scholars;* and Metcalf, *Perfecting Women.* Also see the relevant essays in Sarkar and Sarkar, *Women and Social Reform.*

[7] Charu Gupta, *Sexuality, Obscenity, Community: Women, Muslims, and the Hindu Public in Colonial India* (New Delhi: Permanent Black, 2000); Kenneth A. Ballhatchet, *Race, Sex and Class under the Raj: Imperial Attitudes and Policies and Their Critics, 1793–1905* (New York: St. Martin's Press, 1980); and Banerjee, *Dangerous Outcast.* For the perception of prostitutes and anxieties of sexual deviance in Victorian England, see Walkowitz, *Prostitution and Victorian Society;* and Walkowitz, *City of Dreadful Delight.* For their position in France, see Corbin, *Women for Hire.*

[8] Veena Talwar Oldenburg, 'Lifestyle as Resistance: The Case of the Courtesans of Lucknow, India', *Feminist Studies* 16, no. 2 (Summer 1990): 259–87. Also see Veena Talwar Oldenburg, *The Making of Colonial Lucknow, 1856–1877* (Princeton, N. J.: Princeton University Press, 1984).

the spouse and the mother attending to domestic responsibilities in the
household spaces. In an important article, Richard Williams contests such an
assumption, and argues that the courtesans were an integral component of social
life and that their lives were marked by varying levels of interaction with the elites,
and middle-class men and women in the household.[9] In her study of the courtesans
in Hyderabad, Karen Leonard came to the same conclusion, and argued that the
courtesans were significant participants in sociopolitical developments.[10]

There is an obvious difference in terms of the content and narrative structure
between the representation of the 'veiled women', that is, women who lived in
the inner quarters of the household, and the 'public women' who entertained
customers in their salons or public spaces. At the same time, the boundaries
between the *kotha* and the home were porous and fluid; our *tazkiras* provide
ample evidence of boundary crossing, citing instances of courtesans and prostitutes
getting married and setting up a home of their own. Araish, a public performer,
was 'once a showpiece displaying herself in the market in Delhi', but she later
got married and 'is now lending elegance to someone's house'.[11] In another
instance, Bismillah, who, according to Nadir, belonged to a 'Hindustani lineage'
(*hindī nezād*), abandoned her profession (*pesha*) after the revolt of 1857, married
someone, and 'contented herself with the permitted comforts (*'aish-i mubāh*)'.[12]
Commending her decision, Ranj similarly informs us that 'she was before the
revolt (*ghadar*), given to vices (*pāband-i harām*), but is married to someone now,
and is preparing herself for her life after death'.[13]

Instances of women coming from respectable households becoming courtesans
are also mentioned in the biographical compendia, and our compilers mention
cases of women getting their daughters trained in music and dance as well. Sardar
Begum, inform Ranj and Nadir, was actually a respectable woman who belonged
to a noble household (*sharīf khāndān*) in Lucknow, but after the revolt of 1857,
she lost her spouse and fell on bad days. Finding herself a widow, living in straitened
circumstances, she took her daughter, Kazmi Begum, to Kanpur and then Kannauj
to a training-cum-dwelling centre (*dera*) and got her trained in music and dance.

---

[9] Richard David Williams, 'Songs between Cities: Listening to Courtesans in Colonial North
    India,' *Journal of the Royal Asiatic Society* 27, no. 4 (October 2017): 591–610.

[10] Karen Leonard, 'Political Players: Courtesans of Hyderabad,' *Indian Economic and
    Social History Review* 50, no. 4 (October 2013): 423–48; Karen Leonard, *Hyderabad and
    Hyderabadis* (New Delhi: Manohar, 2013b), 378– 427.

[11] *TN*, 124; *BN*, 99.

[12] *TN*, 129.

[13] *BN*, 107.

With her daughter, she would organize music and dance gatherings (*mujra*), and developed her own clientele. Interestingly, it was her poems that were put to vocal skills by her daughter. The mother–daughter duo was often invited to functions, and at one such function Nadir was also a witness and records listening to Kazmi's melodious voice and her mother Sardar's verses.[14]

Crossing Boundaries: Emotions of Love and Their Transgressive Potential

Our *tazkiras* affirm the active involvement of courtesans and prostitutes in urban life, and not just in the prosperous cities, but also the petty townships or the *qasbas*; and while they certainly indicate the separation between the household and the courtesan's salon, they also provide evidence of crossover and breaches in the boundaries that separated them. Love was indeed an emotion that could, and did, bring the family man into the arms of the courtesan, and took the courtesan into the 'inner' spaces of the family and the household. Interestingly, when these love affairs, which traversed social boundaries, led to tragedies, including deaths, the figure of the prostitute was reinstated and invested with honour and respectability; it is as if the intensity of love re-inscribed her as a 'chaste woman'.

Let us take one such case here, narrated by both Ranj and Nadir with particular relish. This concerns a prostitute (*kasbī*) by the name of Banno, who lived in the city of Delhi.[15] She was in a relationship with a *khatri* merchant, Gulab Singh Ashufta, who lived in the posh colony of high merchants (*mahājans*) in Chandni Chowk. Presumably, a minor tiff between them prompted Banno to cease visiting him, and when her separation became unbearable, Ashufta committed suicide. Heartbroken, she rushed to meet him and see if she could save him but was prevented from doing so by his friends and relations, who found her anxiety and insistence as suggestive of her mental breakdown. Dejected, she found solace in reciting the verses he wrote for her, and gave up her lifestyle and followed him into death a mere six months after his demise. She also wrote couplets in his memory to express her feelings and experience of loss and pain. Both our authors record the following poem that she wrote in memory of the loss of her lover, Ashufta:

---

[14] *TN*, 160–63; *BN*, 152–53.
[15] *TN*, 129–31; *BN*, 107–09.

Death doesn't come to me, nor is life any friend of mine either,

It is true, Ashufta, your death has killed me as well;

I don't control death, for if that were so,

Without you near me, I would surely have rejected life;

Where have disappeared peace (*chain*), comfort (*'aish*) and the bed to sleep (*bistar-i khwāb*);

Even the silken (*makhmal*) bed aches the body no less than the bed of thorns (*bistar-i khāra*);

In the din caused by all the wailing and lamentations,

Why did you not call for me when they [the angels of death] were taking you away?[16]

A Hindu *khatri* merchant in love with a Muslim prostitute makes for a scintillating trope, because it breaks down several boundaries – the ones that separated the household from the bazaar, a Hindu from a Muslim, and a ritually high-caste man from an impure and polluted woman. In recounting the love story, our *tazkiras* recount the ability of love to transcend and dismantle socially sanctioned boundaries, in particular the separation of 'public' from 'chaste' women. This kind of love is described as a 'malady' (*bimār-i 'ishq*) and an 'affliction' (*āzār*), since it is so very impassioned and intense. The feeling of love is described by Banno as leading to the disappearance of peace and comfort, an inner restlessness in which 'even the silken (*makhmal*) bed aches the body no less than the bed of thorns (*bistar-i khāra*)'.[17]

The narrative structure has a purpose: the intensity of feelings serves to legitimate the relationship situated outside the family and household. It also disrupts the dominant social perception of the prostitute as a heartless creature, ruthless and insensitive, and so a threat to the social order. In the emphasis that had come to be placed on family and companionate marriage in the colonial period, it is easy to lose sight of the forces of resistance, and fail to see the space for the existence of relationships outside marriage. Our *tazkiras* celebrate a relationship with a prostitute and describe Ashufta as an 'earnest companion' (*muhib-i sādiq*).[18] Situated outside the realm of the domestic space, Banno's relationship with Ashufta is still considered a cause for celebration, an event worthy of memorialization. Clearly, Victorian domestic ideals were still not a given, but were actively resisted by sections of the literati and people like Ashufta and Banno.

---

[16] *TN*, 131; *BN*, 109.

[17] *TN*, 130.

[18] *TN*, 130.

The point that these *tazkira*s make is not that marriage and family were unnecessary and dispensable institutions, but that they were not equally significant for all sections of society. In the creation of an ethical and responsible selfhood, the primacy of familial relations and conjugal intimacies should not be assumed, and people can constitute their identities, and experience fulfilment, despite and through the rejection of marriage and familial affinities. While narrating the life story of a slave girl (*kanīz*), Chameli, bearing the pen name Yasmin, Ranj informs us that she was averse to the idea of marriage, and when her master, a high noble, Inshallah Khan, succeeded in getting her married to someone, despite her protestations, she died within just three days of her marriage.[19] She did not find marriage as leading to the end of her loneliness, and it is this sense of perennial loneliness that is reflected in her couplets as well:

He came down with speed but only after the news (*khabr*) of my death (*qaza*) reached him,
He left his house [for my place] only after life had departed from my body;
When I saw my house, I was reminded of a desert,
And, when I came across a desert, I remembered my house.[20]

This is interesting because in the reformist literature, an unmarried woman was a potential source of disorder, and marriage was depicted as an institution that served to keep women under appropriate control and protect them from the anarchy of their senses and desires.[21] In our *tazkira*s, on the other hand, marriage is held desirable, for sure, but not a uniform normative ideal for women across class, caste, and personal preferences. Interestingly, in a couple of digressional notes, their authors throw light on the anxieties of the conjugal households, and one such anxiety is captured in the figure of the henpecked husband (*zan murīd*).[22] Nadir refers to a certain 'Hindu who belonged to an elite household (*'ālī khāndān*) and was well versed in Persian and Nagri (Hindi), and had poetic compilations or *diwān*s in Persian, Hindi and Urdu'. This high-profile scholar had prohibited his son from marrying anyone because he feared that 'if he turned out to be a henpecked husband (*zan murīd*), it would ruin him in his old age'. Berating him, Nadir says: 'Even today

---

[19] *BN*, 238; also see *TN*, 207.
[20] *BN*, 238; *TN*, 207.
[21] Metcalf, *Perfecting Women;* Banerjee, *Dangerous Outcast;* Majumdar, *Family Values in Colonial Bengal;* and Mitra, *Indian Sex Life.*
[22] *TN*, 133.

when the light of education has dispelled the darkness of ignorance, in this transitory world, such self-centred and selfish people occasionally come into existence.'[23]

Unlettered Women Poets: Orality in Literary Culture

Interestingly, linguistic skills and aesthetics were not exclusively dependant on social position, or at least that is the impression our *tazkiras* communicate; even as a slave girl (*kanīz*), Yasmin was, says Ranj, 'extremely learned and intelligent' (*nihāyat taba'a aur fahīm*).[24] If class and caste were incidental to literary accomplishments, we also come across evidence of the lack of literacy as of no significance in the making of a gifted poetess. Ranj refers to a sitar-playing courtesan based in Jaipur in Rajasthan, Nazakat, who was unlettered but could still recite poems of high calibre: 'Her poetry is the source of envy for even such accomplished poetesses as Mushtari and Sardar.'[25] Mushtari and Sardar were courtesans known for their skills in poetry.[26] This is interesting for it reveals the persistence of oral traditions and their influence in shaping the literary culture. She was quite a successful courtesan, and Ranj cautions us against treating her, owing to her illiteracy, as a 'riff-raff' (*kachad khalil*); she was quite resourceful and managed her own establishment (*dera*).[27] Her poems are lucid and strike a chord with the sensitive reader, highlighting as it does the theme of love and the consequent loss of freedom; she likens her situation to a wounded nightingale, and even finds the healing touch of Christ inadequate. She says:

> If I am an injured nightingale (*bulbul-i zār*) today, it is because I belong to you,
> If I have lost my freedom today, it is because I belong to you;
> The [strained] relations that I have with the angels these days,
> [And] If they see me as a sinner (*gunehgār*), it is because I belong to you.
> Even the healing touch of Christ has failed to cure me,
> If I am so very sick today, it is because I belong to you.[28]

---

[23] *TN*, 133.

[24] *BN*, 238; *TN*, 207.

[25] *BN*, 231.

[26] For Mushtari, see *TN*, 192–93; and *BN*, 202–05; and for details about Sardar, see *TN*, 120– 23 and *BN*, 152–53.

[27] *BN*, 231; also see *TN*, 203–04.

[28] *BN*, 231; *TN*, 203.

We could take a couple of other instances of female poets who were illiterate but nonetheless accomplished in the skills of poetry. Sardar Begum, who organized music and dance events along with her daughter, Kazmi, was illiterate (*nā-khwāndah*), and she would get her verses written down by scribes or literate acquaintances. Her poetic compositions were sung by her daughter, and their popularity is noted by both Ranj and Nadir.[29] Ranj mentions an illiterate poet, the daughter of a cloth printer by the name of Rawia, and describes her verses as 'neither excellent nor substandard' (*na badtar hai na bahtar*).[30] These instances draw our attention to the deep entrenchment of oral traditions in the literary culture. Literacy co-existed with orality, and women poets who were unlettered found spaces for expression and articulation in the literary sphere. It is quite remarkable that our *tazkira* writers take care to acknowledge them and record their compositions in their compilations.

Representations of Same-Sex Relations: Courtesans Contesting Heteronormativity

The indifference of the beloved is a running theme in the compositions of the courtesans and prostitutes, but while the gender of the beloved in Rekhta is usually undefined and nebulous, in one of the poems of a courtesan, Nazakat, cited by Ranj, it seems, from her description of her beloved applying henna on her hands and feet, that the allusion is to same-sex relationship. The salon of the prostitute was indeed a space where gender identities were fluid, and heteronormativity was not always the norm. Let us cite her poem here:

> She does not kiss (*bosah*) me on my cheek, nor does she let me touch her hair,
>
> A whole lifetime has passed me by with this indifference, day in and night;
>
> What is so special if two to four persons lose their lives owing to the indifference [of their beloveds]?
>
> When my beloved applies henna [on her hands and feet], she causes a bloodbath (*qatl-i 'ām)'.[31]

---

[29] *TN*, 160–63; *BN*, 152–53.

[30] *BN*, 145–46; Nadir also mentions her but expresses his doubts, adding that the verses attributed to her were probably composed by one Rabia, who was the daughter of a physician (*TN*, 151–52).

[31] *BN*, 231; *TN*, 204.

Interestingly, homoeroticism in women's poetry was not specific to the courtesans and prostitutes, but is found in the compositions of elite women as well. Women expressed their homoerotic feelings through their poems, and among those who did so was also one of the wives of the ruler of Awadh, Wajid Ali Shah, Rang Mahal Begum. She wrote in *rekhti* style,[32] and this is how Ranj describes her: 'Her heart is full of fervour and excitement even as her face remains veiled.'[33] She was, it seems, well known in *rekhti* circles, and her verses are found in a couple of compilations of *rekhti* poems.[34] This is how she expresses her intense feelings for her beloved:

> I will not let you go to the house of your in-laws (*susrāl*),
> Your presence here was never a burden;
> You comb and braid my hair,
> For that, I am indebted to you, my loving companion (*do-gāna*)'.

> *Nā bhejungī susrāl men tum ko khānam*
> *Nahin mujh ko dūbar hai khānā tumhārā*
> *Merī kangī, chotī ki letī khabar ho,*
> *Yeh ehsān hai sar par do-gāna tumhārā.*[35]

The choice of the word *do-gāna* for the companion is important here, and suggests homoerotic intimacies. Carla Petievich points out that the word is found in *rekhti* literature to indicate 'an intimate, even erotic, relationship between two women'.[36] *Do* in *do-gāna* means 'two' and refers to an intimate companion, but Begum also refers to *seh-gāna* for the 'third companion'; *seh*, as we know, means 'three'.

---

[32] *Rekhti* was a literary form in which the lover/narrator takes on a feminine voice, and the beloved/addressee also has, not infrequently, a female gender. For details, see Ruth Vanita, *Gender, Sex and the City: Urdu Rekhti Poetry in India, 1780–1870* (New Delhi: Orient Blackswan, 2012); Carla Petievich, *When Men Spoke as Women: Vocal Masquerade in Indo-Muslim Poetry* (New Delhi: Oxford University Press, 2007); Carla Petievich, 'Gender Politics and the Urdu Ghazal: Exploratory Observations on *Rekhta* versus *Rekhti*', *Indian Economic and Social History Review* 38, no. 3 (September 2001): 223–48; Ruth Vanita (ed.), *Queering India: Same-Sex Love and Eroticism in Indian Culture and Society* (New York: Routledge, 2002). For a comparative perspective on same-sex relations between women, see Sahar Amer, *Crossing Borders: Love between Women in Medieval French and Arabic Literatures* (Philadelphia, PA: University of Pennsylvania Press, 2008).

[33] *BN*, 113.

[34] Vanita, *Gender, Sex and the City*, 7.

[35] *TN*, 132; *BN*, 113.

[36] Petievich, 'Gender Politics', 244–45.

The *seh-gāna* was the female lover of the female beloved, and her presence in love poetry points to the complexities in homosocial intimacies in the inner spaces of the household, known as the *zanāna*. Referring to these experiences, Begum says:

> Seeing my *do-gāna* turning up as a guest at the *seh-gāna*'s place,
> I was lit aflame and lost my life.

> *Ghar seh-gāna ke do-gāna merī mehmān gai'*
> *Main ye angāron pe lautī ki merī jān gai'.*[37]

Poetry as a Form of Self Narrative: Language, Emotions, and Selfhood

Women's poetry was a form of 'unveiling', and in the poems found in our biographical compendia, constrained by literary conventions and entrenched practices, the poets nonetheless discovered, constructed, and represented themselves. The poetic compositions of courtesans, prostitutes, and dancer-musicians were particular forms of self-narratives, rich in autobiographical reflections. Of course, 'poetry' is not 'autobiography', but as forms of expression, there is an element of fabrication in both, which goes alongside components of self-presentation, reflexivity, and selfhood. It is true that their verses do not always directly relate to concrete events in their lives, but there are instances where they did. We came across earlier the tragic love affair between Gulab Singh Ashufta and Banno (a prostitute) leading to the former slitting his throat and Banno's death a few months thereafter. It was rare in Persian and Urdu to reveal the subject by name, but in the poem that Banno recited in memory of her lover, she is explicit: 'It is true, Ashufta, your death has killed me as well' (*hai' Āshufta! tērē marnē nē mārā mujh ko*).[38] Struggling to describe her state of mind, following his death, she refers to the loss of 'peace' (*chain*), 'comfort' (*'aish*), and 'sleep' (*bistar-i khwāb*); and in a language marked by excess but still reflective of her feelings, she adds: 'Even the silken (*makhmal*) bed aches the body no less than the bed of thorns (*bistar-i khārā*)' (*nahin makhmal bhi kam az bistar-i khārā mujh ko*).[39] Clearly, an event in the life of the poet provides the context to the elaboration of an excess of emotions, a feat achieved through a rich repertoire of allusions and metaphors.

---

[37]   *TN*, 132; *BN*, 113.

[38]   *TN*, 131; *BN*, 108.

[39]   *TN*, 131; *BN*, 109.

It is obvious that the poems of courtesans, prostitutes, and slave girls were marked by considerable variety in terms of the choice of themes and forms of expression. Even so, a large number of their compositions veered around themes of the loss of freedom, indifference and unrequited love, and sickness and death. We referred to Yasmin, a slave girl, earlier, and in one of her verses, she refers to her death as the moment that awakened her apathetic beloved from the slumber of indifference; he rushed to her house 'only after life had departed from my body' (*ghar sē nikle woh merī jān nikal jānē ke bād*).[40] Interestingly, given the spatial dislocations that these women experienced in their lives, the trope of a ruined and deserted house is not infrequently applied in their compositions. Yasmin, for example, equates her home with a lifeless desert:

> When I saw my house, I was reminded of a desert (*dasht*),
> And, when I came across a desert, I remembered my house.[41]

For the courtesans and public entertainers, it was important to look attractive, and so it is that beauty accoutrements found their way into their language and forms of expression. At the same time, there was also a realization of the meaninglessness of cosmetics and jewellery with advancing age. Araish, who was a public entertainer performing in the Delhi market (*bāzār Dehlī*) before she settled down with an unknown person, expressed this sentiment in the following couplet:

> When I was young, it suited me to get all dressed and decked up,
> In this old age, applying henna (*mehndī*) and dentifrice (*missī*) serve no purpose.[42]

In another instance, reflecting the real lives of the courtesans, Hur, whose compositions were 'tasteful' and performance 'graceful' (*shīrīn adā*),[43] refers to, in a couplet bearing homoerotic associations, the 'gold anklets' (*toda*) of her beloved and the effect they had on her:

> When you, the fairy (*parī*) one, wore the ankle bracelet (*toda*) on your feet,
> Your lover (*dīwāna*) was, with the burden of the heavy chains, crushed under your feet.[44]

---

[40] *BN*, 238.
[41] *BN*, 238.
[42] *TN*, 124; *BN*, 99.
[43] *TN*, 145; also see *BN*, 137.
[44] *TN*, 145; *BN*, 137.

With a vocabulary attentive to cosmetics and ornaments, their compositions described the women's world and the objects that surrounded them. Even so, the transience of beauty was also a part of their consciousness and experience, and was conveyed in such couplets as the following one by Bismillah:

Do not pride yourself in your ephemeral beauty (*husn-i 'arzī*),
And don't ever believe that this is a spring (*bahār*) that has no autumn (*khizān*).

Na kījiyē nāz husn-i 'arzī par
Na samjho ye bahār-i be-khizān hai'.[45]

Within their world, besides the beloved's lane (*kūcha*) and the garden (*chaman*), representations of space also included the locations where courtesans entertained their clients with their dance and music performances; known as *bazm* and *mehfil*, these spaces, and the audience therein, constituted an intricate part of their experience and world views. Describing one such gathering, Pari, one of the 'public beauties' (*hasinān-i bāzārī*) based in Calcutta, says:

Why have these strangers turned up at the gathering (*bazm*),
Will someone tell me, who invited them?
Where was this melodious voice of the nightingale for so long?
Her voice has so stunned Pari that she turned pale.

Ye kyon bazm men ghair āyē huē hain
Batao' to kis ke bulāye huē hain
Kahān thī ye bulbul men naghma-sarāi'
Parī ke ye sab hosh udai' huē hain.[46]

It is interesting that some of the courtesans were conscious of the transactional nature of most relationships, and saw the period as marked by a culture of consumption and display, where a person's worth was defined by her or his material possessions. Giving her take on early modernity, Basti, a dancer (*raqāsa*) based in Agra, says:

---

[45] *TN*, 129. Ranj is not sure if the verses attributed to her were actually composed by her or it is 'the work of one of her lovers' (*BN*, 107).
[46] *BN*, 116–17. Ranj appreciates her poetic skills and believes that there was no one like her when it came to 'playing with words' (*chustī-i alfāz*) and 'disciplining the theme' (*bandish-i mazāmīn*) (*BN*, 116–17).

We need for sure the material goods (*asbāb-i zāhirī*), Basti!
The people of this world go with the directions of the wind.

Bastī, zarūr chāhiye asbāb-i zāhirī
Duniyā ke log dēkhnē wāle hawā ke hain.[47]

Umrao Jan, a courtesan based in Delhi, is expressing a similar sentiment when
she thanks her fate for her newly acquired prosperity; she was a *dēredār*, that is,
a courtesan who managed her own establishment, and her establishment or *dera*
attracted a good number of clients every day.[48] In her own words:

Your good days have arrived, Umrao!
Your days of penury recede with each coming day.

Āe' Umrāo din tēre achē
Din ba-din muflasī jo ghatī hai'.[49]

Marginalization, indifference, and deceit were some of the common themes in
the poems of the courtesans and prostitutes. Hur, for example, expresses the fake
world around her in the following couplet:

To those who were nasty to me, I treated them with kindness,
It is in my temperament (*khū*) to befriend those who are my enemies.

Badī kī jis ne hamsē hamnē us ke sāth nēki ki
Hamārī khū hai ye, hum dostī karte hain dushman se.[50]

Tazkiras and the Apprehension of the Semantic Field: Tutors, Fractured Authoriality, and the Bio-Notes

While these biographical compendia are commendable exercises in the recovery
of women's voices, it is important to be attentive to the textual strategies through
which their authors sought to regulate and discipline them. As mentioned earlier,

---

[47] *TN*, 129; *BN*, 111–12. Ranj had personally met the dancer at a government function in Agra,
and this suggests that she was quite popular as a performer with the elites and government
officials (*BN*, 111).
[48] *TN*, 128; *BN*, 105.
[49] *TN*, 128; *BN*, 105.
[50] *BN*, 137; *TN*, 145.

the poetic compositions are always prefaced with short biographical clippings, which serve as a guide – a gateway, as it were – on how to read and interpret the verses. Second, almost all biographical details take care to mention the tutor of the female poets or the person who improved and corrected their poems. This serves to coeval the poets' subjectivity with that of their tutors, creating an impression of fractured authoriality, and compromised autonomy in literary spaces. The elite women usually had some of the most accomplished scholars as their tutors. Asir, who was one of the 'Chaghtai ladies' (*begumat-i chughtai*), had the famous scholar Shah Fakhruddin Ahmad Dehlawi as her tutor.[51] Jina Begum, the daughter of a high noble, Mirza Babur, was a student (*shāgird*) of another well-known poet, Mirza Muhammad Rafi Sauda (1706–81).[52] Some of the courtesans and prostitutes indeed had quite accomplished scholars as their tutors, but a large number among them, interestingly, learnt the nuances of language and took lessons in poetry from the scribal communities, the *munshi*s. Bismillah, a courtesan turned housewife, whose poems, according to Ranj, were marked by 'simplicity and clarity' (*sāf sāf kalām*),[53] had a *munshi* by the name of Inamullah as her guide in poetry, and she would 'seek his advice in her compositions' (*mashwara-i sukhan*).[54] Similarly, Munni Bai, a courtesan based in Calcutta, took lessons from *munshi* Shaukat in the art of poetry.[55] It seems that the clerical communities had an important role to play in the education of performers and entertainers, and their acceptance and position in the literary sphere was considerably facilitated by the scribal community, who tutored them and 'corrected' their poems.

While the role of the tutor was an important one, if these women stood out in the world of men, it was because of their literary acumen and educational skills. Courtesans and public performers could compose poems in a multiplicity of languages, and our sources provide ample evidence of women reciting them in Braj and Persian, along with Urdu. They were usually also trained in music and dance,

---

[51] *BN*, 99–100; *TN*, 127.

[52] *TN*, 138–39; *BN*, 123–24. For details about Sauda's contribution to Urdu literature, see: Khurshidul Islam and Ralph Russell, *Three Mughal Poets: Mir, Sauda, Mir Hasan* (New Delhi: Oxford University Press, 2006 [reprint]); Khurshidul Islam, *Kalām-i Sauda* (Aligarh: Anjuman-i Taraqqi-i Urdu [Hind], 1964); Muhammad Husain Azad, *Āb-i Hayāt* (Allahabad: Ram Narayan Lal Publisher, 1980); Muhammad Sadiq, *A History of Urdu Literature* (Oxford: Oxford University Press, 1964); Mirza Muhammad Rafi Sauda, *Kulliyāt-i Sauda*, 2 vols. (Allahabad: Ram Narayan Lal Publisher, 1971); and Ram Babu Saxena, *A History of Urdu Literature* (New Delhi: Asian Educational Services, 1990).

[53] *BN*, 107.

[54] *TN*, 129.

[55] *BN*, 134–35.

and instances of courtesans playing musical instruments while singing *ghazals* are repeatedly mentioned in our *tazkiras*. One such multi-talented public performer (*hasīnān-i bazārī*) based in Azimabad (modern-day Patna), was Naz, who, says Ranj, 'is dark complexioned (*sānwala rang*), has alluring lips (*ghuncha dahn*) and is about twenty-five years in age'. Referring to her skills as a vocalist, he says, 'She sings in cyclical intonation (*gol sur*). She is so well versed in the art of music (*'ilm-i musaqī*) that she instructs the masters (*ustād*) about the subtleties (*nikāt*) of music.'[56] She knew Persian and, of course, Urdu well, but what was particularly remarkable was her knowledge of English, mentioned by both Ranj and Nadir.[57] Her poems clearly indicate her literary skills and commendable grasp of Persianate aesthetic traditions. They draw on the trope of the indifferent beloved and the pain and afflictions that result therefrom:

> If he had to leave me eventually, in the end,
> Shouldn't he have shown his face to me one last time?
> Accursed are the frailties, for they don't let me get up,
> I see him leave for his house, and can do nothing;
> In his assemblies there is no place for a pitiable person like me,
> But I still get to see him going to and coming from places.

> *Unko jānā thā mere pās se gar waqt-i ākhir*
> *Shakl ek bār mujhe aur dikhāte jātē*
> *Nā-tawānī kā bura ho nahin uthne deti*
> *Woh gai' kūcha-i dildār men jātē jātē*
> *Unki mehfil men kahān hum se gharībon kā guzar*
> *Dekh lete hain magar rāh men ātē jātē.*

And, she continues:

> Now that I have given up on life,
> Now that I have drowned my heart in the ocean of love;
> Now that I have renounced my kingdom (*bādshāhī*),
> I have turned into a beggar (*faqīr*) sitting at the door of your house.

> *Hāth jeene se jabke dhō baithē*
> *Bahr-i ulfat men dil dibō baithē*

---

56   *BN*, 215.
57   *TN*, 225; *BN*, 215.

Chod kar apnī bādshāhī ko
Terē dar par faqīr ho baithē.[58]

In reading the verses of the courtesans and prostitutes in *BN* and *TN*, we realize the permeability between the body of the poet and her lyrical compositions. It is within this inter-penetrative relationship between text and body that we need to contextualize the emphasis on physical traits, not infrequently bordering on the erotic, in their biographical notes. These notes sought to apprehend the somatic and sensorial context of their lyrics, and the entanglement of lyrics with embodied performance. Let us take a few instances here. Describing Umrao, 'a beautiful courtesan' (*tawai'f*) who resided in Delhi, Ranj says that she was 'skilled in the art of deceit' (*fan-i 'ayyarī men fahīm*).[59] And, this is how Nadir describes her: 'She is in the prime of her youth, and is the spring of enchanting youthfulness' (*uthtī jawānī, nai' joban ki bahār hai*).[60] What we notice here is that our authors are describing the poet in a rhetorical language usually reserved for the 'beloved' in Persian poetry; the lovers/poets often describe their beloved as 'deceitful', and their beauty 'youthful' and 'enchanting'.

To take another instance, this is how Nadir describes Dhab, a courtesan: 'She was intoxicated with the wine of beauty, but was still averse to the pleasures of worldly life.'[61] And then again: 'Her beauty was without blemish; she was created by God with his own hands' (*kyā qayāmat kā husn pāyā thā; aap Allāh ne banāyā thā*).[62] She was, adds Nadir, 'faithful' and 'pious' by disposition.[63] The poet and the subject of poetry – the beloved – are rendered identical, and like the beloved of Persian poetry, she or he is created by God 'with his own hands'; her beauty is without blemish and intoxicating. Putting the dark complexion of one of his favourite poets, Badla, to good use, Ranj equates her to Laila, the legendary beloved of the iconic lover, Majnun. He says:

'She is dark-complexioned (*sānwali*), but she is still a delightful beloved. What is the meaning of 'but' here? What is wrong with a dark-complexioned face? After all, it was the colour of Laila [Majnun's beloved] that took Majnun into the wilderness.[64]

---

[58] *BN*, 215–16.
[59] *BN*, 105.
[60] *TN*, 128.
[61] *TN*, 150.
[62] *TN*, 150.
[63] *TN*, 150–51.
[64] *BN*, 114–15.

There were indeed more direct descriptions too, but they were also inserted within an understanding of an identification of the lyrics (text) with the poet (body) and to gently goad the reader into a predetermined semantic field. About Basti, a famous dancer (*raqāsa*) in Agra, Nadir says: 'Even as she was not very attractive, she still bore a charming disposition.'[65] And, Achpal, a prostitute in Saharanpur, is thus described by Ranj: 'Her job is to rip off the wealthy and naïve [lit. 'blind'] persons, through deceit.'[66] Citing the famous newspaper *Oudh Punch*, he goes on to add: 'She is the pathway to the city of ruination (*shahr-i barbādī*).'[67]

These biographical notes were powerful literary devices through which the *tazkira* writers sought to control meaning, and gently cajoled the reader into reading women's verse in predetermined ways. Working under the assumption of the mutually constitutive relations between the person's biography and her work, these notes, brief and succinct, served to exclude certain potential meanings and encourage certain others; they were thus crucial to the shaping of the semantics and aesthetics of women's literary contribution. Just as much as these *tazkiras* served to 'unveil' women's voices, at the very moment of doing so, they also sought to control, even appropriate, their voices. Even so, they remain commendable sources for the recovery of women's creative pursuits and lyrical compositions.

Representation of an Inclusive Literary Sphere: Articulations of Gender within an Intersectional Frame of Reference

The *kotha*s of the courtesans were not isolated islands separated from social life, and women had varying levels of interactions with the men visiting them. These relations were not always instrumental, and occasionally led to intense love affairs as well. Some of these affairs led to tragic consequences, such as the one between Gulab Singh Ashufta and Banno, mentioned earlier, in which both paid the price of their love with their lives. British officials and soldiers visited the courtesans and prostitutes,[68] and among the poets described by Ranj and Nadir, we come

---

[65] *TN*, 129.

[66] *BN*, 106.

[67] *BN*, 106.

[68] For an understanding of the anxieties that the encounters between British officials and soldiers with Hindustani women evoked, see Ballhatchet, *Race, Sex and Class under the Raj*; Durba Ghosh, *Sex and the Family in Colonial India: The Making of Empire* (Cambridge: Cambridge University Press, 2006); and William Dalrymple, *White Mughals: Love and Betrayal in Eighteenth Century India* (New Delhi: Viking, 2002).

across instances of those who were born out of their relationships. Badshah Begum, who bore the pen-name 'Khafi' ('the concealed'), was one such poet; she was the offspring of a British official, Blake, and a courtesan, Choti Begum, who had her establishment (*dera*) in the locality of Yusufwalian in Delhi. Her British father refused to accept her as his daughter, even as she left her mother's vocation and settled down with a British official living in India.[69] She was a woman of multiple talents, and, besides her skills as a poet, she excelled in English and Persian calligraphy: 'She is well versed in English, and quite accomplished in Persian and calligraphy (*khush khati*). I have seen texts in English and Persian written by her in elegant hand (*jail qalam*).'[70] In an unusual role reversal, she also provided instructive guidance to men composing poems.[71] Like several other compositions found in our *tazkiras*, her poems have an overbearing sense of pain caused by faithlessness and indifference:

> Those with whom I develop relationships,
> Are also the ones who cheat me;
> Listen Khafi, my tears that remain unheeded (*ashk-i be-tāsīr*)
> Are mocked without remorse by the people in this world.[72]

The range and variety among the 'women of the market' (*bāzāri 'aurat*) is amazing: a courtesan in love with her client, a slave girl who was averse to marriage, an illiterate courtesan who composed heart-wrenching verses, and an illegitimate daughter whose father was a British official and mother a courtesan. Adding to the richness in variety, both Ranj and Nadir have an interesting entry on the famous courtesan – described by Ranj as a 'prostitute' (*randī*) – in Hyderabad, Mahlaqa Chanda. Believed to be the first woman to have a *diwān* of her own, she was a woman of multiple talents; a gifted poet, she was also a trained wrestler, an accomplished archer, and a skilled horse rider. This is how Ranj describes her:

> Chanda, a prostitute (*randī*) was the first woman to have a *diwān* of her own. She was based in Hyderabad Dakhan, and also bore the name Mahlaqa. Owing to her opulence, she led a life of considerable splendour. There were five hundred soldiers (*sipāhis*) under her service (*namak khwār*). She lavishly patronized poets. She was a wrestler (*pahlwān*) of such excellence

---

[69]   *TN*, 147–48; *BN*, 139.
[70]   *TN*, 147; *BN*, 139.
[71]   *TN*, 147.
[72]   *TN*, 148; *BN*, 139.

that she earned the appreciation of renowned wrestlers. She was an excellent archer (*tirandāz*), so adroit and skilful that her targets were never found amiss. She was such an excellent horse rider that no cavalier, however skilled, could withstand her.[73]

It is, of course, understandable that someone so opulent and resourceful should find a place in the *tazkiras*, but along with her, Ranj and Nadir also mention someone like Kamman, a poet who had a small outlet in the market in Bharatpur (in Rajasthan) where she served an intoxicating drink, *bhāng*,[74] to men seeking to unwind themselves and experience pleasure after an exacting day's work.[75] This is how Ranj describes her:

> Kamman was both her poetic and real name. She would sit in a market (*bāzār*) in Bharatpur and sell *bhāng*. In the evening, her much-admired shop attracted a crowd of *bhāng* addicts. Once they got intoxicated, these regulars bonded well. Her stall had earned popularity and was pretty well known. She was well behaved and courteous [towards her customers]. She had learned to read and write and could compose appealing poetry as well.[76]

One cannot but appreciate the narrative strategies that the compilers adopted to emphasize the diversity and inclusiveness in the literary sphere; in their biographical compendia, someone like Kamman cosily co-exists with Mahlaqa, and both find a place alongside the spouses and daughters of rulers and high nobles, such as Akhtar who had the 'Chengizid lineage'[77] and Asir who is described in the *tazkiras* as one of the women of the Mughal household (*begumāt-i chughtai*').[78] In *TN*, there are three women bearing the nom de plume Umrao; two of them were 'public women' (*shāhid-i bāzārī*) and the third was a 'chaste woman' (*pardah nashīn*) coming from an elite family living in Delhi.[79] Alongside the poems by Rashk Mahal Begum, one of the wives of the ruler of Awadh, Wajid Ali Shah,[80] and Bahu Begum Jani, the wife of Asaf-ud

---

[73] *BN*, 127–28; also see *TN*, 139–41.
[74] *Bhāng* is an intoxicating drink that is prepared from hemp leaves.
[75] *TN*, 183; *BN*, 186.
[76] *BN*, 186.
[77] *TN*, 124–26.
[78] *BN*, 99–100; *TN*, 127.
[79] *TN*, 127–28.
[80] *BN*, 113; *TN*, 132.

Daula of Awadh (1775–97),[81] there are verses of someone like Rawia who was, insists Ranj, the daughter of a 'cloth printer' (*chepi*).[82]

Clearly, beyond suggesting that women were an integral component of the literary sphere, these *tazkiras* also draw attention to its diffused and inclusive personality – a cloth printer, a *bhāng* seller, an Englishman's illegitimate daughter, and a street performer were as much a part of the sphere as an elite courtesan, the wife of the ruler, and the daughter of a high noble. Women poets occasionally wrote as artists and littérateurs rubbing shoulders with men in raising new standards of aesthetic refinement and literary expression. Indeed, they wrote as women, but their gendered experiences were moulded by their class, caste, and community identities. They were just as crucially shaped by their spatial locations; a street performer dancing in the streets, a public entertainer singing in the marketplace, and an aristocratic woman composing poetry in the relatively tranquil and segregated spaces of her home held very different experiences of their lives and gender. Gender was never quite the primary marker of identity, but emerged as a fluid and tenuous formation, enmeshed with the other markers of social difference in the lives of the poets and their audience.

In view of this, we need to be careful about the meanings of gender in early modern South Asia. For one, while gender was certainly 'a useful category of historical analysis', the tendency to envision it in uniform and undifferentiated terms is both reductionist and ahistorical.[83] In the Persianate world, in particular, it was certainly not defined in oppositional male–female binary, and these texts indeed draw our attention to the fluidity and multiplicity of gender identities in the literary culture. Furthermore, reading these biographical compendia, we are even less convinced of the primacy of gender in shaping relations of power; in Hindustan for sure, as in other parts of the Persianate world, gender was entangled with other markers of difference, and was not, as suggested by Scott, 'a primary way of signifying relations of power'.[84] Before European modernity had come to transform the culture in Iran, as has been shown in an important study by

---

[81] *BN*, 121; *TN*, 137.

[82] *BN*, 145–46; Nadir doubts that, and his research leads him to believe that Rawia was actually Rabia, the daughter of a physician, who was particularly skilled in English styled embroidery (*TN*, 151–52).

[83] Scott, 'Gender: A Useful Category'; Also see Scott, *Gender and the Politics of History*.

[84] Scott, 'Gender: A Useful Category'. For critical evaluations of her work, see Boydston, 'Gender as a Question of Historical Analysis'; Judith M. Bennett, 'Feminism and History', *Gender and History* 1, no. 3 (September 1989): 251–72; Joan Hoff, 'Gender as a Postmodern Category of Paralysis', *Women's History Review* 3, no. 2 (1994): 149–68

Afsaneh Najmabadi, gender relations there were similarly articulated in the arts around the axis of normative manhood, and not through rigid and oppositional binaries.[85] The fluidity of gender boundaries and the collusion of gender with other forms of social hierarchies is probably a shared feature of the Persianate literary culture during our period of study.

It is, therefore, important to bear in mind that gender is not, as is rightly pointed out by Jeanne Boydston in her critique of Joan Wallach Scott, a fixed 'category of analysis', but a historical process whose nature and meaning is historically contingent and ever-shifting. It is equally important not to treat it as a 'primary' marker of difference as a generalized principle, for that risks isolating gender from the social processes. It is instructive for our study here to remember Boydston's words of caution:

> Dispensing with [gender as] the overarching category might encourage us to set aside the historically unproductive insistence on the primary-ness of gender and focus instead on the complex fabric of processes and meanings that constitute a social or cultural history. We know that 'gender' never exists as a self-sufficient or self-realizing category. In the abstract, at least, we know that there is no social subject whose experience is solely constituted through the processes of gender (however we define gender) or whose continuing *sole* identity (experienced or attributed) is gendered. Although the complexity of social processes is seldom the main point of historical gender studies, in fact virtually all of the work on gender to date demonstrates that even an identity as male or female is in constant and inseparable interplay with other processes of status and identity.[86]

Conclusion: 'Can the Courtesans and Prostitutes Speak?'

This raises the question of how to read women's poetry and to what extent, if at all, could these women speak. Following the influential work of Gayatri Spivak, scholars have argued that women cannot actually speak, and within certain strains of feminist scholarship, this is assumed to be an axiomatic truth. It has been argued by Spivak that the subalterns, including women, lack autonomy and agency; constituted in and through disciplinary discursive processes, they are not sovereign subjects of their consciousness, but are unwitting reproducers of the dominant culture and its structures of difference and hierarchy. Following her influential

---

[85] Najmabadi, 'Beyond the Americas'; Najmabadi, *Women with Mustaches*.
[86] Boydston, 'Gender as a Question', 576.

piece, historians have argued that in the modern period, language was so deeply embroiled with power and, in the case of women, forces of gender hierarchies, that it was incapable of articulating the voices and concerns of those 'on the other side of silence'. The silences that were introduced by the discursive formations have been described by Spivak, following Foucault, as instances of 'epistemic violence', and for women, the only means of resisting the violence of speech was to descend into silence.[87] Surely, women did talk but were not listened to; their voices fell into spaces of silences, and could never become an act of speech – a discourse. Entrapped in the logic of 'hegemonic listening',[88] women could not speak; their voices were quickly dismissed by the reason of language or were appropriated to reproduce the patriarchal order. Women's alleged counter-discourses only served to reinforce the dominant episteme, buttressing up the very discourse that they seemed to challenge.

Indeed, there were multiple constraints to women's speech, but we should pause, I think, before concluding from them the impossibility of speech. As suggested earlier, women litterateurs did not write as 'women', but their gendered experiences were enmeshed with their multiple identities that they so often shared with men as well. Of course, they could not dislodge the dominant episteme, nor could they speak from outside the reason of language. Even so, as the fast-expanding literature on women's writings reveals, when they wrote on a sheet of paper or composed a poem or recited a couplet, they were asserting their subjectivities and, not too infrequently, challenging social norms, including those that reproduced gender iniquities. In doing so, they had to surely negotiate the terrains of reason and language, but literate women, such as the ones mentioned in our *tazkira*s, still succeeded in expressing their emotions and sensibilities, and their experiences and concerns.

As acts of self-presentation, women's poetic compositions were important writing practices through which women constituted their selfhood and redefined their relations within their households and communities. Their life stories – memoirs, autobiographies, letters, and diaries – marked a conscious effort on their part to reclaim their agency and participate in spaces of social communication. Scholars have noticed that through their writings, women appropriated literacy

---

[87] Spivak, 'Can the Subaltern Speak?'; and Gayatri Chakravorty Spivak, *A Critique of Postcolonial Reason: Toward a History of the Vanishing Present* (Cambridge, MA: Harvard University Press, 1999).

[88] Nikita Dhawan, 'Hegemonic Listening and Subversive Silences: Ethico-political Imperatives', in *Destruction in the Performative*, ed. Alice Lagaay and Michael Lorber, 47–60 (Amsterdam: Rodopi, 2012).

to critique and redefine community norms and the position of women within their communities.[89] It has rightly been argued by Anshu Malhotra and Siobhan Lambert-Hurley that women's autobiographies in South Asia were performative acts of self-representation, in which women appropriated the resources of language – the power of words, narrative choices, metaphors, and allusions – to fashion their identities and subjectivities.[90] Describing women's autobiographies as 'speaking of the self', their work draws attention to the presentation of the 'self-in-performance' in women's writings in South Asia.[91] While Spivak is right in cautioning us against ignoring the epistemic and discursive violence and the ordered and elusive silences in language, it would nonetheless be ahistorical to deny agency and subjectivity to women in speech (and text).

Even so, women wrote from a multiplicity of social locations, and while the complexities of gender were ever present, these were, as earlier argued, mediated by their community ties, social position, class and caste considerations, and distance from the networks of patronage and political authority. In this context, Siobhan Lambert-Hurley's study of South Asian Muslim women's autobiographies is particularly relevant.[92] She disputes the widely shared assumption that autobiographical writings were an exclusively European invention, which were later imbibed, to varying levels of finesse and perfection, by the literate communities in Asia during the late nineteenth and twentieth centuries. On the contrary, even as autobiographies emerged as a distinctive genre of writing only in the colonial period, her work argues that in their growth and expansion, it was the social and cultural developments taking place in South Asia that were of primary significance – the development of printing presses, expansion in literacy, social reform activities, restructuring of the household spaces, and the qualitatively greater participation of merchant groups and service gentry in social communication.[93] In the case of Muslim women's autobiographies, her work found gender to be entangled with

---

[89]   In addition to the literature cited earlier, see the following compilation of women's writings in India: Susie Tharu and K. Lalit (eds.), *Women Writing in India, Vol. 1: 600 B.C. to the Early Twentieth Century* (New York: Feminist Press, 1991); Susie Tharu and K. Lalit (eds.), *Women Writing in India, Vol. 2: The Twentieth Century* (New York: Feminist Press, 1993).

[90]   Malhotra and Lambert-Hurley, *Speaking of the Self*.

[91]   See 'Introduction: Gender, Performance, and Autobiography in South Asia,' in Malhotra and Lambert-Hurley, *Speaking of the Self*, 1–30.

[92]   Lambert-Hurley, *Elusive Lives*.

[93]   Lambert-Hurley, *Elusive Lives*. Also see David Arnold and Stuart Blackburn (eds.), *Telling Lives in India: Biography, Autobiography, and Life History* (Bloomington, Indiana: Indiana University Press, 2004); and Vijaya Ramaswamy and Yogesh Sharma (eds.), *Biography as History: Indian Perspectives* (New Delhi: Orient Blackswan, 2018)

community identities, educational attainments, and the anxieties of their 'noble' or *ashraf* background. Even so, 'the collectivities to which women in Muslim South Asia belonged – clan, community, country – did not undermine a sense of self so much as frame their multiple and varied expressions of interiority'.[94] In this, their experiences were very similar to what the Islamic feminist scholarship suggests was the case in the Islamic world as well.[95]

Appendix 3A.1

Yasmin, a Slave Girl[96]

Yasmin was her pen name (*takhallus*), and her real name was Chameli. This lady was a slave (*kanīz*) of the late Inshaallah Khan, and was extremely learned and intelligent (*nihāyat taba'a aur fahīm*). She was averse to the idea of marriage. It is said that when Inshaallah Khan, after repeated admonitions, finally got her married to someone, she died after just three days of her marriage. Nobody knows the reasons [that caused her death].

Verses of Yasmin

He came down with speed but only after the news of my death reached him,
He left his house [for my place] only after life had departed from my body;
When I saw my house, I was reminded of a desert,
And, when I came across a desert, I remembered my house.

Āye kyā jald khabar ko qaza āne ke bād
Ghar se niklē woh merī jān nikal jāne ke bād
Yād āya mujhe ghar dekh ke dasht
Dasht ko dekh ke ghar yād āyā.

---

[94]   Lambert-Hurley, *Elusive Lives*, 25.

[95]   See Margot Badran and Miriam Cooke (eds.), *Opening the Gates: An Anthology of Arab Feminist Writing* (Bloomington and Indianapolis: Indiana University Press, 2004 [second edition]); and Margot Badran, *Feminists, Islam, and the Nation: Gender and the Making of Modern Egypt* (Princeton: Princeton University Press, 1996). Also see Farzaneh Milani, *Words, Not Swords: Iranian Women Writers and the Freedom of Movement* (Syracuse, NY: Syracuse University Press, 2011); and Booth, 'Locating Women's Autobiographical Writings'.

[96]   *BN*, 238; also see *TN*, 207.

Appendix 3A.2

Nazakat, a Sitar Maestra[97]

Nazakat is her poetic name (*takhallus*), and her real name is Kandu. She is the daughter of one Husaini and lives in Jaipur. She is charming (*tarhdār*) and is fond of playing the sitar. She is no riff-raff (*kachad khalil*), but has her own well-known establishment (*dera*). She is not educated, but her poetry is the source of envy for such accomplished poets as Mushtari and Sardari.[98] She got her ghazals corrected (*durust*) from Mir Wajid Ali Lakhnawi Shagufta, and his suggestions served her well.

Verses of Nazakat

(1)

If I am an injured nightingale (*bulbul*) today, it is because I belong to you,
If I have lost my freedom today, it is because I belong to you;
The [strained] relations that I have with the angels these days,
[And] If they see me as a sinner (*gunehgār*), it is because I belong to you.
Even the healing touch of Christ has failed to cure me,
If I am so very sick today, this is because I belong to you.

Bulbul-i zār hun to terā hun,
Main giraftār hun to terā hun;
Un farishtōn kā wāsta mujh sē,
Main gunehgār hun to terā hun;
Hun na achā kabhī masihā sē,
Main jo bīmār hun to terā hun.

(2)

She does not kiss me on my cheek, nor does she let me touch her hair,
A whole lifetime has passed me by with this indifference, day in and night;
What is so special if two to four persons lose their lives owing to the indifference [of the beloved]?
When my beloved applies henna [on her hands and feet],[99] she causes a bloodbath.

---

[97] *BN*, 231; also see *TN*, 203.

[98] Mushtari and Sardari were courtesans who were well known for their poetic compositions. For details about Mushtari, see Chapter 4.

[99] *Mehndi*, or henna, was applied by women on their hands and feet to give them an alluring appearance. It turned the hands and feet endearingly red, and served to emit a pleasant smell. *Henna* was also used by women and men to dye their hair as well.

Na bosah rukh kā dētē hain na gēsū chūne dētē hain,
Yūn hī ek 'umr guzrī hai ki subh-o shām kartē hain;
Hue do chār khungar nāgahānī se 'ajab kiyā hai,
Woh jab mehndi lagāte hain to qatl-i-'ām kartē hain.

Appendix 3A.3

Araish, a Retired 'Public Performer'[100]

Araish was her pen name, and her real name is not known. Once she used to lend her charm to the Delhi market (*bāzār Dehlī*). Now, she is illuminating someone's house [is settled and living in a house]. The following verse by her describes her life (*hasb-i hāl*):

> When I was young, it suited me to get all dressed and decked up,
> In this old age, applying henna (*mehndī*) and dentifrice (*missī*) serve no purpose.

> *Jawāni men bhali ma'lūm hotī thīye Ārā'ish*
> *Budhāpe men to mehndī missī ki hai khāk zebā'ish.*

Appendix 3A.4

Banno, a Concubine, and Her Mortal Love Story[101]

Based in Delhi, Banno was in a relationship (*rabt zabt*) with Gulab Singh Ashufta. A respectable gentleman from his community has informed us that she was a prostitute (*kasbī*). Ashufta belonged to the community (*qaum*) of the *khatri*s, and resided in the colony of the *mahājan*s in the Chandni Chowk market....

Distressed by her momentary absence (*mufāriqat*), Ashufta slit open his throat and ended his life. Look at the intensity of love (*jazba-i 'ishq*) that his beloved (*dilbar*) immediately rushed to save him, but was prevented by his near and dear ones from reaching him on the pretence that she had lost her mind. Feeling weak and helpless, she found solace in the following verse of her lover:

> Those who are afflicted with the disease of love (*'ishq*) stand no chance of survival,
> Oh Lord! Let no one suffer this affliction of love.

---

[100] *TN*, 124; also see *BN*, 99.
[101] *TN*, 129–31; also see *BN*, 107–09.

Bachta nahīn hai koi' bhī bimār-i 'ishq se,
Yā rab! Nā ho kisī kō ye āzār 'ishq se.

And so it is, this poetess repented for her excesses, and within six months or so went on to meet the soul of her earnest companion (*muhib-i sādiq*).

Verses of Banno

(1)

Leaving me alone, where forth do you, the wayward idol, depart?
Wherever you go, my heart will accompany you;
In the death caused by your mortal glances, I have found release from sorrows,
Why don't you, the source of my affliction, [release me and] cut my throat with the knife (*churī*).

Chod kar mujhkō kahān Ae but-i gumrāh chalā
Tū chalā kyā ki yeh dil bhī terē hamrāh chalā
Chūt gayā gham se merā kushta-i abru mar kar
Ek churī merē galē par bhi meri āh chalā.

(2)

Death doesn't come to me, nor is life any friend of mine either,
It is true, Ashufta, your death has killed me as well;
I don't control death, for if that were so,
Without you near me, I would surely have rejected life;
Where have disappeared peace (*chain*), comfort (*'aish*) and the bed to sleep (*bistar-i khwāb*);
Even the silken (*makhmal*) bed aches the body no less than the bed of thorns (*bistar-i khārā*);
In the din caused by all the wailing and lamentations,
Why did you not call for me when they were taking you away?

Nā maut āti hai', nā zīst ka yārā mujh ko
Hai' Āshufta, tere marne ne mārā mujh ko
Maut par bas nahīn chaltā hai karūn kyā, warnā
Tū nahīn hai to nahīn zīst gawārā mujh ko
Ab kise chain, kahān 'aish, kidhar bistar-i khwāb
Nahīn makhmal bhi kam az bistar-i khārā mujh ko

Kyā hoī, hāi' fughān kī terē shor angezī
Lē chalē tujh ko tō tūne na pukārā mujh ko.

Appendix 3A.5

Mahlaqa Chanda, a High-Class Prostitute and a Wrestler[102]

Chanda was a prostitute (*randī*). She is known as the first woman poet to have her own *diwān*. She was affluent and led a life of ease and comfort. She had five hundred soldiers in her employ, and lavishly patronised the poets as well. She was an excellent wrestler (*pahlwān*), and her skills were appreciated by the well-known wrestlers. She was an accomplished archer (*tirandāz*), and her targets were never amiss. An excellent horse rider, she could not be beaten by the most accomplished among them. She was an intelligent student (*shāgird-i rashīd*) of Sher Muhammad Khan, and no one at the time had seen or heard a better poetess than her. This was the time when Arastu Jah was the governor of the Deccan, and Alamgir-II the sovereign. Her physical charms and skills as a poet were a hot topic of discussion everywhere. The author of *Tabaqātush Shu'arā* has written that she had presented her *diwān* to an influential English official at a function in 1799. Her *diwān* was believed to be preserved at the Qaisari library, but her poetic compositions are no more extant (*mafqud*).

Mahlaqa's Verses

Unless you became conscious of [the limitations of] your disposition,
You would have conceited views about yourself.

Akhlāq se to apne wāqif jahān rahegā
Par āp kō ghalat kuch ab tak gumān rahegā.

Appendix 3A.6

Hur: A Public Performer Based in Lucknow[103]

This Hur is Hur-II (*hūr-i sānī*), and she is the student (*shāgird*) of Muhammad Raza bearing the pen name (*takhallus*) of Tur. She is a graceful performer (*shīrīn adā*) and her verses are tasteful as well.

---

[102] *TN*, 139–41.
[103] *TN*, 145; also see *BN*, 137.

Verses of Hur

When you, the fairy (*parī*) one, wore the gold anklets (*toda*) on your feet,
Your lover (*dīwāna*) was, with the burden of the heavy chains, crushed under your feet;
To those who were nasty to me, I treated them with kindness,
It is in my temperament (*khū*) to befriend those who are my enemies.

Jo pahnā pāon men sonē kā todā, ae parī tūne
Masalsal pāi' dīwana huā zanjīr-i āhan se
Badī kī jis ne hamse hamne us ke sāth nēki ki
Hamārī khū hai ye, hum dostī karte hain dushman se.

Appendix 3A.7

Khafi: A Half-British Poetess[104]

Khafi is her pen name (*takhallus*); her real name is Badshah Begum, and she is the daughter of Choti Begum.[105] Her seat (*dera*) is known as Yusufwalian in Delhi. It is believed that she is the granddaughter [from her maternal side] (*nawāsī*) of the Kashmiri merchant (*saudāgar*), Muhammad Yusuf; and was born out of the illicit relations [of her mother] with a high British official (Sahib Bahadur)[106] called Blake. Leaving the vocation of her mother, she is now living with an Englishman, but Sahib Bahadur [her father] still doesn't accept her [as his daughter]. She is well versed in English and quite accomplished in Persian and calligraphy (*khush khati*). I have seen texts in English and Persian written by her in elegant hand (*jail qalam*). God be praised! She writes with such elegance and also provides guidance (*islāh*) to select men.

Khafi's Verses

[Durga Prashad Nadir admits to lifting her verses from Fasihuddin Ganj's *Bahāristān-i Nāz*.]

---

[104] *TN*, 147–48; also see *BN*, 139.
[105] It is interesting to note here that the lineage of Khafi, as was the case with prostitutes and low-caste performers, is traced along her maternal side.
[106] High British officials were addressed, out of respect and in recognition of their authority, in Persian and Urdu sources as *sahib bahadur*.

(1)

In the love for captivity (*shauq-i asīrī*), I allowed myself to be entrapped in the trap set up by the hunter,

I was not tempted by even a single grain [that he had sprinkled to capture me].

Khud shauq-i asīrī se phanse dām men saiyād
Sharmindah tere ek bhi dāne ke nahin hum.

(2)

Those with whom I develop relationships,
Are also the ones who cheat me;
Oh Khafi! My tears which remain unheeded,
Are mocked without remorse by the people in this world.

Jin se hum āshnāi' karte hain
Hum se who bewafāi' karte hain
Ae Khafi! Apne ashk-i be-tāsīr
Muft men jag hansāi' karte hain.

Appendix 3A.8

Naz: A Public Performer of Lucknow [107]

Naz is her pen name (*takhallus*), and her name is Amir Jan. She is the daughter of Gauhar Jan. She is one of the public performers (*hasinān-i bāzārī*) in Lucknow.

Naz's *Ghazal*

In his assembly (*mehfil*), he offered me the seat next to him,
Now that I am without a heart (*be-dil*), he seeks to comfort my [missing] heart;
Bearing the qualities of an angel (*hūr-i shamā'il*), he took me to the rooftop,
Once there, I saw myself ascending to heaven (*mi'rāj*);[108]
After slaughtering (*bismil*) me with the sword of his coquettish glances (*tegh-i nigāh-i nāz*)
My assassin kept [ruefully] looking at me for a very long time;

---

[107] *BN*, 219–20.

[108] In Islamic theology, *me'rāj* refers to Prophet Muhammad's alleged journey to heaven.

I shall depart from this world in just a few moments (*dam*), so stay with me for a few more minutes,

Will you leave me now when I am slaughtered [and just about to leave this world]?

In my presence, my companion (*yār*) enjoyed the heat of intimacies (*garmiyān*) with a stranger,

Like a candle, he lit me [and burned me out] at the assembly (*mahfil*);

The respect that my friends have for me would increase,

If you were to address me with frankness and insolence [lit. 'call me *tū* (instead of *tum*)'];[109]

I wrote this *ghazal* at the insistence of my friends,

Even as my heart was never into it.

Apnē pahlū men jagāh di sar-i mahfil mujh ko
Dil dehi yār ne dekh ke be-dil mujh ko
Lē gayā bām pe woh hūr shamai'l mujh ko
Aaj me'rāj kā rutba huā hāsil mujh ko
Karke tegh-i nigāh-i nāz se bismil mujh ko
Dēr tak ghaur sē dekhā kiyā qātil mujh ko
Aur mehmān hun koi' dam kā zara thairō to
Kyā chale jāoge ab chod kē bismil mujh ko
Garmiyān yār ne kin ghair sē mērē āge
Sifat-i shama' jalāyā sar-i mahfil mujh ko
Chashm-i ahbāb men afzūn merī 'izzat ho jai'
Tum jo tū keh kar pukārō sar-i mahfil mujh ko
Nāz ahbāb ki khatir se likhī main ne ghazal
Go ki deta thā ijāzat na merā dil mujh ko.

Appendix 3A.9

Nazakat: An Affluent and Gifted Singer[110]

Ramju was her name, and her pen name was Nazakat. She lived in Narnaul, and had a melodious voice (*khush go*). For a very long time, she led a life of comfort and affluence in Faizabad and Shahjahanabad. She rubbed shoulders with the lovers

---

[109] In the Urdu language, both *tu* and *tum* mean 'you', but the former expression is considered impolite and/or candid.

[110] *BN*, 221–22; also see *TN*, 202–03.

of literature from dusk to dawn. She was lost in the world of poetry, engrossed in finding forms of appropriate expression. She died on the day of her marriage. She had a house at Charkhawalan in Delhi, which can still be seen.

Nazakat's Verses

(1)

Since my beloved (*yār*) resides in my eyes,
The vision of my eyes is impaired with agitation;
In the assembly of rose-faced damsels, that trickster,
Stole my heart before a thousand watchful eyes;
Blessed am I that the dust of his feet (*khāk-i pā*) has become my collyrium (*surma*),
For the dust [from his feet] has reached my eyes.

Bas ki rahtā hai yār ānkhon men
Hai' nazar be-qarār ānkhon men
Mehfil-i gul-i rukhsān men woh 'aiyār
Lē gayā dil hazār ānkhon men
Surma-i khāk-i pā 'ināyat ho
Āgayā hai ghubār ānkhon men.

(2)

He asks me if my love for him is just an artifice,
For love these days has disappeared from the world;
How many ordeals have I borne in this dungeon of love (*andoh-i 'ishq*),
Nazakat, there's nothing left in me now, except my name.

Kahtā hai āp ki bhī hai kyā 'ashiqi ghalat
Gar kahiyae terē 'ahd men ulfat nahin rahī
Kyā kyā 'azāb uthai' hain andoh-i 'ishq men
Juz nām ab to kuch bhī Nazakat nahin rahī.

(3)

Even as you, my indifferent idol, commits such injustices (*na-munsifī*),
There would still be others who would be drawn to you, but surely none like me;
If this is the retribution for desiring you, Oh tyrant (*zālim*),
This transgression would never be committed again.

Nā-munsafi aur āye but-i bedād gar aisī
Chāhat terī ghairon ko bhī hogī magar aisī
Harmān hai agar chāh ki ta'zīr to zālim
Taqsīr na hogī kabhī bār-i dīgar aisī.

Appendix 3A.10

Shararat: A Kanchani *in Chawri Bazaar*[111]

Her name is Amir Jan, and her pen name Shararat. A *kanchan-i dehlavi* (a *kanchan* living in Delhi), she is the daughter of Chote Khan.

[Nadir on the *kanchani*s: An ethno-linguistic interlude:]

While reflecting on the meaning of the word *kanchan*, it came to my mind that the common people (*'awām-un-nas*) refer to *kasbī*s as *kanchī*s, and the people in Punjab call them *kanjars* (*kanjariyan*). In the region of Dehradun, and the adjoining places, they are called *patar*s, and at some other places, *ramjunya*. None of these descriptions takes us to the reality of their origins. My investigations revealed to me that in Hindustan, before the arrival of Islam, there were Hindu dancers (*Hinduan raqāsa*) who were variously called *pātra*, *gāinan*, *bichur*, *kandharbunya*, and so on. In the Sanskrit texts, they are mentioned as *barīd*. When the Muslims arrived in this country (*mulk*), they allowed their women to practise this vocation, and Muslim women dancers created their own groups that were identified with the communities (*firqa*) they came from; and so it is that we have today several dancing communities: *kanchan*, *kanjar*, *nat*, *ramjani*, *pātar*, *rāwat*, *dhiwat*, *dhiye*, and so on.

Besides them, there are those shameless women (*chināl*) who desert their homes and take to prostitution (*kasb-i 'ām*), and they are called *khāngī*. They take willing women within their community only after an elaborate feast, and until she [a prostitute] becomes a member of their community, she is treated with disdain, even if she is wealthy or talented.

Over and above them both are the community of *chinalun*; neither are they seen in state surveys nor do they ever visit the hospitals [presumably, for medical check-ups for sexually transmitted diseases]. Hidden [from the gaze of the state], they enjoy life, and vilify them both [the *kanchani*s and the *khāngī*].

[Returning to Shararat, the author further adds:]

Returning to the topic, this *kanchanī* has come back here after a long sojourn during which time she visited Mathura, Agra, Tonk, and other places. One of

---

[111] *TN*, 163–65; also see *BN*, 161–62.

her poems has been published in *Majmu'at-ul ash'ār* published from Agra. The second *ghazal* [recorded by Nadir here] was recited by the poet herself at a poetic gathering (*mushā'ira*), and is recorded in this *tazkira*. She has herself admitted, 'I recited verses earlier too, but it was only after I became the student (*shāgird*) of Amir Khan Sahib Mirza Akbarabadi, who resides in Mathura, that I have been able to compose about fifty to a hundred *ghazals*.'

She is today above thirty years of age. She is unconcerned with knowledge and is barely literate (*harf shanās*). She is both a singer and dancer, and resides at a *kotha* in Chawri Bazaar. She is apparently well behaved.

Verses of Shararat

(1)

My slayer turned my night of separation into a nightmare,
I had several painful deaths before the arrival of the dawn;
The night turned dark with the lamp in the assembly,
For the flowers withered away when they saw the slayer in that assembly.

Aisi mujh par rāt mushkil furqat-i qātil ne ki
Sāth mere subh mar mar kar merī mushkil ne ki
Rū-siyāhī shab ko apnī mash'al-i mahfil ne ki
Hō gayī sāq wājib bazm men qātil ne ki.[112]

(2)

I have no control over my life! What should I do, my God, I am helpless,
My Beloved ['my heart'] has done something that he should not have done to me;
The ship of my existence is drowned in such a river of misfortune,
That even the shore (*sāhil*) shudders from giving me refuge.

Bas nahīn chaltā hai' yā-rab! kyā karen, nāchār hain
Jo na karnī thī hamāre sāth woh us dil ne ki
Aisī daryā-i balā men gharq hai' kashtī merī
Tauba jis ke nām sē aye nā-khudā sāhil ne ki.[113]

---

[112] *TN*, 165; *BN*, 121.
[113] *TN*, 165; *BN*, 121.

Appendix 3A.11

Kamman: A Bhāng Seller Who Writes Poetry[114]

Kamman was her name, and this was also the name she used in her poetry. She had a shop in a market in Bharatpur where she sold *bhāng*. Late in the evening, her popular shop attracted a good number of *bhāng* addicts. Once intoxicated, these regulars bonded well with one another. Her stall was quite popular, and was well known there. She was quite well behaved and courteous. She had taught herself reading and writing, and was now composing poetry.

Kamman's Verse

> If I were with Shabbir [in his battle with Yadith],[115]
> I would have killed Shimr[116] through my stratagems.

Appendix 3A.12

Farhat: A Singer Who Enticed Tansen's Soul[117]

Farhat is her pen name, and her name is Farhat Baksh. She comes from a family of prostitutes in Faizabad. She was in the service of a *nawab*. She was so brilliant in music that when she sang, the soul of Tansen would come and attend her performance (*mujra*). She was fully devoted to the art of poetry.

Verses of Farhat

> I have fallen for your braided hair; shouldn't you reciprocate,
> I have provoked a snake, for God's sake let there be a response;
> I will never let go of the enticing hair of my idol, Oh preacher,
> Why should you be concerned about me; just leave me alone.

> *Dil lagāya hai' terī zulf-i dota se, kuch ho*
> *Sānp ko ched liyā ab to balā se kuch ho*
> *Main na chodungi sar-i zulf-i butān ae wā'aiz*
> *Merī kyā tujh ko padī teri balā se kuch ho.*

---

[114] *BN*, 186; also see *TN*, 183.

[115] The reference is to the battle between the grandson of Muhammad, Husain, and the son of Muawiya, the governor of Syria, Yadith, at Karbala in Iraq.

[116] Shimr was the military commander who defected to Muawiya and, at the battle at Karbala, slayed Husain.

[117] *BN*, 180; see also *TN*, 181.

4

Representing the *Kothas*

The Two Sisters in the Literary Sphere

In this chapter, we look at, with a focus on two sisters, both courtesans – Zuhra and Mushtari – the meaning of and constraints on the participation of women entertainers in the literary sphere. We hear them 'speak' and from their speech-acts explore their construction of selfhood, articulation of subjectivities, and resistance to dominant social and literary norms. At the same time, we make an effort to unravel the anxieties that their literary talents evoked in the sociocultural spaces, and the reasons for their immense popularity in social memory. We also ask how their agency in the cultural domain was represented in the literary sphere, in particular the biographical compendia of the time.

The Courtesans as Models of Literary Emulation: The Pre-eminence of the Sisters in Cultural Spaces

Why these sisters? My reason for choosing them is because their literary acumen was widely accepted, and critics often measured the compositions of other women poets against the depth and range of their poems. The sisters had, it seems, set the standards that other poets were expected to aspire to and emulate. Nazakat, 'an endearing public performer' (*mahbūba-i bāzārī*) based in Bombay, wrote a couplet and a *ghazal* as an accompaniment to (and in the same meter as) one of the poems of Mushtari; comparing her effort with the literary skills of the two sisters, Nadir found her endeavour no more than 'meaningless verbosity' (*tūl-i fazūl*), and decided not to include the *ghazal* in his *tazkira*.[1] Ranj was blunt, and saw her attempt to imitate Mushtari as ridiculous. He says:

---

1   *TN*, 204.

She [Nazakat] wrote this *ghazal* which she visualized as an aesthetic response to one of the poems of Mushtari Lucknawi. How can the Sun be compared with a tiny particle (*kahān zarrah kahān āftāb*)? How can the shoddy distich (*bhadde ashʿār*) of Nazakat be an answer to the *ghazal*s of Mushtari?[2]

In the case of another courtesan by the same name, Nazakat, Ranj expressed his appreciation of her poetry by comparing her with Mushtari (and Sardar). This courtesan, based in Jaipur, could, says Ranj, get the likes of Mushtari envious.[3] Clearly then, in matters of literary expression and aesthetics, Mushtari, and her sister, Zuhra, were held out as models against whom other poets were assessed, and their compositions evaluated. A study of their literary compositions could help us better understand the critical standards by which women's poems were assessed, and hopefully provide us clues about the conditions under which their lyrical compositions earned such respect and popularity.

Zuhra and Mushtari were sisters who had their salon in Chowk Bazaar in Lucknow. They were both accomplished courtesans and counted among their clients the respectable gentlemen or the *mirza*s living in the city.[4] The former was popularly known as Bi Chuttan, but her real name was Umrao Jan.[5] Describing her, Ranj says that she was 'skilled in composing verses, and her insolence (*shokh tabʿī*) was famous everywhere'.[6] From a note (*tahrīr*) by Mushtari, Ranj had come to know that she had left her profession and had married and settled down with an established aristocrat (*raʾīs ʿalā khāndān*), and, away from the public, was now living in seclusion as a 'chaste lady' (*pardah nashīn*).[7] Her sister, Mushtari, was perhaps better educated and, along with Urdu, composed poems in Persian as well. Nadir discusses her in two places, once in the section on Persian poets and then again in the section on Urdu poets.[8] Her real name was Qamran Jan, but she was popularly known as Bi Manjhu.[9]

---

[2]   *BN*, 232.

[3]   *BN*, 231.

[4]   For references to Zuhra, see *TN*, 155–59; *BN*, 146–47; and for Mushtari, see *TN*, 87, 192–93; *BN*, 202–05.

[5]   *TN*, 155; *BN*, 146.

[6]   *BN*, 146.

[7]   *BN*, 146.

[8]   *TN*, 87, 192–93.

[9]   *TN*, 192; *BN*, 202. *Manjhu* in Urdu refers to the daughter or the son who is neither the eldest nor the youngest but placed in between. *Chuttan*, on the other hand, means the youngest child. In all likelihood, Mushtari (Manjhu) was Zuhra's elder sister.

The Trope of the Tutor in Love: The Sisters' Instructor, Their Mother's Lover, and Intimate Spaces

What made these women such exceptional literary figures? For the *tazkira* writers, it was the close and diligent guidance of their tutor, Mir Agha Ali Shams, that was the main reason behind their extraordinary success and popularity. Ranj and Nadir are unequivocal in believing that the richness in language, depth of expression, and attentiveness to allusions and metaphors in the work of these sisters was a result of their education and training at the hands of Shams. In his entry on Mushtari, Ranj generously praises her for her literary skills and aesthetic niceties, and commends her for her 'distinctive imagination' (*khyāl-i be-misālī*), 'sharp intellect' (*tez*), and 'reflective mind' (*fikr-rasā*), but immediately qualifies his appreciation by adding that she had acquired her education from Shams.[10] In an effort to communicate an impression of dependant agency while, at the same time, drawing attention to the immense appeal and crowd-pulling abilities of the two sisters, Ranj goes on to add:

> God be praised! Just like their teacher (*ustād*), Zuhra and Mushtari are famous (in the literary circles). Why should that not be the case? After all, when the teacher provides instruction with such concern, how would the student (*shāgird*) be prevented from becoming a household name (*ghar ghar shuhrat pāyen*)? The fact is that Shams has glistened both these sparks of light (*parkāla-i ātish*) in such a way that Zuhra and Mushtari shine like stars in the sky. If she continues to receive instruction (*ta'līm*) from him in the future as well, the fame of Mushtari would reach the skies. Since the age of seven, this poetess was fond of reading and writing, and this brilliant star (*sitara-i jalwa rez*) has since then been receiving her education from honourable Shams, and has now emerged as the full moon (*chaudhwi rāt kā pūrā chānd*).[11]

Recounting her success story, Ranj informs us that Mushtari was a property holder and owned a mosque, a Shi'ite place for ritual mourning (*imāmbārah*), a garden, and a hereditary house in Khairabad. She was, it seems, quite well read, and was particularly accomplished in Persian and Urdu literature, history writing, and calligraphy – both free-hand (*khati jali*) and ornate (*khazi jali*) – and enjoyed 'worldwide popularity in the art of literary imagination (*pindār*)'.[12] For all her skills and achievements, Ranj is emphatic in placing the credit at the door of her teacher, Shams:

---

[10] *BN*, 202.

[11] *BN*, 202–03.

[12] *BN*, 203.

Thanks to the efforts of her sincere teacher (*ustād-i shafīq*), there was scarcely any subtlety in linguistic expression that was unknown to her. There was scarcely any poetic gathering (*bazm-i mushā'ira*) bereft of audience clamouring for Shams, Zuhra, and Mushtari. Why shouldn't this poetess [Mushtari] be an expert (*kāmil*) in so many skills; after all, her *ustād* is himself an accomplished man (*sahib-i kamāl*).[13]

The teacher–student dyad is a recurrent theme in the biographical notes of women poets, and it serves to communicate the author's dependence and her lack of autonomy; more importantly, it creates an impression of multiple authorial presences in women's poetic compositions. Sticking to the two sisters, Ranj describes Zuhra in much the same way as he describes Mushtari, as someone whose poetic talents were carefully honed by their tutor, Shams:

She is the student (*shāgird*) of Mir Agha Ali Shams, and he is the one who has made her what she is today. Mir's accomplishments outshine the sun, and he is the one who has perfected Zuhra's language. If the student is good, then it is a source of pride for the teacher. Thanks to Zuhra, Mian Shams is remembered every moment of the day [in the poetic gatherings].[14]

Like Ranj, Nadir also emphasizes the role of Shams in the literary achievements of Zuhra and Mushtari, and we could have skipped those details here, but he complicates his narrative by introducing the sisters' mother into the picture. In his captivating story, the student–teacher dyad is actually a triad, and includes, besides the sisters and their tutor, their mother (also a courtesan) as well. We need to pursue his story not for its salacious content, but to recover the complexities that informed the presence of courtesans in literary culture. Like Ranj, Nadir acknowledges the extraordinary talents of Zuhra and Mushtari but is severely condemnatory of their arrogant, blunt, and irreverent attitude, which, he believes, mars the quality of their literary compositions. Modesty and politeness of speech were an important component of the literary *adāb*, or norms of etiquette, and by violating them, they were damaging the literary culture, but, more importantly, their place therein. Nadir describes Zuhra as a 'babbler' (*munh-phat*) and 'loudmouthed' (*munh-zor*),[15] but what really disturbs him is the insolence with which they poke fun at the accomplished scholars in the field: 'These prostitutes (*randiyān*) are loudmouthed, and often Urdu newspapers carry their critical comments.

---

13 *BN*, 203.
14 *BN*, 146.
15 *TN*, 154–55.

They ridicule (*ta'n*) the accomplished scholars and, perhaps misguided by their names,[16] see themselves as strolling in the skies.'[17]

What we see here is not just the articulation of the norms of appropriate behaviour or *adāb*, but also the anxieties that their infringement caused for the literate public in the nineteenth century. These norms governed the teacher–student relations as well, and it is here that the sisters committed the most unforgivable offence; contrary to the expected deference due to a teacher, Zuhra and Mushtari had earned quite a reputation for belittling him and treating him in public gatherings with uncharacteristic indifference and rudeness. It was believed that Shams patiently bore their taunts and disdain, and was deeply involved in their education because he was in love with their mother; Nadir describes his feelings for her as a kind of 'exclusive attachment' (*rabt-ba ikhtisās*).[18]

It seems that this was a much-discussed issue in the literary gatherings, and this was a view that was shared not just by our authors but by other littérateurs as well. Nadir reproduces a versified letter on this issue from the *diwān* of Amirullah Taslim, and we shall take that poem here to gain a better grasp of the social perceptions of women poets who came from the social margins, and delve deeper into the teacher–student relations in the lives of the courtesans.[19] The poet describes the sisters as 'the shining stars of the literate world', and if that was not enough of a compliment, further adds: 'They shine forth like the illustrious sun and the moon' (*Ze mehrah khudāwand-i khurshīd-o māh*).[20] They reached the height of success because of their education, and the close attention of their teacher, Mir Shams; and yet they have not only ignored his many acts of kindness but have also immensely hurt him by treating him at times with indifference, and other times with disdain. They were 'unkind' (*nā-mahrbāni*) to him, and 'stabbed him with the dagger of cruelty' (*tegh-i sitam*).[21]

In doing so, they had clearly disrespected one of the significant components of literary etiquette, or *adāb*, and Taslim terms it as constituting the 'rights of the teacher' (*haq-i ustād*):

They have ignored the rights of the teacher (*haq-i ustād*),
And have blackened their face in the eternal abode.

---

[16] 'Zuhra' is Venus, and 'Mushtari' means Jupiter in the Persian language.
[17] *TN*, 154.
[18] *TN*, 155.
[19] *TN*, 155–56.
[20] *TN*, 155.
[21] *TN*, 155.

Farāmosh kardan haq-i ustād
Bua'd ru-siyāhi badar-ul-ma'ād.[22]

Hinting at Shams' attachment to their mother, Taslim blames him for his pitiable condition; after all, he should have carried himself with more dignity and grace, and refrained from wastefully spending long hours at their *kotha* in the company of music, dance, and the woman he loved:

> May God, the protector of this world, forgive him [Shams],
> For his indulgence was unworthy of his position;
> He should have reflected on the implications of his activities,
> And should have, for a moment at least, felt ashamed (*sharm*) about his actions;
> All the time, he was busy with dance and music (*raqs wa sarūd-o ghanā*),
> Every night, he would indulge in debauchery and adulterous activities (*fusūq-o fujūr-o zinā*);
> We should follow the instructions of our auspicious Prophet [Muhammad],
> Where in the Koran are these activities considered permissible (*halāl*)?[23]

Adāb in Cultural Spaces: The 'Rights' of the Teacher and Reverence for the Masters

Following this anecdote, we are reminded of the *adāb* in literary spaces, and the kind of anxieties their infringement aroused among the literati and laymen alike.[24] It was expected that the poet should be humble and down to earth, and the sisters lost their credibility once they assumed airs and behaved in a haughty and conceited manner. It was also against the prevailing *adāb* for the student to ignore and disrespect her teacher, and to refuse to extend formal courtesies to him. A teacher had certain 'rights' (*huqūq*), and one such right was to receive deferential treatment from his students. At the same time, it was also not expected of a teacher to fall in love with a courtesan or a prostitute, and to indulge in a

---

[22] *TN*, 156.
[23] *TN*, 156.
[24] For a detailed exposition of the *adāb* in the Persianate world, see Kia, *Persianate Selves*; and Barbara Daly Metcalf (ed.), *Moral Conduct and Authority: The Place of Adab in South Asia* (Berkeley: University of California Press, 1984. Also see Kia, '*Adab* as Literary Form'; and Arley Loewen, 'Proper Conduct (*Adab*) Is Everything: The *Futuwwat-namah-i Sultani* of Husayn Va'iz-i Kashifi', *Iranian Studies* 36, no. 4 (December 2003): 543–70.

life given to pleasure and entertainment, an offence for which Shams paid dearly. Like a 'gentleman' or the *mirza*, he should have a taste for the good things in life but should avoid excess or intemperance; life was to be enjoyed in moderation. He should be a connoisseur of the arts and letters, and extend patronage to artists, but should refrain from developing intimacies with them. The transgressions of Zuhra and Mushtari actually did not end there, but they were also known to censure and berate the work of established literary scholars as well; referring to Mushtari, Nadir says: 'She loves to roast them [the poets] like someone roasts a fish.'[25]

The discussion on the two sisters in the accounts of Ranj and Nadir indicates contestations within the literary sphere and shifting perceptions of literary *adāb*, or norms of appropriate language and civil behaviour. For Nadir, their insolence and disrespectful behaviour towards their teacher and other well-known poets was outrageous and could not be ignored even with their exceptional skills and talents. Ranj, on the other hand, was quite light-hearted about it, and, even as he found their arrogant behaviour 'hurtful', he found the attacks on them excessive. In his entry on Mushtari, he says:

> God be praised! Her imagination could reach the skies; and the reader is free to trust or doubt her. After all, how do we know the truth of her heart? The fact of the matter is that I enjoy her poetic compositions (*kalām*).[26]

Ultimately, the important thing, according to Ranj, is the quality of her lyrics, and while social norms and *adāb* are important, a poet's place is purely based on her literary aesthetics and command over language. Mushtari's insolence and 'haughtiness' (*nakhwat*) 'was a black wart (*tika*) that warded off the evil spirits (*nazr-i bad*)'.[27] The primacy that Nadir assigns to the ethical norms is absent in Ranj's work, and this probably reveals to us the contestations over *adāb* in the literary spaces, with some scholars now beginning to see literary aesthetics as independent of norms of social behaviour and politeness. Of course, from the fact that these sisters earned a reputation for their arrogant behaviour and disrespectful treatment of their teacher and were still considered as the 'shining stars' from whom other poets could learn about language and aesthetics, it would seem that the literary *adāb* were fluid and contested. This is important because so very often when we discuss the *adāb* in the Persianate

---

25   *TN*, 87.

26   *BN*, 203.

27   *BN*, 203.

world, we ignore their malleable character, and the contestations that continually reshaped them.

What made Mushtari and Zuhra such exceptional poets? How does one explain their unusual success in the literary spaces? For one, their salon was visited by influential local elites, and some of the powerful aristocrats (*rai's*) and gentlemen (*mirza*) were among their clientele. Their relations with some of them were certainly quite warm and friendly, and they would share lighter moments with them, crack jokes, or enjoy light banter with them. Narrating one such incident, Nadir informs us that once 'a respectable and influential aristocrat of Lucknow' (*Lukhnau ke waz'-dār ba-wiqār*), Niaz Ahmad Mahzun, dropped in at Zuhra's place, and on meeting him, she recited the following line: 'I won't visit the heavenly skies all alone' (*sair-i falak ko hum kabhī tanhā nāj āyenge*). In a humorous exchange of words, Mahzun retorted thus: 'I would do so [and visit the skies] in the company of either Zuhra or Mushtari' (*Zuhra ke sāth jāyenge yā Mushtari ke sāth*). Durga informs us that Zuhra was so enthralled by his hemistich that she kissed him, and 'this is how she returned the favour'.[28]

Listening to the Verses: Rhetorical Choices and Language Strategies

Of course, the relative edge that these sisters enjoyed over most other women poets came from their ability to write and recite poems that related to and found resonance with their community of readers, but, more importantly, their audience in the music and dance gatherings in their establishments (*kotha*). For them to do so, their knowledge of Persian and vernacular literature, and the norms of literary aesthetics, which they acquired under the guidance of their teacher, Shams, must have been quite useful. Even so, it was the ease with which they deployed rhetorical devices, in particular imagery, metaphors (*isti'āra*), analogy (*tamthīl*), and similes (*tashbih*), to generate intense emotions and particular states of mind (*inf'ālāt*) that made them so very popular in Indo-Persian literary circles. In the Persianate literary world, the science of rhetoric (*'ilm-ul balāgha*) was a very well-developed discipline, and creative works were assessed on the basis of the success with which they applied it to their work. It included semantics (*ma'ānī*), allegorical or metaphorical speech (*bayān*), and

---

[28] *TN*, 159.

literary embellishments (*'ilm-ul badī'*).[29] In the poems of Zuhra and Mushtari, these literary devices are certainly used to good effect, and the creative mesh of existing metaphors and imageries to create new ones must have certainly helped them become praiseworthy women poets in a culture where the laurels as a rule went to male poets. To take an example here, in a poem reproduced by Nadir, Zuhra describes her rival in love (*raqīb*) as a 'wrong word' (*harf-i ghalat*) who should be erased (*mitānā*) out of the picture. She says:

> I entreat you not to write a letter to that evil-faced rival of mine,
> S/he is a wrong word (*harf-i ghalat*) that surely deserves to be erased.[30]

The figure of the *raqīb* (the rival/competitor in love) is a standard trope in Persian and Urdu, and fidelity to established poetic conventions was considered by critics as a necessary component of a successful *ghazal*; at the same time, a successful poem should succeed in articulating new ideas and forms of expression, and, above all, generate wonder (*t'ajjub*) and pleasure (*lazzat*) among the readers or listeners. Zuhra accomplishes these objectives, perhaps, in the above verse by introducing the metaphor of the 'wrong word' to refer to her rival in love. Incidentally, this particular metaphor reflects the expansion in literacy and encourages us to consider how the greater circulation of paper and pen had intruded upon literary consciousness. In other instances of the creative use of metaphors and imageries for rhetorical effects, in the same poem, Zuhra equates the henna on her hand with blood, and her world with a cage; similarly, she represents herself as a bird with broken wings:

> You should surely colour your hands with my blood,
> This [my blood] is the dye (*mehndi*) worth applying [on the hand];
> My whole life, I was imprisoned in a cage (*qaid-i kanj-i qafas*)
> Wherefrom will I have the strength to flap my feathers and wings.[31]

---

[29] For the intricate nuances in literary compositions in the Persianate world, see Paul E. Losensky, *Welcoming Fighani: Imitation and Individuality in the Safavid-Mughal Ghazal* (Costa Mesa, CA: Mazda Publishers, 1998); Prashant Keshavmurthy, *Persian Authorship and Canonicity in Late Mughal Delhi: Building an Arch* (London: Routledge, 2016); Ali Asghar Seyed-Gohrab (ed.), *Metaphor and Imagery in Persian Poetry* (Leiden: Brill, 2012); Sunil Sharma, *Mughal Arcadia: Persian Literature in an Indian Court* (Cambridge, MA: Harvard University Press, 2017); Kia, *Persianate Selves*; and C. M. Naim (ed.), *Urdu Texts and Contexts: The Selected Essays of C. M. Naim* (New Delhi: Permanent Black, 2004).

[30] *TN*, 158.

[31] *TN*, 158.

It is certainly impossible to point to anything specific to explain the widespread popularity of the sisters, but surely the rhetorical effects that they successfully introduced in their compositions played an important role in establishing their position in the literary world. In creating imageries they also invoked stories about the prophets, in particular, Moses and Joseph. In one of her poems, Zuhra constructs an analogy between Moses' quest for divine light with her search for her lover. In the same poem, she also builds a contrast between the demand for Joseph in the market where his brothers were plotting to sell him as a slave and her loneliness emanating from the failure to find a buyer who could purchase her with love:

> Is there anyone whose sight doesn't bear the light emanating from the friend's face (*rukh-i yār*)?
> Is there anyone who is not desirous of the vision (of the Beloved)?
> The habit (*'adat*) of your company doesn't ever go away,
> Even though I may utter your name in silence;
> There is a bizarre demand for Joseph in the market,
> But the star in the sky [my Beloved] is not interested in purchasing Zuhra.

> *Kis ki ānkhon men tajalli-i rukh-i yār nahīn*
> *Kaun Musā ki tarah tālib-i dīdar nahīn*
> *Nahīn jātī, nahīn jātī ye tumhārī 'ādat*
> *Hān jo ek bār zubān par hai to sau bār nahīn*
> *Hai 'ajab garmi-e bazār mere Yusuf kī*
> *Mushtarī charkh ba Zuhra kī kharīdar nahīn.*[32]

Amid the excess of metaphors, analogies, and tropes, Zuhra weaves a narrative of unrequited love, an indifferent beloved, and the anguish of loneliness. These are standard motifs in Indo-Persian poetry, but could easily relate to and be identified with the lives of the courtesans as well. In one such *ghazal*, Zuhra says:

> My heart saw you as a fairy (*parī*),
> And your tresses a source of affliction (*balā*);
> You give a willing ear to everyone,
> But do you ever care to listen to me;
> People say all sorts of things,
> But no one ever understood my afflictions.

---

[32] *BN*, 146.

And then again:

> Everyone who hears my life-story feels grief-stricken,
> But for my disloyal friend (*yār-i be-wafā*), who dismisses it with indifference.[33]

Language and Emotions: Love, Loss, and Quotidian Practices

Indeed, the search for love (*'ishq*) and the grief of separation (*firāq*; in Braj: *viraha*) are the topoi around which littérateurs perfected their poetic skills in the Persianate and Indic worlds. For women poets, in particular the performers among them, to establish their literary credentials, they had to experiment with new forms, metaphors, and literary expressions centred on these themes. However, in doing so, they expressed not only their emotions and feelings but also their routine day-to-day experiences; this was reflected in their choice of expressions and construction of imageries and metaphors. We chanced upon some of these expressions earlier. Zuhra, to take an instance, describes her failures in love as the absence of her love's purchasers in the *bazār*, putting a spin of a market transaction to her failed love life. Her sister, Mushtari, in the verse we cite below, perhaps has an indifferent customer among her audience in mind when she scoffs at the indifference of her beloved to her seductive graces, and asks him not to play God. In the same poem, reflecting on her own liminal status and her popularity, she describes herself as someone who neither lives in the skies nor on the earth, but in the hearts of the people. She says:

> To feign disinterest in the coquetry of the beautiful one (*nāz-i husn*) is so dishonest,
> For you, my benefactor (*bandah nawāz*) shouldn't play God;
> Those from whom I expected a bouquet of flowers,
> They did not even bring thorns at my burial;
> There are those who live high in the skies and there are others, who embrace the dust of the earth,
> But I am a tempest (*ghubār*) that lives in the hearts (*dilon*) of the people.[34]

There is an obvious correlation between their quotidian practices and versified compositions. The ornaments they wore, the cosmetics they applied on their face and body, and their relations with the 'clients' they entertained are all expressed

---

[33]   *TN*, 158.
[34]   *BN*, 203–04.

and portrayed, with intensity and sensitivity, in their poems. Even so, it should be borne in mind that the primary objective of their lyrical compositions was to enthral and entertain; perhaps, entertainment is not the appropriate word here, but the more pertinent expression would be the ones found in the sources of the period, in particular the literary treatises and expositions on arts and aesthetics. Like music, a good *ghazal* was supposed to kindle and satisfy the taste for refined sentiments and emotions, known to the connoisseurs as *zauq*. A shifting signifier, *zauq* refers to a range of significations – from the love of God in Sufi parlance, to appropriate emotions and taste for arts and aesthetics in courtly cultures. In the literary world, it reflected a taste for intense emotions, and their sensorial inscription on the body. It is the element of sensoriality that Mushtari describes as the contraction and expansion of the heart:

> At times owing to your infidelity (*be-wafāi'*) and other times because of my sincerity (*wafādarī*);
> My heart (*dil*) has sometimes experienced expansion [joy], other times contraction [sorrow].[35]

It is the tactile apprehension of the emotions of love and the pain of separation that are captured by Mushtari by invoking the imageries of rain to represent the tears in her eyes, and the darkness of the night as a metaphor for her state of mind. Clearly, behind the rich invocation of metaphors and imageries, the effort is to use language to generate strong, intense emotions in the heart of the audience; this is what is termed as *zauq*, but in certain treatises and commentaries also as *lazzat*, or 'taste'. Indeed, to let the connoisseur experience the taste for emotions was the primary objective of these poetic compositions, and it is this that explains the success of Zuhra and Mushtari as poets. In the poem from which we cited a verse earlier, Mushtari says:

> When the world-cherished beloved (*'azīz-i 'ālam*) stepped out to sell himself,
> The price (*nirkh*) of the moon-like beauties of Levant diminished;
> The clouds come and bring rain, and then depart,
> The ever-flowing rain from my moist eyes continues unabated;
> Mushtari, the night of separation (*hijr ki shab*) has brought forth the storm of sorrows,
> The stars have brought light, and would someone ask them to shorten the darkness of the night (*shab-i tār*).[36]

---

[35]   *BN*, 204.
[36]   *BN*, 204–05.

The audience is taken to various emotional states amidst such tantalizing imageries and expressions as 'the world-cherished beloved', 'moist eyes' that are constantly replenished with never-ending tears, 'the night of separation', and the 'darkness of the night'. This is indeed one of the successful *ghazals* of Mushtari, and its success inheres in its ability to use words to inculcate feelings and invite the audience to 'taste' the emotions of beauty, love, and separation. Recited in poetic gatherings and dance performances, the verses of these two sisters served to create within an enclosed space a lived emotional community. Barbara Rosenwein defines 'emotional communities' as 'groups in which people adhere to the same norms of emotional expression and value – or devalue – the same or related emotions'.[37] The 'emotional community' that was created in the courtesan's literary and music gatherings was unlike any other: temporarily brought into existence in a particular space and time, it transcended social distinctions and hierarchies, and brought together the connoisseur and the artist, the patron and the client, and the audience and performer together in a shared emotional space wherein the 'taste' (*lazzat*) of feelings were savoured and consumed by all those present in the *kotha* of the courtesan.

Texts and Performance: Words and the Non-verbal Means of Communication

In a significant contribution to the history of emotions, William Reddy has drawn attention to the constructed nature of emotions, pointing out the role of language in shaping them. As he highlights, 'emotion speech-acts' are the necessary instruments for the social construction and elaboration of emotions.[38] Clearly, it is through the act of speaking (and listening) that societies have historically created and reproduced emotions, differentiated them, and invested some of these emotions with sociocultural, medicinal, and transcendental meanings, and dismissed some others as anarchic, destructive, and evil. Through their poetic compositions, Zuhra and Mushtari, like any other courtesan and performer mentioned in these *tazkiras*, participated in the economy of emotions in and through which the social elites and the respectable gentlemen articulated their manliness and perceived their selfhood.

---

[37]   Barbara Rosenwein, *Emotional Communities in the Early Middle Ages* (Ithaca and London: Cornell University Press, 2007), 2. For an instance of the application of this concept to South Asian history, see Margrit Pernau, 'Feeling Communities: Introduction', *Indian Economic and Social History Review* 54, no. 1 (March 2017): 1–20.

[38]   William M. Reddy, *The Navigation of Feeling: A Framework for the History of Emotions* (Cambridge: Cambridge University Press, 2001). See also William M. Reddy, 'Emotional Liberty: Politics and History in the Anthropology of Emotions', *Cultural Anthropology* 14, no. 2 (May 1999): 256–88.

While Reddy's 'emotion speech-acts' help us realize the constructed nature of emotions, they are still inadequate in grasping the complexities of emotions' history, particularly when it is the courtesan's poetry that is the subject of study.[39] The primacy of language in Reddy's formulations fails to take into account the non-verbal means of communication and their entangled relations with the text.[40] The poems of Zuhra and Mushtari, like that of any other public entertainer, were actually performed; they were sung to the accompaniment of music and dance at *mehfils* or assemblies organized in the spaces of their salons or the 'men's quarters' (*mardān-khāna*) of their patrons. Their meanings were apprehended within an inter-medial mode in which the auditory, visual, textual, and tactile forms and experiences coalesced together into an integrated whole. It is, of course, quite impossible to revisit that experience today, but it is important, while reading the verses of a courtesan writing in that period, to be attentive to the routines, performances, and music that accompanied their recitation. Their meanings were contingent on their consumption, and these compositions were consumed amidst dance and music, in assemblies where refreshments and fragrances provided an additional aromatic and olfactory mode for the reception of these compositions.

The relationship of music to emotional states, or *rasa*, has been explored in detail by Katherine Butler Schofield, but I feel that her arguments can be fruitfully applied to the lyrical compositions of the performing women as well, particularly when the sensorial effects of their *ghazals* were reinforced with music and/or dance performances.[41] One of the important points that Schofield makes is that

---

[39] For a critical engagement with Reddy's formulations, see Rosenwein, *Emotional Communities*, 16–25.

[40] Margrit Pernau and Imke Rajamani, 'Emotional Translations: Conceptual History Beyond Language', *History and Theory* 55, no. 1 (February 2016): 46–65; also see Imke Rajamani, Margrit Pernau, and Katherine Butler Schofield (eds.), *Monsoon Feelings: A History of Emotions in the Rain* (Delhi: Niyogi Books, 2018); and Margrit Pernau, 'Studying Emotions in South Asia', *South Asian History and Culture* 12, nos. 2–3 (2021): 111–28.

[41] See the following articles by Katherine Butler Schofield: 'Emotions in Indian Music History: Anxiety in Late Mughal Hindustan', *South Asian History and Culture* 12, nos 2–3 (2021): 182–205; 'The Courtesan's Tale: Female Musicians and Dancers in Mughal Historical Chronicles, c. 1556–1748', *Gender and History* 24, no. 1 (April 2012): 150–71; and 'Learning to Taste the Emotions: The Mughal *Rasika*', in *Tellings and Texts: Music, Literature and Performance in North India*, ed. Francesca Orsini and Katherine Butler Schofield, 407–21 (Cambridge: Open Book Publishers, 2015). For an appreciation of the music in the Persianate world, see Laudan Nooshin, *Iranian Classical Music: The Discourses and Practice of Creativity* (Farnham and Burlington: Ashgate, 2015); and Rachel Harris and Martin Stokes (eds.), *Theory and Practice in the Music of the Islamic World: Essays in Honour of Owen Wright* (London: Routledge, 2017).

in the Sanskritic (and the vernacular) knowledge of music, based on the *raga* system, the objective of music, and the singular sign of its success, inhered in its ability to arouse intense emotions; and it is for this reason that in music treatises of the period, specific musical modes were linked to one or the other of the nine emotional essences, or *rasas*.[42] In Mughal court culture, the Persian elites imbibed the Indic theory of music, and assessed and appreciated music in terms of its ability to arouse emotions; and among all the nine emotions,[43] it was the emotion of love (*'ishq*) and the *rasa* of longing and separation (*firāq* or *viraha*) that were the most cherished and sought after. Actually, a successful *ghazal* was supposed to do the same, and while the poets were surely composing poems on a wide range of themes, their mettle as a poet was tested against their ability to arouse emotions of love and the pain of separation from the beloved. Like a good piece of music, lyrical compositions were 'tasted' by the connoisseurs, and were believed to bring 'inner peace' and equanimity which were, in the prevailing medical knowledge, understood as ensuring humoral balance in the body.[44]

This is particularly relevant when we read the verses of the courtesans and other entertainers. In their assemblies (*mehfils*) they sang their poems, to the accompaniment of music and dance performances. It would surely be historically incorrect to disengage one from the other, and words, instruments, and bodily gestures have to be seen in terms of their mutual engagement (and 'conversations') to recover their meanings and experience. Indeed, the *ghazals* of the sisters, like any other poem recited by a 'public entertainer', should be read within a framework in which language, music, and dance constituted a continuum; their meanings were contingent on the music and performance that accompanied their recitation. The courtesans were usually multi-talented, and combined their literary skills with their expertise in dance and music as well. Badla, a courtesan living in the locality of Madar Darwaza in Aligarh, was, according to Ranj, an accomplished poet (*shā'ira*); she was also a gifted singer, and her voice 'enraptured the soul of Baiju Bawra [a legendary *dhrupad*[45] musician]' (*gāne men baiju bawre*

---

[42] Schofield, 'Emotions in Indian Music History'.

[43] The nine *rasas* are: *shringara* (desire), *karuna* (grief), *hasya* (humour), *raudra* (rage), *vira* (courage), *bhayanaka* (fearful), *bibhatsa* (revulsion), *adbhhuta* (wonder), and *shanta* (peace). Sheldon Pollock (ed.), *A Rasa Reader: Classical Indian Aesthetics* (New York: Columbia University Press, 2016).

[44] Katherine Butler Schofield, 'Music, Art and Power in 'Adil Shahi Bijapur, c. 1570–1630', in *Scent Upon a Southern Breeze: Synaesthesia and the Arts of the Deccan*, ed. Kavita Singh, 68–87 (Mumbai: Marg, 2018).

[45] *Dhrupad* is a form of north Indian classical vocal music.

ki ruh ko bāwra banā diyā).[46] Moreover, when Tansen (the court musician at Akbar's court) felt like stretching his vocal chords in his grave, he would first respectfully take her name.[47] She was also an unusually talented dancer, and 'the well-known dancers of the time quarrelled with their rivals over her'.[48] She was certainly not the only one to be so appreciated for her multiple talents; this is the general strain within which the talented courtesans are described in *BN* and *TN*. In the last chapter, we mentioned Nazakat, a poet who was well recognized for her skill in playing the sitar.[49] We also earlier came across the mother–daughter duo where the mother, Sardar Begum, composed the poems and her daughter, Kazmi, recited them in the gatherings (*mehfils*) they organized at their place (*dera*).[50] Nadir mentions a public woman by the pen name of Sharm in Lucknow who was an accomplished dancer; he was actually so impressed by her dancing skills that he attributed to her graceful bodily movements the ability to bring the dead back to life:

> The clanging of your anklets have brought the dead back to life,
> With every movement of your feet you cause tumult and commotion.
>
> *Murde zinda ho gaye pāzeb kī jhankār se*
> *Har qadm par hashr barpā hai terī raftār se.*[51]

In an important study of the roles of courtesans in reproducing the norms of civility and performing arts in the aftermath of the revolt of 1857, Richard David Williams argues that the reception of their poetic compositions was confounded with the 'multi-sensorial and multi-medial forms of interpretation'.[52] As he puts it:

> Experiencing a courtesan's poetry was not a matter of silent reading, but involved embodied voices, performance (recitation, singing, dancing), specific forms of sociability, material objects (relating to the salon of the printed page), and larger political considerations. The audience or consumer of the poem was not

---

[46] *BN*, 114–15.
[47] *BN*, 114–15: 'Even today, before stretching his vocals in his grave, Tansen takes her name, and holds his ear [a sign of respect]' (*Tansen ab tak qabr men tān lete waqt in hīn kā nām lekar kān pakadte hain*).
[48] *BN*, 114–15.
[49] *BN*, 231; *TN*, 203.
[50] *TN*, 160–63; *BN*, 152–53.
[51] *TN*, 166.
[52] Williams, 'Songs between Cities'.

a passive recipient of these experiences, but responded through active listening (entailing gesture and response), and supplementary actions, perhaps including eating, drinking, and sex, all of which had transformative potential in terms of emotional impact.[53]

Historians of emotions have rightly alerted us to the multiple media of meaning apprehension when reading a text; their work encourages us to look for inter-penetrative spaces between the verbal and non-verbal means of communication.[54] Their insights are, as we argued earlier, particularly relevant when we are reading the poems of the dancers and courtesans, for these were performed in spatial settings in which the sonic, the visual, and the tactile came together to set the stage for the consumption of the text by the audience.

At the same time, we should also consider the semantic shifts that come with the movement of a literary text from one domain to another. It is obvious that the compositions of the courtesans lost much of the richness in their meaning when they were transposed from their sites of performance and ensconced in texts of cultural memorialization. Surely, they could have developed new forms of signification in the process of their textual inscription, that is, in their relocation from orality to literacy.[55] These are difficult issues, and given the dearth of evidence, our interpretation is bound to be partial and provisional. Even so, we can be quite certain about the incompleteness of the process; the poetic compositions of the courtesans imbibed performance and oral traditions. Even as texts, in terms of

---

[53] Williams, 'Songs between Cities', 593.

[54] Heidi Pauwells, 'Cultivating Emotions and the Rise of the Vernaculars: The Role of Affect in "Early Hindi-Urdu" Song', *South Asian History and Culture* 12, nos. 2–3 (2021): 146–65.

[55] For an understanding of the sociocultural effects of the replacement of orality with literacy, see Walter J. Ong, *Orality and Literacy: The Technologizing of the Word* (London and New York: Routledge, 2002 [reprint]); Jack Goody, *The Logic of Writing and the Organization of Society* (Cambridge: Cambridge University Press, 1986); and Jack Goody (ed.), *Literacy in Traditional Societies* (Cambridge: Cambridge University Press, 1975). For a critical engagement with their formulations, see Keith Thor Carlson, Kristina Fagan, and Natalia Khaneko-Friesen (eds.), *Orality and Literacy: Reflections across Disciplines* (Toronto: University of Toronto Press, 2011). For the impact of literacy in the Islamic world, see Jonathan Bloom, *Paper before Print: The History and Impact of Paper in the Islamic World* (New Haven, CT: Yale University Press, 2001); Brinkley Messick, *The Calligraphic State: Textual Domination and History in a Muslim Society* (Berkeley: University of California Press, 1993); and Brinkley Messick, *Shari'a Scripts: A Historical Anthology* (New York: Columbia University Press, 2018).

their phonetics and rhythmic structure, and language and semantics, their verses combined literacy with orality and performance.[56]

The problem is actually confounded when we realize that these memorializing texts – our *tazkira*s – were about women and the memories of their presence in the cultural domain; and in the process of recording their verses (and life stories), they not only highlighted the richness of the literary culture but also the significance of the role of women in shaping and reproducing it. The collection of women's poems in these biographical compendia served to constitute an archive of women's voices, and while they did not cease to remember their expertise in music and dance, the relocation of their voices into 'texts', imprinted on paper in ink, facilitated a certain level of standardization and fixity that one associates with the written word. More interestingly, the lyrical compositions of the 'public women' were now interpreted, and their meanings derived from the intertextual practices of the literate world.

Redefined as 'texts', their compositions were quickly appropriated, as earlier mentioned, for the reformist project of the upwardly mobile middle class; for both the authors of *BN* and *TN*, the objective that informed their efforts was to promote women's education, and by recollecting memories of women poets – past and present – they hoped to inspire women (and men) to take to education and develop interest in literature. And, so it is that at a time when the colonial state and educated Indians were developing new anxieties about dancing girls and courtesans,[57] scholars like Ranj and Nadir were citing their versified compositions as evidence of the long history of women's literary talents and education in Hindustan. The appropriation of the voices of courtesans, as also other women mentioned in the *tazkira*s, for the modern reformist project did not end with women's education, but encompassed other issues as well. Reiterating the need for education, Nadir refers to the practice of female infanticide (*dukhtar kashī*) that the people in Hindustan considered 'permissible' (*jā'iz*) because they were 'uneducated and totally illiterate' (*be-'ilm aur jāhil-i mutlaq*).[58] Quite unusually,

---

[56] For studies that explore the interstitial spaces between literacy and orality and Performance, see Orsini and Schofield, *Tellings and Texts*; Hasan, *Paper, Performance, and the State*.

[57] Mitra, *Indian Sex Life*; Philippa Levine, *Prostitution, Race, and Politics: Policing Venereal Diseases in the British Empire* (New York: Routledge, 2003); Sumanta Banerjee, *Under the Raj: Prostitution in Colonial Bengal* (New York: Monthly Review Press, 2000); Banerjee, *Dangerous Outcast*. See also, Williams, 'Songs between Cities'. Our *tazkira*s contest the prejudices against prostitutes and other public women, but there were other voices later in the period that also contested the dominant narratives about them. See, for example, Sarah Waheed, 'Women of "Ill Repute": Ethics and Urdu Literature in Colonial India', *Modern Asian Studies* 48, no. 4 (July 2014): 986–1023.

[58] *TN*, 133.

while discussing the courtesan Badla, Ranj refers to her dark complexion and condemns those who berate her because of her colour.[59] What we have here is an instance of the condemnation of the prejudice of colour within an Indo-Persianate frame of reference.

Clearly, the lyrical compositions of the courtesans and other female performers were shifting signifiers, and were consumed in multiple settings with varied significations. In reading literary pieces, we often ignore the relations of texts to space and the extent to which shifts in spatial settings impinge on their meanings. Recited as songs in the *kothas*, along with dance and music, the compositions of the courtesans formed an intricate part of the aural–visual–tactile continuum, and derived their meanings from a complex inter-medial and multi-sensorial mode of communication. They served to arouse emotional states and feelings and, in the process, created an 'emotional community' that cut across, if only temporarily, social and economic distinctions. Removed from their performative contexts, and placed in written and published forms in the poetic compendia, their versified compositions, in addition, also became literary pieces that derived their meanings from intertextual practices. Circulated within a wide 'reading public', they were appropriated to further the newly emergent middle class sensibilities.

Conclusion

Reared and educated in the *kotha* of a courtesan, Zuhra and Mushtari rose to become influential poets, and the extent of their popularity is suggested from the fact that the other women poets were compared (and measured) against their literary skills. Erased from cultural memory by literary critics and commentators, they have been restored to history by the authors of our *tazkiras*, and had these scholars not made the effort, their voices would probably have been lost forever. The appreciation of their literary talents was matched with the condemnation of their arrogant and self-absorbed behaviour, and Ranj and Nadir were expressing a popular perception when they accused them of deriving sadistic pleasure from belittling male littérateurs. They were censored for violating *adāb*, or the norms of ethical behaviour, but were still appreciated as poets, and this probably reflects the development of a new aesthetics marked by a developing fissure between literary skills and norms of appropriate behaviour. The most outrageous act of indiscretion – a violation of one of the most important *adāb* in the literary culture – was the indifference, even disdain, with which they treated their teacher, Shams.

---

[59] *BN*, 114–15.

This was an issue that was much discussed in the contemporary literary circles and even prompted some poets to compose *ghazals* on teacher–student relations and the betrayal of the sisters. In the Perso-Arabic tradition of knowledge, the scholar-teacher was not just the medium for the transmission and instruction of knowledge, but was knowledge-incarnate. Within an anthropomorphic perception of knowledge, the teacher imbibed knowledge. In a marked shift in literary practices, the cruel indifference to Shams by these sisters was indicative of a claim to autonomy in the literary field. That they could repudiate their teacher and yet be accepted as exceptional poets is probably reflective of a shift, however gradual and intermittent, from an anthropomorphic to a bibliocentric view of knowledge.

Even so, the figure of the teacher was a necessary trope in the construction of the life stories of women poets. This was one of the devices through which the literary critics and compilers constrained the agency of women poets and undermined their claim to autonomy in the literary field. What we notice in biographies of women poets, particularly in texts such as *BN* and *TN*, is the enactment of a paradox: they reveal the women poets' agency and subjectivities, and their exceptional literary acumen and linguistic skills, and yet situate them in a dependant relationship with their teachers. While their teachers usually came from elite aristocratic families, in the case of the courtesans and prostitutes, we notice an interesting change; many of their teachers came from the clerical communities. This indicates changes in the nature and composition of the literary sphere, but, more importantly, the shifts in the support networks of the performing women as well.

Reading the lyrical compositions of Zuhra and Mushtari, it became evident that they were cognitively consumed and aesthetically experienced within a multi-sensorial mode of reception in which the sonic, the visual, and the tactile media came together to communicate new meanings, shared feelings, and states of mind. Their poetic compositions, just like those of any other 'public woman' mentioned in the *tazkiras*, were 'performed' in spatial settings where music, dance, and words formed a continuum in facilitating their consumption by the discerning audience. Like music, therefore, these compositions were judged and scrutinized for the emotions (*jazba* or *rasa*) they evoked, and the intensity with which they succeeded in doing so.

However, there is more to these lyrics than their performative contexts and their spatial location in the courtesans' salons. The compositions of the courtesans and prostitutes also entered the 'print community' through the biographical compendia, and let us not forget that some of these courtesans also compiled their own *diwāns*, or collections of poems. Once they reached the 'reading community', they were appropriated for modern reformist projects, and served the sensibilities of the newly emergent, upwardly mobile middle classes.

Appendix 4A.1

Zuhra: A Brash and Disrespectful Courtesan[60]

Her name is Umrao Jan, and her pen name is Zuhra, and she is popularly known as Bi-Chuttan. She lives in Chowk Bazaar in the city of Lucknow. She was the favourite student (*shāgird-i khās*) of Mirza Agha Ali Shams, and this was because, as suggested by a gentleman of Lucknow, he was deeply attached (*rabt ba-ikhtisās*) to her mother. He took special interest in the education of Zuhra and [her sister] Mushtari.

In the *diwān* of Amirullah Taslim, there is a letter addressed to Zuhra and Mushtari, and its contents bear out the fact that these brash (*munh-phat*) sisters turned against (*munharif*) their kind-hearted teacher (*shafīq ustād*). The content of the letter is reproduced below, and it proves beyond doubt that Shams was attached (*lagāo*) to someone in that house. God knows best!

[The versified letter in Persian addressed to Zuhra and Mushtari]:

The shining stars of the literate world,
Who are like Nuri and Anwari in their mastery of language;
They shine forth like the illustrious sun and the moon,
And have reached the pinnacle of success with admiration;
And so it is that this vagrant and frail Taslim,
Has heard this [about them];
That their sincere friends (*yār-i wafādār*) should be wary,
Of both these pleasant looking women;
They turned against [their tutor], Agha Ali Shams,
And gave him a lot of grief and pain;
From their lush and comfortable dwelling,
And their felicitous mansion as well;
They committed unkind deeds against him,
And stabbed him with the dagger of cruelty (*tegh-i sitam*).

---

[60] *TN*, 155–59; also see *BN*, 146–47.

'Utārid raqm Zuhra wa Mushtarī
Ba ūj-i sukhan Nurī wa Anwarī
Ze mehrab khudāwand-i khurshīd-o māh
Ba-mānd bar ūj-i iqbāl-o jāh
Ze Taslīm āwārah wa khasta tan
Ba-sam'a-i razā ba-shanūd in sukhan
Ki in-nak ze yār-i wafādār-i khesh
Shunīdam ke ān har-do farkhandah kesh
Ze manzil gāhe 'aish-o ārām-i khesh
Ze aiwān farkhandah farjām-i khesh
Ba na-meherbānī barūn karde-and
Ze tegh-i sitam khūn darūn karde-and.

[Deeply perturbed by how the sisters had treated their teacher, Nadir accuses them of ignoring 'the rights of the teacher.' He says:]

They have ignored the rights of the teacher (*haq-i ustād*),
And have blackened their face in the eternal abode.

Farāmosh kardan haq-i ustād
Bua'd ru-siyāhi badar-ul-ma'ād.

[Interestingly, the author of the versified letter holds the tutor, Shams, himself responsible for his pitiable condition. He says:]

May God, the protector of this world, forgive him,
For his indulgence was unworthy of his position;
He should have reflected on the implications of his actions,
And should have paused for a moment, and realized how shameful were his activities;
All the time, he was busy with dance and music,
Every night, he would indulge in debauchery and adulterous activities;
We should follow the instructions of our auspicious Prophet [Muhammad],
Where in the Koran are these activities considered permissible?

Ghafūrest parwardigār-i jahān
Shumā rā ta'assub na-zebad chunān
Gāhe fikr bāyad ba af'āl-i khwesh

Dame sharm bāyd ze ā'māl-i khwesh
Hame waqt raqs wa sarūd-o ghanā
Hame shab fusūq-o fujūr-o zinā
Bajā guft paighambar-i nēk fāl
Ba qurān kujā kard īzid halāl.

[Lending his support to the contents of the letter, which he cites in full, Nadir further adds his observations:]

Everywhere, these prostitutes (*randiyan*) are known for bad mouthing, and details of their literary discussion are recorded in the Urdu newspapers. They freely ridicule some of the best scholars, and just as their pen names suggest, they are arrogant and put on a lot of airs.

Zuhra's *Ghazals*

(1)

If he can't come over and visit me out of coyness,
I can't come down and visit him owing to fear;
You should surely colour your hands with my blood,
This [my blood] is the dye (*mehndi*) worth applying [on the hand];
My whole life, I was imprisoned in a cage,
Wherefrom will I have the strength to flap my feathers and wings;
It was you [referring to God] who gave grandeur to Alexander,
[Thanks to you] he could look at his image in the mirror with pride;
I entreat you not to write a letter to that evil-faced rival of mine,
He is a wrong word (*harf-i ghalat*) that surely deserves to be erased;
The coral in the shell is shame-faced before you,
It is in on position to compete with your beauty;
The lovers are hungrily seeking the illusion of union,
They deserve to suffer the pain and the sorrows of separation.

Hyāse jo nahīn woh jo āne ke qābil
To hum khauf se kab hain jāne ke qābil
Karo khūn se mere tum hāth rangīn
Ye mehndi hai sahib lagāne ke qābil
Rahe 'umr bhar qaid-i kanj-i qafas men
Kahān bāl-o-par hum hilāne ke qābil

Sikandar ko di ābru tum ne sāhib
Huā ā'ina munh dikhāne ke qābil
Raqīb-i siyāh-ru ko nama na-likho
Woh harf-i ghalat hai mitānēke qābil
Lahu men hain tar sharam se dast-i marjān
Nahin tum se panjāh milāne ke qābil.

(2)
[Nadir claims to have obtained this *ghazal* by post from one of his acquaintances]:

My heart saw you as a fairy (*parī*),
And your tresses a source of affliction;
You give a willing ear to everyone,
But do you ever care to listen to me;
People say all sorts of things,
But no one ever understood my afflictions;
I swear on God, whenever you, my beloved (*sanam*), came to see me,
I believed the medicine for my ailments had arrived;
Everyone who hears my life story feels grief-stricken,
But for my disloyal friend (*yār-i be-wafā*), who dismisses it with indifference;
I swear on God, I was only praying to God to bless you,
Why did you find it so hard to believe! God knows!
Accursed me! I destroyed myself for no reason,
Mistakenly believing that love was the pinnacle [to a meaningful existence];
Your friend (*yār*) carries so many misgivings against you, Zuhra!
He reads even your expressions of gratitude as taunts.

Dil men tujh ko parī laqā samjhā
Zulf ko terī main balā samjhā
Tūne har-ek ki sunin bāten
Merā matlab bhi kuch bhalā samjhā
Apnī apnī har-ek kahtā hai'
Koī merā na mudd'aā samjhā
Tere āne ko ae-sanam wallāh
Dard ki apnī main dawā samjhā
Sab merā hāl sun ke hain pur-gham
Tū na kuch yār-i be-wafa samjhā

Main ne wallāh dī du'ā tum kō
Tū khuda jāne dil men kyā samjhā
Hai be-fā'ida kharāb huā
'Ishq ko maine intihā samjhā
Bad-gumān tujh se yar hai Zuhra
Shukr ko tere woh gilā samjhā.

Appendix 4A.2

Mushtari: 'Her Insolence Protects Her from Evil Eyes'[61]

Mushtari is her *takhallus* (pen name), and her name is Qamran Jan, but she is famously known as Manjhu. She lives in Lucknow, and her poetic leap of imagination (*khyāl*) is simply unprecedented (*be-misāli*). She is quite bright and creative; and she has received her education from Mian Shams. Zuhra and Mushtari are just as renowned as their teacher (*ustād*), and, why should that not be so? When the tutor teaches his students with such close attention, it is obvious that the fame of the students [Zuhra and Mushtari] would spread far and wide. Undoubtedly, the respectable (*hazrat*) tutor, Shams, polished these sparkling sisters to such an extent that the skies resonate with the colours of Zuhra and Mushtari....

Since she was seven years old, this poetess has been fond of reading and writing. Trained and educated by *hazrat* Shams, this sparkling little star has now evolved into an illuminating full moon. She is well served in her material needs, and God has blessed her with property as well. She has a mosque, an *imāmbāra*, a garden, and a house in Khairabad. She is proficient in composing poems in Persian and Urdu, and in prose and history-writing (*tārikh goi*); and she has a calligraphic hand, and writes in style both plain and cursive letters (*khati khafi wa jali*). She is also famous for her arrogance and conceit. Owing to the efforts of her kind-hearted *ustād*, she is well versed in the subtleties of poetry; there is scarcely any poetic assembly (*mushā'ira*) where the audience is not enthralled by the recitations of Zuhra and Mushtari. Why should this poetess not excel in her skills, for her *ustād* is the pinnacle of perfection? For her to be so sharp and talented when she is just twenty-three years old reflects on the excellence of her teacher. God be praised! She has a mind that strives to reach the skies. You may believe or disbelieve me, and people can have different opinions about her, but insofar as I am concerned, I find her compositions enjoyable. It is rather unfortunate that despite

---

[61] *BN*, 202–05; also see *TN*, 192–93.

her talents, she is very distant from humility that comes with education. A person who is both talented and humble is the most luminescent of the luminescent selves (*nūr ʿalā nūr*).... But then, her insolence is not without a purpose. In my opinion, it serves to protect her from evil eyes. To sum up this discussion, she carries herself well.

Mushtari's Verses

(1)

To feign disinterest in the coquetry of the beautiful one is so dishonest,

For you, my benefactor shouldn't play God;

Those from whom I expected a bouquet of flowers,

They did not even bring thorns at my burial;

There are those who live high in the skies and there are others, who embrace the dust of the earth,

But, I am a tempest that lives in the hearts of the people.

Nā-ḥaq hain nāz-i ḥusn se ye be-niyāziyān
Bandah nawāz āp kisī ke khudā nahīn
Thī jin se mujhe phūl chadhāne ki tawaqquʿ
Kānte bhī woh le-kar mere madafn pe na-āye'
Yān ʿarsh par dimāgh hai aur khāksār hain
Jis ki jagah dilōn men hai woh hum ghubār hain.

(2)

From the heart, sincerity, joy, and love became scarce,

But your dalliance, my shrewd idol, did not diminish;

At times owing to your infidelity, and other times because of my sincerity,

My heart has sometimes experienced expansion [joy], other times contraction [sorrow];

When the world-cherished beloved stepped out to sell himself,

The price of the moon-like beauties of Levant diminished;

The clouds come and bring rain, and then depart,

The ever-flowing rain from my moist eyes continues unabated;

Mushtari, the night of separation has brought forth the storm of sorrows,

The stars have brought light, and would someone ask them to reduce the darkness of the night.

Dil se ikhlās ghatā lutf ghatā pyār ghatā
Par nā woh nāz tera ae but-i 'ayār ghatā
Be-wafāi sē terī apnī wafādāri se
Dil kai bār badhā aur kai bar ghatā
Khud-faroshī ko niklā woh 'azīz-i 'ālam
Nirkh husn-i māh-i kun'ān sar-i bāzār ghatā
Gayin bhi, āyin bhi barsin bhi ghatāyen barson
Bārish-i didah-i tar ka na kabhi tār ghatā
Mushtarī hijr ki shab umda hai tūfān-i 'ālam
Tāre bijlī nazar āte hain, shab-i tār ghatā.

5

Commemorating Women Poets

Memory, Gender, and the Literary Culture in the Persianate World

In recreating women's literary spaces, the *tazkira*s not only mention the poets of their time but also refer, in interesting details, to the life stories and lyrical compositions of women poets from the historical and imagined pasts. In the process of commemorating them, these texts portray them as exemplars in terms of their literary skills and aesthetic qualities for the littérateurs of their generation. As commemorative texts, both *BN* and *TN* memorialize their literary precursors, but, in the process of doing so, they remind us of the historical presence of an inclusive literary space in which were ensconced memories of lyrics allegedly composed by women. The poets from the multiple pasts claimed an undying existence, an enduring and ever-inspiring presence, in the literary public sphere. It should be emphasized here that even as these *tazkira*s are exclusively concerned with women poets, the literary community they seek to reproduce and represent is not gender-specific; the community of women poets, writing and reciting poems in Persian and Urdu, did not constitute an exclusive social group, but were seen as a crucial component of the larger Persianate literary culture. In fact, the overwhelming interest of Ranj and Nadir in publishing their compendia was to draw the attention of the reader to the significance of women literati in shaping the norms of aesthetics and appropriate expression in art and literature.

*Tazkira*s as Commemorative Exercises: Memorializing Women and Their Words

In the last several decades, there have been quite a few insightful studies on the tradition of biographical commemoration in the Persianate world, and scholars have looked at the complex ways through which remembrance – repeated and constructed – served to structure a moral community, and circulating within networks of communication, reinforced ethical norms and appropriate practices.[1] It is for this reason that some scholars have described the *tazkira*s as 'memorative communications'[2] wherein memories were restructured by forms of communication and vice versa. The appropriate ethical norms and behaviour, and aesthetic tastes and expression constituted the Persianate *adāb* (singular: *adab*),[3] which were reiterated and reformulated in and through the remembrance of the lives and work of exceptional persons. Of course, *tazkira*s were of different types, and while some focused on the political elites, others the Sufis and theologians, and still some others the poets and the literati. Irrespective of the choice of subject, each of the life stories in the biographical compendia reminded the reader/audience of the ways within which the *adāb* were to be practised and pursued in real life. In cultivating the traits of *adāb*, as has been argued by Mana Kia, articulations of place and origins were crucial, but within the literary culture, these were grasped in terms quite different from our modern sensibilities.[4] The meanings of a place were not restricted by conceptions of territoriality, but included the sociocultural identifications of the physical space with the poets and their assemblies, religious men and their circle of followers, and places of worship and pilgrimage, among other variables. Of course, these forms of identifications were realized through the circulation of texts in existing networks of communication, creating text–space correlations that were crucial to the representations of place in the

---

[1] Kia, *Persianate Selves*; Marcia K. Hermansen and Bruce B. Lawrence, 'Indo-Persian *Tazkiras*'; Shivangini Tandon, 'Mooring the Mughal Tazkiras: Explorations in the Politics of Representation', NMML Occasional Paper, History and Society (New Series), No. 40, Nehru Memorial Museum and Library Publications, New Delhi, 2013; Shivangini Tandon, 'Remembering Lives in Mughal India: Political Culture and Social Life in Indo-Persian *Tazkiras*, 16th–18th centuries' (Ph.D. dissertation, University of Delhi, New Delhi, 2016). For a discussion on the representation of women in these *tazkira*s, see Sunil Sharma, 'From 'A'isha to Nur Jahan: The Shaping of a Classical Persian Poetic Canon of Women', *Journal of Persianate Studies* 2, no. 2 (2009): 148–64.

[2] Hermansen and Lawrence, 'Indo-Persian *Tazkiras*', 150.

[3] Kia describes *adab* as 'the proper form of things and of being in the world'. In the Persianate cultural world, it referred to 'proper aesthetic and ethical forms, of thinking, acting, and speaking, and thus of perceiving, desiring, and experiencing' (Kia, *Persianate Selves*, 5).

[4] Kia, *Persianate Selves*.

literary culture.[5] Similarly, unlike modern perceptions of origins that are either natal or territorial, lineages of origins were multiple, and included associations based on service, education, and spiritual training as well. Within the Persianate world, a person's origins were always varied, and while natal connections mattered, people often identified their origins with places associated with their teachers, spiritual guides, and employers.

Within contexts informed by multiple sources of origins, and inclusive and enlarged understanding of places, the commemorative texts created social collectives, and persuaded and prompted the reading communities and aural audiences to discover their sense of selfhood therein. Unlike the modern autonomous selves, the Persianate selves were relational, a necessary component of one or the other, more often a combination of several social collectives together. Social identifications and perceptions of selfhood were marked by heterogeneity, and engaged with differences within a relational frame of reference. Within a culture in which alterity was largely eschewed, differences were contingent and negotiable, and this helped create a literary universe marked by heteroglossia, or what Mana Kia, taking cue from Derrida, terms as 'aporia'.[6]

These are certainly important points to ponder when studying the *tazkiras* as commemorative and communicative exercises, but with reference to the *tazkiras* of women poets, they assume an added significance in view of the fact that these texts not only revitalize the living memories of poets but also restructure the literary spaces by bringing women's voices from the historical and mythical pasts in conversation with existing literary trends and norms of aesthetics. The element of construction is important here, because a large number of lyrical compositions attributed to poets of distant pasts might actually be of more recent provenance, but they still serve to provide a pretence of continuity to the existing literary culture. Emerging from the interactions between the literary and the performative public sphere, these recollections served to create spaces for negotiations with the literary *adāb*, in particular, the norms of linguistic expression, the limits of

---

[5]   On the modes of place-making in early modern India, see Nile Green, *Making Space: Sufis and Settlers in Early Modern India* (New Delhi: Oxford University Press, 2012). For a discussion on the construction of place in the Islamic world, see Zayde Antrim, *Routes and Realms: The Power of Place in the Early Islamic World* (Oxford: Oxford University Press, 2012); also see Ali Mozaffari, *Forming National Identity in Iran: The Idea of Homeland Derived from Ancient Persian and Islamic Imaginations of Place* (London: I. B. Tauris, 2014).

[6]   Kia, *Persianate Selves*, 10–11, 13–14, 92–93.

rhetoric, and forms of appropriate aesthetics.[7] Historians have, as mentioned earlier, highlighted the significance of *adāb* in the reproduction of Persianate culture, and in the commemorative texts, in particular, the construction of life stories were intended to serve as embodiments of ethical life and appropriate behaviour – as instances of *adāb* in practice. The important point that is so often missed in the discussion on *adāb* is that people both followed and contested them; as a sociocultural space, it was open and susceptible to dialogue and negotiations, and conflicts and contestations.

It is here that our *tazkira*s assume significance for they suggest that this space was not gender-specific, and was dotted with women all along in Hindustan. The literary *adāb* were not the exclusive prerogatives of men, but were articulated and practised, and contested and modified by women as well. Memorializing the women scholars from multiple histories, both Ranj and Nadir seem to be making the point of the antiquity of women's participation in literary spaces, and, in doing so, they subtly subvert the European post-Enlightenment understanding of civilizational hierarchies. There is a political context to commemoration here, for the larger point that they make through their memorializing exercises is that women's education, including their skills in language and aesthetics, is ingrained in their civilization – this is what defines Hindustan as a civilization.[8] If women's education were the trope around which civilizations were to be assessed and hierarchized, then Hindustan should claim a position of pre-eminence and should certainly be placed alongside western civilization.

Representations of the Literary Space: Memories from Distant 'Hindu' and 'Islamic' Pasts

Striking a feminist tone, Nadir initiates the discussion by arguing that women in his time were deficient in education not because of any lack of effort on their part but because of the arrogance of men who believed that their honour and 'prestige' (*iftikhār*) were dependant on keeping their women in ignorance. In doing so, they were actually going against the spirit of their civilization in which there were women like Parvati and Sita composing verses in Sanskrit. It is interesting that Parvati, the spouse of Lord Shiva, and a goddess of devotion and motherhood, and Sita, the dutiful wife of Lord Rama, are invoked here not for

---

[7] For a discussion on the public sphere, see Francesca Orsini, *The Hindi Public Sphere, 1920–1940: Language and Literature in the Age of Nationalism* (New Delhi: Oxford University Press, 2000); and Hasan, *Paper, Performance, and the State.*

[8] See Chapter 2.

their wifely duties and devotion but for their literate skills and command over language. As he says:

> In these times, men prefer to keep their women in ignorance (*be-'ilm*) with a view to enhance their prestige (*iftikhār*), quite oblivious of the fact that in the past, among the Hindus, there were Parvatiji and Sitaji, and so many other Sanskrit-knowing (*Sanskrit-dān*) women; some among them composed poems (*kabitā*) too.[9]

In the ancient period, says Nadir, women did not only compose poems in Sanskrit but also in Prakrit and Bhasa.[10] And, as a representative example of the ancient period, he specifically mentions the reign of Raja Bhoj, an early eleventh-century ruler in the region of Malwa, in whose reign several schools for women's education, *zanān-e madrase*, were established in his kingdom. Every village and district – the word he uses is *pargana* – had educational associations (*'ilm-i majlis*), and taking a dig at the British reformers, Nadir adds: 'The associations (*anjumans*) and the societies that are budding these days owing to the efforts of the government (*sarkār*) are its imitations.'[11]

It is evident that the memories that the authors of *BN* and *TN* invoked were motivated by contemporary politico-ideological concerns, and it is for this reason that the poets, their life stories, and couplets allegedly rescued from distant pasts were a part of an 'invented tradition'. Even so, they collectively served to create a commemorative space, or what Pierre Nora terms as *lieux de memoire*, or 'realms of memory',[12] within which women's literary skills were celebrated and constructed, and invoked and memorialized with a view to reframe Hindustan as a civilization where women were educated and well-read, enjoying considerable command over the arts and norms of aesthetics. At the same time, for both Ranj and Nadir, it was equally important to represent Hindustan as an inclusive and expansive space, and that is why Nadir does not end his introductory prelude with Parvati and Sita, but proudly mentions legendary Muslim women from the early history of Islam as well; they are celebrated not for their piety or saintly status, but for their literary qualities and high education. In this list of Muslim women, he mentions Aisha, the wife of Prophet Muhammad, reciting verses to

---

[9]   *TN*, 45.

[10] *TN*, 45

[11] *TN*, 45.

[12] Pierre Nora and Lawrence D. Kritzman (eds.), *Realms of Memory: The Construction of the French Past, vol. 1- Conflicts and Divisions*, trans. Arthur Goldhammer (New York: Columbia University Press, 1996).

the Prophet; and Fatima, his daughter, composing elegies.[13] In the same vein, he mentions Khadija, the Prophet's first wife, and Zubaida Khatun, the wife of the famous Abbasid caliph Harun Rashid (766–809 CE), as a 'scholarly poet' (*fāzila shā'ira*).[14]

Hindustan was after all an integral part of the larger Persianate world, and so it is that the women precursors who inspired the contemporary literati included legendary figures from the pre-Islamic past as well. Nadir mentions Zulaikha, the lover of Prophet Yusuf (Joseph), composing couplets expressing her love for Joseph.[15] Asiya, the wife of Firaun (Pharaoh), is remembered in collective memory as a respectable female scholar (*fāzila*).[16] And in the 'age of ignorance' (*jāhiliyah*), that is pre-Islamic Arabia, there was a princess called Zibba, who was remembered in the Persianate world as 'a poetess (*shā'ira*) who was well known among the poets in the Arab world'.[17] Also remembered in the Persianate literary space was Ummiya, the daughter of Abdul Mutalib, the grandfather of Prophet Muhammad, who, like her sisters, was a respectable poetess, and her elegies were well known in Arabia.[18]

Within the Persianate 'realms of memory', commemoration was certainly a creative activity, and the literary skills of these poets were represented as emanating from their life stories. Qatila, the daughter of one Nasr, wrote a poem in remembrance of her father who died fighting the Prophet at the famous battle of Badr (624 CE). When the Prophet heard the poem, he was deeply moved and told his followers that if he had heard her poem earlier, he would have saved his life; Nadir adds, 'See how very effective is poetry; an appropriate poem can generate such intense emotions'.[19] Islam was clearly not a boundary marker, and women poets were remembered across their religious affiliations; women who joined the fold of Islam along with their fathers or their spouses are remembered for sure, but so are those who came from households that contested the expansion of Islam and fought battles against Muhammad.

---

[13] Nadir cites a verse in Arabic that is attributed to Fatima, and translates it thus: 'My afflictions are so sorrowful indeed; they could convert broad daylight into the darkness of the night' (*TN*, 49).

[14] *TN*, 48–49.

[15] *TN*, 54.

[16] *TN*, 54.

[17] *TN*, 54.

[18] *TN*, 54.

[19] *TN*, 55.

Indeed, a large number of Arab women poets in Nadir's compendium come from the early history of Islam when bloody conflicts and warfare were common; their poems appear to be part of the ritual mourning for those who died in the battlefield. The mother of Umm-i Musallam wrote elegies (*marsiye*) on the death of her son in 'the battle of the camel' (*jang-i jamal*) and in the same battle, Abdul Qais also lost his life, and his spouse wrote elegiac verses when she saw the dead body of her husband.[20] The daughter of the military commander Hujr Adi Kindi (died: 660 CE) was a poet, and she composed elegies to commemorate the assassination of her father by Muawiya (602–80 CE), the founder ruler of the Umayyad caliphate; he was killed, informs Nadir, owing to his loyalty and allegiance to Ali.[21]

Nadir mentions several other Arab women poets composing elegiac verses to commemorate the death of members in their households. His detailed discussions about them enables him to draw attention to the creative intervention of women in mourning rituals; they were not just passive participants reciting *marsiya*s to the accompaniment of wailing and chanting, but composed some of these elegies themselves. The martyrdom of Prophet Muhammad's grandson, Husain, at Karbala in modern day Iraq at the hands of the Umayyad ruler Yazid in 680 CE is commemorated among the Shiite Muslims, and scholars have studied the grieving rituals in terms of their role in constructing community ties and enforcing ethical and moral values; their work also examines how the event is reinterpreted in rituals and elegies within changing political and sociocultural contexts.[22] The point that *TN* makes then is that some of these elegies were composed by women, and some others derived their inspiration from them. Elegies were an important literary form in the Persianate culture, and in mentioning women composing elegiac verses, Nadir seeks to bring to the forefront the historical contribution of women's creativity in enriching the contemporary literary culture.

This provides the context to the main body of discussion on women poets and enables the positioning of women's literary activities within an inclusive

---

[20] *TN*, 55. The battle of Jamal (Camel) took place in 656 CE between Ali, the fourth caliph and the Prophet's son-in-law, and Khadija, the wife of Muhammad. The battle is known as 'the battle of the camel' because Khadija fought Ali's forces riding a camel.

[21] *TN*, 55.

[22] Syed Akbar Hyder, *Reliving Karbala: Martyrdom in South Asian History* (New York: Oxford University Press, 2006); Juan R. I. Cole, *Roots of North Indian Shi'ism in Iran and Iraq: Religion and State in Awadh, 1722–1859* (Berkeley: University of California Press, 1988). Also see Epsita Haldar, *Reclaiming Karbala: Nation, Islam and Literature of the Bengali Muslims* (London and New York: Routledge, 2023); and Nishat Zaidi (ed. and trans.), *Karbala: A Historical Play by Premchand* (New Delhi: Oxford University Press, 2022).

cultural space, which was polyvalent and accommodative. In this, as we know from the work of Mana Kia, our *tazkiras* were not any different from the other commemorative texts that were in circulation in the Persianate world, wherein perceptions of selfhood and community were aporetic, and differences were contingent, relative, and negotiable.[23] Within such an aporetic cultural space, Nadir commemorates both Parvati and Sita, and Aisha and Fatima with the same enthusiasm; they were all integral to the shaping of the literary heritage, and their poetic compositions were a source of inspiration for both women and men across religious demarcations.

More than anything, these figures should inspire women to acquire education, and men to encourage their women to do so. To reiterate the point, interestingly, Nadir again draws on the resources of co-existence, and communication across difference, and invokes both the Islamic legal-sacral system (*shari'at*) and the Vedas to exhort the people of Hindustan to vigorously pursue women's education. Referring to the Muslims in Hindustan, he says:

> What should I say about the Muslims? It is enjoined in their *shari'at* that they should educate their women, and indeed among several respectable households women have access to education. Even when they have not had proper education, they still learn to read the Koran (lit. 'the God's word': *kalām Allah*) from the time they turn four years, four months, and four days old. They are thus instructed in one of the sayings of the Prophet (*hadith*): 'It is obligatory on all Muslim men and women to search for knowledge (*talab-ul'ilm*)'.[24]

Hindu women are similarly exhorted in the Vedas to acquire education, and Nadir cites the following excerpt addressed to women allegedly from the Atharvaveda:

> O pious woman! You should always provide comfort to your spouse. Don't be ever neglectful towards him. You should manage the affairs of the household in accordance with the best principles, and provide adequate protection to the animals in your house. *You should strive to acquire best skills and education.* You should give birth to healthy children, and should rear them well.[25]

It is interesting that in a compendium devoted to Urdu and Persian women poets, there is, in the introductory section, quite a detailed discussion on women writing in classical and vernacular Indic languages. For Nadir, linguistic boundaries

---

[23]   Kia, *Persianate Selves.*

[24]   *TN*, 47.

[25]   *TN*, 48, emphasis added.

were porous, and he was certainly writing at a time when signs, metaphors, and ideas traversed easily from one language to another.[26] Drawing on the multi-lingual literary heritage, he mentions Kargi, who used to have 'scholarly debates' (*mubāhis-i 'ilmī*) with a *rishi* ('an enlightened scholar') during the reign of Raja Janak, who is mentioned in the Hindu epic Ramayana as the king of the kingdom of Videha (Mithila) and the father of Ram's wife, Sita.[27] Nadir refers to Mandudri, the wife of Ravana, the king of the island of Lanka, as a scholar and the inventor of the game of chess.[28] Also mentioned in the list of 'Hindi [Hindustani] female scholars' are Sankarmati, the daughter of the Mauryan ruler Asoka (268–32 BCE), who was, says Nadir, 'a highly regarded woman scholar, intellectual and administrator' (*fāzila wa 'ālima wa 'āmila*) and well versed in the Pali language.[29] He also refers to Kalidas' wife, Vidyatama, as 'a great scholar-intellectual who defeated many renowned pundits of her time'.[30] And then there were in the ancient period Lilawati, an expert mathematician, Khona, a renowned astrologer, and Bagya, a scholar of classical Sanskrit.[31]

Later in time, during the fifteenth and sixteenth centuries, there was Mirabai, whose devotional compositions in Braj are, says Nadir, 'recited by the people of Hindustan even today'.[32] He does not forget the charismatic Rupmati either, and refers to her transformation from being a 'public entertainer' (*shāhid-i bāzārī*) to being a queen, married to the ruler of Malwa, Baz Bahadur. He also recalls her heroic skills in the battlefield when she was defending the kingdom from the assault of the imperial Mughals.[33] Nadir also cites songs (*geet*) and couplets that are popularly attributed to Rupmati. One such popular song goes as follows:

> Let those who are rich take pride in their wealth,
> My wealth of happiness (*sarmāya-i nishāt*) comes from love that is exclusive;
> I keep my wealth safely locked within my heart,

---

[26] For a discussion on the literary culture before the Hindi–Urdu linguistic divide, see Francesca Orsini (ed.), *Before the Divide: Hindi and Urdu Literary Culture* (New Delhi: Orient Blackswan, 2011); also see Walter N. Hakala, *Negotiating Languages: Urdu, Hindi, and the Definition of Modern South Asia* (New York: Columbia University Press, 2016).

[27] *TN*, 58.

[28] *TN*, 58.

[29] *TN*, 58–59.

[30] *TN*, 59.

[31] *TN*, 59.

[32] *TN*, 60.

[33] *TN*, 60.

I keep a watchful eye on the person I love more than my life;

He is protected from the [evil] eyes of the others, and I fear not losing him,

For I alone possess the key of access to him, and that is the real truth;

My wealth keeps on increasing with each passing day,

How can this immense wealth ever decrease?

My heart has decided, unconcerned with considerations of gains or losses,

I have to stand by the side of Baz Bahadur for the whole of my life.

Karne do fakhr unko jo hain sāhib-i daul,

sarmāya-i nishāt hai yahān 'ishq-i be-dakhl.

Mazbūt qufl dil kā hai, is ganj par lagā,

uski nigāh rakhti hun main jān se siwā.

mahfūz chashm-i ghair se hai aur be-khatr.

Kunjī hai' uski bas men merē qissa mukhtasar.

Sarmāya hotā jātā hai har roz kuch siwā,

is ganj-i sha'igān ko hai' ghatne se kām kyā.

Ab dil men thān lī hai ki ho nafa' yā zarar,

denā hai sāth Bāz Bahādur ka 'umr bhar.[34]

Constructing a Cosmopolitan Heritage: Memories of Poets in Distant Pasts and Places

Looking for the first woman Urdu poet in Hindustan, Nadir shares a sentiment in popular memory that credits the multi-talented and influential wife of the Mughal emperor Jahangir (1605–27 CE), Nur Jahan,[35] as being the first woman who composed poems in that language. He cites some of her couplets in popular circulation, but immediately dismisses the popular belief for the simple reason that Urdu was non-existent as a language in the seventeenth century, and there is no evidence of Nur Jahan composing poems in any other language besides Persian.[36] Even so, in citing the fabricated Urdu verses attributed to Nur Jahan in social memory, Nadir indicates the depth of feelings for Nur Jahan in popular imagination, and the element of construction that was so crucial to commemoration in memory sites. While the first woman poet cannot be ascertained, the first woman to have a *diwān* of her own was the courtesan Chanda Deccani; in reconstructing

---

[34] *TN*, 60–61.

[35] For a reliable and detailed study of her life and achievements, see Lal, *Empress*. Also see Findly, *Nur Jahan*.

[36] *TN*, 57.

a gender-inclusive literary heritage, he compares her with Wali Deccani, and points out that just as he was the first man to have composed a *diwān* of his Urdu poems, Chanda was the first woman to do the same. They should both be remembered and acknowledged in shaping the literary heritage.[37]

Scholars working on collective memories usually draw a distinction between 'memory' and 'history', but this distinction is based on an erroneous attribution of facticity to history, and the location of memories exclusively within the realm of popular imagination removed from the real facts of history. In actual fact, 'memory' and 'history' are mutually imbricated categories, and serve to enrich each other.[38] In the biographical note that Nadir provides about Nur Jahan, there is obviously an effort to rewrite history along with the commemoration of her skills and talents. It is with a view to rewrite history that Nadir, in his note on the Maratha queen Ahilyabai Holkar (1725–95 CE), refers not only to her scholarship but also her administrative skills, and places her alongside the Mughal emperor Akbar: 'Just as Jalaluddin Muhammad Akbar is considered as the best known ruler of Hindustan, and for that matter the whole world, she should be considered as enjoying the same station among the women, for there was none like her.'[39]

In the case of several women poets, the biographical details are confusing, but, interestingly, the image in one entry after another communicates a picture of strong, talented, and multifaceted personalities. Women are commemorated not only for their literary skills but also their sharp intellect and refined temperament, and for the fact that they could easily outwit men, even when these men happened to be rulers and high officials. In his entry on Aram, a poet of the Mughal period, Nadir is certain about her royal status, but is quite confused about her spouse; sharing the confusion, he informs us that some believe that she was the wife of the Mughal emperor Jahangir, while others are convinced that she was married to his son and successor, Shahjahan, and yet several others think that she was the spouse of a Safavid ruler in Iran.[40] Ranj is, however, quite certain that she was one of the wives

---

[37] *TN*, 57.

[38] Siobhan Kattago (ed.), *The Ashgate Research Companion to Memory Studies* (London and New York: Routledge, 2016); Susannah Radstone, *Memory and Methodology* (London and New York: Routledge, 2020); Jeffrey K. Olick, Vered Vinitzky-Seroussi, and Daniel Levy (eds.), *The Collective Memory Reader* (New York: Oxford University Press, 2011); Anna Lisa Tota and Trever Hagen (eds.), *Routledge International Handbook of Memory Studies* (London and New York: Routledge, 2016). Also see Jeffrey K. Olick, *The Politics of Regret: On Collective Memory and Historical Responsibility* (London and New York: Routledge, 2013).

[39] *TN*, 61.

[40] *TN*, 69.

of Jahangir.[41] In both *TN* and *BN*, she is remembered as a highly educated woman, and while the former, in addition, describes her as 'an influential scholar' (*badī 'allāma*),[42] the latter finds her 'exceptionally intelligent and creative' (*nihāyat taba' aur khush fikr*).[43] In both texts, she is presented as a particularly talented chess player, certainly better than her husband. Referring to her skills in the game, Ranj praises her for the quickness with which she anticipated the moves of her adversary and the unique strategies she deployed to win the games. As he says:

> She was well versed in the game of chess. She had, with practice, reached such a level of perfection that many astute players were scared of playing against her. She had developed thousands of brilliant strategies, and could quickly anticipate the moves of her adversary.[44]

In their discussion on Aram, Nadir and Ranj narrate an interesting anecdote. The king was once playing chess with a prince,[45] and came close to losing the game, and with it also one of his wives, for the king had promised to part with one of his spouses if he lost the game. At that moment, it was Aram who suggested to him the right moves and saved the game for the king.[46] The intention in inserting this anecdote is obvious; it is to represent women as smarter than men, and certainly brighter and more intelligent. It is this element of gender inversion – and the representation of women as empowered and sharp-witted persons – that is so characteristic of the commemoration of women scholars in our *tazkiras*.

Discussions around poetic exchanges and witty banter in entries concerning royal women poets and, interestingly, even their servants and slaves serve the same purpose. Aqa Begum, a poet from Herat in present-day Afghanistan, was once attending a gathering where wine flowed freely; she had given up alcohol, and when the wine was still offered to her, with insistence, she instantly came up with the following verse; note the poet's wit and humour evident from the characterization of the one offering alcohol as the 'preacher of rightfulness'.

> Now that I have renounced wine, Oh preacher of rightfulness,
> Why don't you give up [tempting me by] offering it to me?[47]

---

[41] *BN*, 101.
[42] *TN*, 69.
[43] *BN*, 101.
[44] *BN*, 101–02.
[45] Nadir is not sure if he was playing against a prince or a merchant (*TN*, 69–70).
[46] *TN*, 69–70; *BN*, 101–02.
[47] *TN*, 72.

Of course, in constructing the literary heritage, the authors of *BN* and *TN* remember the women poets from Iran and Central Asia as well. They are represented as extremely gifted scholars, and in order to favourably equate them with the celebrated male poets, there are in these *tazkiras* episodes of witty poetic exchanges with some of them. Jahan Khatun, the wife of the *wazir* of the ruler of Shiraz and Isfahan in the fourteenth century, met up with the iconic Persian poet, Hafiz (1325–90),[48] in Shiraz (in present-day Iran), and Hafiz recited a *ghazal* to her, and one of the verses in that poem read as follows:

Don't trust the ways of this world
The wheel of fortune has both its highs and lows.

A'itimād nest bar-kār-i jahān,
Balke bar gardūn-i girdān nez hum.

Believing that this was a dig at her, the quick-witted Khatun retorted with the following distich, wherein she takes him to task for his pessimism, even as his poetry is a celebration of love, described here as 'wine-worship':

Oh Hafiz, what kind of wine-worship (*mai' parasti*) is this?
That you are both fed up (*bezār*) and intoxicated (*mastān*) too.[49]

In presenting Jahan Khatun as a poet to whom Hafiz recited his *ghazal*s, and with whom he had poetic exchanges, these *tazkiras* obviously intend to suggest that women poets occupied the centre stage in the Persianate literary culture, and that they were just as good, if still unrecognized and uncelebrated, as the influential and well-known poets celebrated across the Persianate world. Incidentally, if Hafiz recited poems to her, the other well-known poet in Shiraz, Zakani, was deeply in love with her and wanted to marry her; she rejected him, and chose to marry the *wazir* instead.[50]

Similarly, Nadir refers to banter and witty exchanges between Bijah Munjimah and the famous Persian poet in Herat, Abdur Rahman Jami, during the

---

[48] For an understanding of his poetry, and his influence over the Persianate world, see Leonard Lewisohn, *Hafiz and the Religion of Love in Classical Persian Poetry* (New York: I. B. Tauris, 2010); J. T. P. De Bruijn, *Persian Sufi Poetry: An Introduction to the Mystical Use of Classical Poems* (London and New York: Routledge, 2013); and A. J. Arberry, *Shiraz: Persian City of Saints and Poets* (Norman, Oklahoma: University of Oklahoma Press, 1960).

[49] *TN*, 76; *BN*, 127.

[50] *TN*, 76; *BN*, 127.

fifteenth century.[51] Details of these exchanges serve a purpose, and that is to depict Munjimah as enjoying a social standing that was equal to that of Jami, and her scholarship comparable to that of this influential poet and theologian. She was not just a poet but also an expert in astrology and gnosis. She was quite rich, and liked to spend her wealth in constructing public and religious buildings, an interest she shared with Jami who also built mosques, educational institutions (madrasas), and public baths (*hamām*).[52] In an incident narrated by Nadir, she once invited Jami to come and offer prayers in one of her mosques, but Jami refused, saying that the mosque was not sacred and was impure, perhaps referring to the objectionable sources of her income. This infuriated her and she tried to remind him that all mosques were sacred, and if his mosque was 'a source of blessing' so was hers: 'What is Mullaji saying? If he has built a mosque, so have I, and the qualities (*faza'il*) that he has, I have too. Why is he then behaving with such arrogance?' Harking on his spiritual attainments (and probably also gender), Jami reminded her that what he possessed, she certainly did not; and in banter with sexual connotations, she, referring to her seductive charms, retorted with the following note: 'I also have something which he doesn't have! He is actually at my mercy (*muhtāj*).' Jami was amused and decided to visit the mosque.[53]

In commemorating women from distant pasts and lands, the effort all along is to depict them as sharp and quick-witted individuals with interesting stories to tell. They are also remembered for their generosity and the patronage they provided to the cash-starved poets. Aqa Begum (who was earlier mentioned as a poet from Herat who had renounced but was still tempted by alcohol) was well known for giving food grains to poets in lieu of their stipends.[54] And, when Khwaja Asifi, a poet, was once ignored and he petitioned her through a quatrain, she, according to Ranj, not only restored but enhanced his stipend.[55] As patrons, these women played a crucial role in enriching the literary culture, and Ranj and Nadir memorialized their contribution in their commemorative texts. Some among them were remembered for their construction activities, and, as mentioned earlier, Bijah Munjimah was known for building mosques and madrasas.[56]

---

[51] *TN*, 74. For details about his life and work, see Hamid Algar, *Jami* (Oxford: Oxford University Press, 2013).

[52] *TN*, 74.

[53] *TN*, 74.

[54] *BN*, 98–99; *TN*, 71–72.

[55] *BN*, 98.

[56] *TN*, 76; *BN*, 127.

Described as 'chaste' and 'secluded' (*pardah nashīn*), these women were, of course, remembered for their piety and chastity. We have, for instance, the case of Padshah Khatun (1256–95 CE), the daughter of Sultan Qutbuddin Muhammad, the ruler of Kerman (in Iran).[57] She was, according to Ranj, 'a model of perfection in piety and devotion' and 'wakefulness was a habit with her, and in remembrance of God, she prayed from dusk to dawn every day'.[58] Even so, if her poems were a part of the collective memory, so were the compositions of Buzurgi, a prostitute (*kasbi*) turned social recluse in Jahangir's time.[59] For her though, the baggage from the past was hard to dispose of, and the poets who once visited her house accused her of following the path of sin and sorrow when they saw an Arab male entering her quarters without interruption. In Ranj's account, the Arab male is described as her 'lover' (*'āshiq*), but Nadir is circumspect and calls him 'an Arab kid with boorish disposition' (*'arab bacha, aubāsh waza'*).[60] Realizing that they were casting aspersions on her character, she had to assure them of her disinterest in him as in other men, and claimed to live 'in peace with both the Arabs and the non-Arabs (*'ajam*)'.[61] In inserting this particular anecdote, probably in circulation in cultural memory, our authors draw the attention of the reader/audience to the indifference with which she treated male poets, and the confidence with which she combated their insinuations. These poets – four in number – are shown to be smaller persons and certainly in no way better poets than a woman who came from a socially suspect background.

Of course, in representing women's memories in literary spaces, it is the powerful women in Hindustan that take centre stage. One such woman was Reziya Sultan (r. 1236–40), the only female ruler in the Delhi Sultanate, and we get to know from *BN* and *TN* that she was also a talented poet composing poems under the pen name Shirin.[62] The stories about her bravery and military exploits were a part of the collective memory, and our authors refer to her military engagements with her brother Ruknuddin Firuz, who had 'abandoned

---

[57] For details on Padshah Khatun, see Karin Quade-Reutter, 'Pādsah Kātun', *Encyclopaedia Iranica*, online edition, 2016, http://www.iranicaonline.org/articles/padshah-khatun (accessed 18 April 2016). Also see Fatima Mernissi, *The Forgotten Queens of Islam* (Minneapolis: University of Minnesota Press, 1997 [reprint]).

[58] *BN*, 109; also see *TN*, 73.

[59] *TN*, 73. Ranj does not mention that she was originally a prostitute but refers to her leading a life of 'contented seclusion' (*BN*, 110–11).

[60] *TN*, 73.

[61] *TN*, 73–74; *BN*, 111.

[62] *BN*, 157–58; *TN*, 79.

the affairs of the state, and indulged in a life of vice and excess'.[63] They also refer to her relations with her Abyssinian slave, Yaqut, who, much to the resentment of the nobles, 'was known to place her on the horse by lifting her with his hands under her arms'.[64] This is how Ranj describes her:

> This woman was delicate in constitution, and attractive and beautiful. Besides these qualities, nobody had seen or heard of someone so brave and courageous. She snatched the crown from her brother with force, fought several tough battles, and ascended the throne. In addition, she was wise and talented as well. In poetry, no poet, however eloquent, could match her.[65]

Even so, for both Ranj and Nadir, it was her poems that had made her immortal. Her compositions are fine specimens of Persian poetry, and, as in the following quatrain, hold the contradictions of love aesthetically together; in addition, one also notices a clever application of allusions and metaphors that are shared across the Persianate literary world; note in particular the characterization of the beloved as both a source of life and the reason for death. Just as much as the face of the beloved is a source of sustenance, her/his looks are like a 'dagger' that slays the lover:

> What is life but wallowing in the light of the face of the beloved (*nūr-i rukh-i khurshīd*)?
> And so it is, I have been killed by the dagger of his looks (*tegh-i nigāh-i ghazab*).[66]

Memorializing the Mughal Women: Remembering the Imperial Harem as a Cultural Place

There is an impressive discussion in both our *tazkiras* on the women in the Mughal imperial harem, and there are entries on Nur Jahan, the wife of Jahangir (r. 1605–27), co-sharing sovereignty with him, Jahanara, the daughter of Shahjahan (r. 1628–58), known for her overseas trading interests,[67] and Zebun

---

[63] *TN*, 79.
[64] *TN*, 79.
[65] *BN*, 157.
[66] *TN*, 79; *BN*, 158.
[67] For details about her life and work, see Afshan Bokhari, 'Masculine Modes of Female Subjectivity: The Case of Jahanara Begum', in *Speaking of the Self*, ed. Anshu Malhotra and Siobhan Lambert-Hurley, 165–202 (Durham and London: Duke University Press, 2015); Bokhari, 'Imperial Transgressions and Spiritual Investitures'; Shadab Bano, 'Jahanara's Role in the Public Domain', *Proceedings of the Indian History Congress* 74th session, New Delhi, 2013, 245–50.

Nisa Begum, the eloquent and articulate daughter of Aurangzeb (r. 1658–1707), among others. Not to be missed from the discussion are the literate female slaves in the domestic establishments of the Mughal rulers, and one such character, mentioned in both *BN* and *TN*, is the sharp-witted 'exclusive slave-girl' (*kanīz-i khās*) of Zebun Nisa, Amani.[68] Impressed by her literary skills, Ranj describes her as 'the heart of Delhi' (*dillī ka dil*) and 'the crème de la crème of literary specialists' (*khwāson men khwās*).[69]

Women in the Mughal harem were quite well educated, and clearly the imperial women made efforts to educate their servants and slaves as well. Scholars have commented on the literate skills of Mughal women,[70] but it is certainly remarkable that their couplets, authentic and fabricated, were on the lips of tasteful connoisseurs and aesthetically inclined people, and were a part of the memories circulating in the literary public sphere. Reflective of the impressive educational background of women in the Mughal harem, our authors indulge in the exaggerated and hyperbolic expressions to emphasize their literary and aesthetic skills. The excess in language is not merely an aesthetic form of expression, but serves to emphasize the need to memorialize their literary contribution and reprimand the tendency among literary critics to ignore them. Hayatun Nisa Begum, one of the wives of the Mughal emperor Jahangir, is described by Ranj as endowed with 'pleasant thoughts' (*khush fikr*), 'aesthetic imagination' (*nāzuk khyāl*), and 'sweetness in expression' (*shīrīn maqāl*); and this was because she was an accomplished scholar of Persian and Arabic literature.[71] In much the same way, Zebun Nisa Makhfi, the daughter of Aurangzeb, reminded people of Sahban Wa'il[72] when it came to eloquence; and when they saw her intelligence, they were reminded of the legendary Persian poet of the twelfth century, Khaqani. She could with her 'wit' (*shōkhī*) embarrass the other poets in poetic meetings, and 'in the battlefield of eloquence she was counted among the men'.[73]

Interestingly, parables of divine intervention that are a standard trope in the hagiographies of rulers, warriors, prophets, and saints are found for Mughal

---

[68] *BN*, 104; *TN*, 72–73.

[69] *BN*, 104.

[70] Lal, *Domesticity and Power in the Early Mughal World*; Lisa Balabanlilar, *Imperial Identity in the Mughal Empire: Memory and Dynastic Politics in Early Modern South and Central Asia* (London: I. B. Tauris, 2012); and Rekha Misra, *Women in Mughal India (1526–1749)* (New Delhi: Munshiram Manoharlal, 1967).

[71] *BN*, 130–31; also see *TN*, 77

[72] He was an orator, particularly famous for his eloquence.

[73] *BN*, 199.

women as well. While discussing the life story of Nur Jahan, Jahangir's queen consort, Ranj informs us that her parents, living in abject poverty, had, soon after her birth abandoned her at a deserted place but when they decided to take her back, troubled by 'motherly affection' (*ulfat-i mādirī*), they discovered that she was protected by a mysterious snake.[74] He also discusses Jahangir's intense attachment for her but makes clear that he loved her both for her enchanting beauty (*husn-i dil fareb*) and scholarship (*qābliyat*).[75]

It is, of course, reasonable to presume that a substantial corpus of poems that were attributed in cultural memory to the Mughal imperial spouses, princesses, and slaves were latter-day fabrications, but even as their reliability is suspect, they serve to convey a picture of popular constructions of powerful women wherein, besides their literary accomplishments, they are celebrated for their sense of humour, strength of character, and combative aesthetic sensibilities. And so it is that these women are remembered not just for their poetic compositions but, more interestingly perhaps, for their alleged literary exchanges and banter with the rulers. These anecdotes inserted in their biographical details serve to highlight their empowered subjectivities, and claim for imperial women a position of near, if not total, equivalence with the rulers and ruling aristocracy.

Interestingly, in their verbal duels we also notice a modest rejection of disciplinary constraints, and the desire to celebrate life and its pleasures. Let us take a couple of instances here. When Jahangir recited a hemistich welcoming the Muslim festival of Eid, after a month of ritual fasting, Nur Jahan completed it into a couplet by adding to the hemistich a line mentioning a return to the pleasures of life, metaphorically described as the opening up of the gates of the tavern: 'The lost keys to the tavern (*kalīd-i maikada gum gashta*) have been found again.'[76] One cannot miss the element of humour in these anecdotes, but there is, in these literary exchanges, a polite mockery of disciplinary forces, and an insistence on the need to enjoy the pleasures of life. In another instance cited by Ranj, Makhfi, Aurangzeb's daughter, was once strolling in the garden along with her father, and charmed by the lush greenery, beds of flowers, and the running streams of water, she composed an instant couplet which referred to the charms of wine and beauty:

What are the four things that captivate the heart?
These are wine, greenery, flowing streams (*āb-i rawān*), and beautiful faces (*rū-i nigār*).

---

[74]   *BN*, 223–24.
[75]   *BN*, 224.
[76]   *BN*, 225.

Incensed by what he had heard, the emperor asked her to repeat what she had just said. She immediately changed the couplet, and, in order to suit the emperor's predilections, mentioned the four things that bewitched the heart as prayers (*namāz*), fasting (*rozah*), rosary, and repentance.[77] These anecdotes not only highlight the literary wit and humour in imperial women but also reflect their contestations with patriarchal norms and ritual conformism. In the social memory, clearly the Mughal women were memorialized not for their passive obedience but for creative engagements with the rulers, and certainly not for their acceptance but contestations with dominant patriarchal norms. It is, of course, not the case that any of these events demonstrate a willingness to subvert the patriarchal order, but they do indicate an effort to push its boundaries, and modify its excesses and disciplinary aspirations.

How do we read the poems and verses that were attributed to these imperial women? How did their Persian compositions become a part of cultural memory, and if they were not their compositions but were attributed to them in cultural memory, then what is it about literary heritage that these compositions served to remember and memorialize? For one, their poems adhered to literary canons and constraints of expression but still succeeded in articulating new emotions and experiences. In this they compare favourably with some of the best compositions by the best-known masters of the art, and yet they fell out of cultural memory later in the period and were shunned by the modern critics as well. There would be many explanations for this act of forgetting, but modern notions of gender division of labour and familial honour were certainly important reasons. At the same time, our *tazkiras* indicate that these perceptions were dominant but not hegemonic; and there were voices within the literary culture that challenged and contested them.

In order to disclose the aesthetic components and linguistic complexities of the literary compositions of Mughal imperial women, let us take a look at the verses of Aram, who, we mentioned earlier, was a woman of multi-talents, adept in the game of chess and the skills of poetry. Her compositions were a part of the cultural memory, and while there is no way one can verify their authenticity, her poems are marked by a creative deployment of Persianate symbols and metaphors: the heart as 'a sacred space' (*farsh-i haram*), the beloved as a hunter and the lover his prey, love as wine (*sharāb*), and the lover as akin to the legendary Majnun[78] meandering

---

[77] *BN*, 199–200.

[78] In the Persianate literary world, Majnun was a legendary lover deeply in love with his beloved, Laila.

in wilderness in search of his beloved.[79] These symbols are used to invoke emotions of love and articulate its intense and embodied nature within the constraints of the literary *adāb*, or the norms and accepted textures of artistic expression. As is the case with Persian poetry, there is a range of meanings to her compositions, and concealed within an excess of allusions, the careful reader can notice the embodied articulations of love. Among other ways of reading, the following verse conveys, within the constraints of the literary *adāb*, the erotic experiences – with wine-drinking suggestive of love-making, and the stained dress loss of virginity:

> After I drank the red wine (*sharāb arkhwānī*) in the early hours of the dawn,
> I spoiled my dress of purity (*libās-i pārsaī*) with the wine spilling over.[80]

It is perhaps this embodied articulation of the emotion of love that is characteristic of women's poetry as remembered in literary spaces during the early modern period. At the same time, love is presented as an entity – almost a person – that eludes and transcends all identities, differences, and contradictions. This is, for example, borne out from the following *ghazal* attributed to Nur Jahan; the 'I' in the poem is an anthropomorphic representation of 'love':

> I am light (*nūrum*) and fire (*nāram*) and an orchard and the rose garden,
> I am the temple and the idol, and the Brahman and his sacred thread (*zunnār*);
> No! No! I am not whatever you have been hearing about me,
> I am the scent of the rose (*bu-i gulam*), one that bears the disposition of the garden;
> If I reveal my thread of love (*zunnār-i ʿishq*), the roses in the garden will burn with envy,
> If I wail in loneliness, the candle in the gathering (*shamʿa-i anjuman*) will burn in pain.[81]

Conclusion

In cultural memory, Mughal imperial women were remembered as multi-talented and educated persons, enjoying considerable agency and spaces for autonomous reflection. They were represented as scholars skilled in the aesthetic use of language, particularly well versed in articulating emotions of love, and the

---

[79] *TN*, 70–71; *BN*, 102–03.
[80] *TN*, 70–71. *BN*, 103.
[81] *BN*, 226; also see *TN*, 95.

experiences of life in sensitive and affect-laden forms. In the poems that were
attributed to them and those of their compositions that were recited and read
out in marketplaces, poetic assemblies, coffee houses, and courtesan's quarters,
we notice a thrust towards corporeal love and tactile means of apprehension of
emotions. The palpability of love is something that is certainly emphasized in their
compositions, but, interestingly, even as it leads to an appreciation of sensoriality,
it also enables these imperial women poets to draw attention to the entangled
proximity of love with violence over women's bodies.

In one of the poetic exchanges between Jahangir and his queen-consort, Nur
Jahan, recorded by both Ranj and Nadir, the emperor asked Nur Jahan what it
was that her 'delicate body' (*nāzuk badan*) was concealing within her clothes. Her
response is suggestive of the coalescence of love with force, but the experience of
intimate violence is communicated within the constraints of Persianate aesthetic
tradition. Her garments, she replied, were concealing 'the traces (*naqsh*) of the
hoof of the antelope (*sum-i āhu*) on the petals of the jasmine (*barg-i saman*)'.[82]
In an astute appropriation of Persianate allegorical system, the 'hoof of the
antelope' represents the nature of her sexual relations with Jahangir – violent
and aggressive, and so forceful indeed as to leave bruises on her body. Her body,
delicate and fragile, is metaphorically described as the 'petals of jasmine'. The
poet does not quite elaborate if the violence is physical or emotional, but it is still
experienced in somatic, embodied terms and is likened to 'drops of blood, as red as
the roses in Badakhshan' oozing out from the open, lacerated wounds.[83]

It is perhaps this rootedness in real-life experiences that marks women's
compositions as characteristically remarkable. It is through their concrete
experiences – tactile and violent – that they discovered their bodies. Women's
bodies were certainly constructed in and through performative exercises, and
literature was a significant site for performance, but corporeality was pre-reflexive;
the materiality of the body experienced in intimate, as also violent moments,
was resilient and obdurate. It was extra-discursive but found new meanings
and possibilities from compositions of queens and princesses that were etched
in popular memories, and found new significations in changing contexts of
time and space.

The poetic heritage was, of course, not restricted to Hindustan, but
encompassed the larger Persianate world; as mentioned earlier, women poets
whose compositions were remembered in cultural memory included those that
came from quite many well-known centres of literary efflorescence and education:

[82] *BN*, 225–26.
[83] *BN*, 226.

Shiraz, Isfahan, Bokhara, Nishapur, Herat, Balkh, and Samarqand.[84] All along, women artists are represented as strong-willed characters, imbued with wit and humour, command over language, and the art of eloquence. Their banter and riposte with their rulers, fathers, and spouses aptly served to demonstrate that they did not see their gender as a constraint, and were certainly popularly remembered as enjoying parity with men in the realm of culture and literary expression. We have discussed earlier in this chapter instances of poetic exchanges that highlighted their wit and sharp intellect, but we could, in order to close the argument, take one further instance here. Our sources refer to a blind woman poet, Daulat Bibi, in Samarqand who had been captured by the soldiers of Amir Timur (1336–1405). His attention was drawn to her when he heard her loudly reciting her poems, and he immediately summoned her. When it was revealed to him that her name was 'Daulat', which means 'wealth', he blurted, 'Is wealth without sight?' In a befitting reply, Daulat retorted: 'If she were not blind, how could she have come into the hands of a lame (*langde*) ruler?'[85] Timur was lame having injured his right leg and right hand in a battle encounter.

The ability of women to stand up to people in power, in particular the sovereign ruler, is something that appears to be commemorated in cultural memory. In an interesting anecdote attributed to Janan Begum, the daughter of the well-known multilingual scholar and patron of music and literature, Abdur Rahim Khan-i-Khanan,[86] we are informed that 'hearing of her fame' (*shohra*), Prince Salim (later emperor Jahangir) was drawn to her, and expressed the intention of marrying her. She was so repulsed by the idea that she persuaded her father to break her teeth and cut her hair, and then she was presented before the prince; seeing her, the prince relented, and apologized for making the matrimonial offer.[87]

The responsibility for maintaining the household was placed on the shoulders of women, and this was an important reason for the movement for their education in the nineteenth century. Among other things, this entailed having to keep their spouses under sexual restraints, and prevent those so inclined from pursuing pederasty. It is by way of celebrating the intelligence and literary skills of women in

---

[84] Let us take some more instances not mentioned earlier: Rabia-Isfahan (*TN*, 107), Rabia-Shiraz (*TN*, 107), Bint-Isfahan (*TN*, 103), Pari-Nishapur (*TN*, 104), Tuti-Iran (*TN*, 105), and Daulat-Samarqand (*TN*, 106–07).

[85] *TN*, 106–07.

[86] For an interesting piece on him, see Corinne Lefevre, 'The Court of 'Abd-Ur-Rahim Khan-i Khanan as a Bridge Between Iranian and Indian Cultural Traditions', in *Culture and Circulation: Literature in Motion in Early Modern India*, ed. Thomas de Bruijn and Allison Busch, 75–106 (Leiden: Brill, 2014).

[87] *TN*, 105.

this context that Nadir mentions a woman poet of Iran, Tuti. Her spouse was fond of boys (*amrad parasti*); tired of seeing him slip out of the home in their pursuit, she sent him the following pair of couplets:

> That impudent person (*shokh*) who imbibes the beauty of the world,
> Oh God! If only I could sleep with him in the night;
> My Lord! Come and let's resolve this issue between us peacefully,
> You embellish his world, while I take care of his dick (*kīr*).

> *Ān shokh ki hast husn-i 'ālam gīrash*
> *Yā rab! che shawad shab-i ba-khwābam zerash*
> *Ae khwāja! Be-yā tā man wa tu sulh kunem*
> *Tū ba-kaunash ba-sāz wa man ba-kirash.*[88]

The note from his wife shocked him, and so the legend goes, he gave up his 'illicit activities' (*f'al-i nā-jā'iz*) and 'spent the rest of life with his wife in peace and comfort'.[89]

Appendix 5A.1

Aram: Poet Who Played Chess[90]

Aram was her pen name and her real name was Dil Aram. She was the spouse of some ruler. She was a bright poet and a renowned scholar (*'allāma*). Some scholars have suggested that she was the wife of emperor Jahangir,[91] but the author of *Mir'āt-ul 'Āshiqīn* (The Lovers' Mirror) refers to her as the wife of Emperor Shahjahan. And, the author of *Malahāt-ul Maqāl* (Elegant Utterances) argues instead that she was married to the Shah of Iran....

It is narrated that the ruler [her husband] had three more wives: Jahan, Hiyat, and Fana. Once, he was playing a game of chess with a prince of some other kingdom, or perhaps a merchant, with the condition (*shart*) that the loser would part with one of his wives to the winner. Just when the king was close to losing the match, he went inside his fort, assembled his four wives, and informed them

---

[88] *TN*, 105.
[89] *TN*, 105.
[90] *TN*, 69–71. Also see *BN*, 101–03.
[91] He is probably referring here to Ranj who mentioned her as one of the wives of Emperor Jahangir (*BN*, 101).

about the bet and enquired which one of them would be willing to accompany the winner....

[Of course, none of them agreed to desert their king, but it was Aram who asked him to lay the board before her, and suggested the moves with which to win back the game. In a verse, she asked him to:]

Oh King, give away your rook, and rest in peace,
Bring your pawn and the bishop forward, and checkmate with the knight![92]

The King returned to the playroom (*bāzīcha khāna*), and followed her suggestions and won the game.

Appendix 5A.2

Aqa Begum: A Poet from Herat Remembered in Hindustan[93]

Known by her pen name Aqa Begum, she was a poet from Herat, and during the reign of Sultan Husain Bahadur Khan, her fame reached the elites and the common folk alike. Every year she gave food grains to poets as their stipend. It so happened that once the stipend did not reach Khwaja Asifi, and he thus reminded her about it:

Do tell me, the one who forgives mistakes, and conceals sins,
Why has my stipulated stipend not reached me?
Whenever you order the release of grains in my favour,
I bow my head in gratitude at the threshold of your door.

The author of *Jawahir-ul 'Ajaib* (The Priceless Jewels) says, perhaps rightly, that her name was Afaq Jala'ir. From the same book, we get to know that she was the daughter of Mir Ali Jala'ir and belonged to the lineage of Emperor Sultan Ahmad Baghdadi. She was the wife of Amir Ali Darwesh.

Once she was present before Mirza Zahid Badi-uz Zaman and wine was freely flowing in the gathering. She had quit drinking, after enjoying it for so long, and so she explained her condition through the following verse:

Now that I have renounced wine, O preacher of rightfulness,
Why don't you give up [tempting me by] offering it to me?

---

92 *TN*, 70.
93 *TN*, 71–72.

[Ranj provides quite similar details about her life but ignores the drinking episode mentioned by Nadir. He adds a small detail when discussing the incident with Khwaja Asifi, and mentions that Aqa Begum liked his quatrain so much that she not only restored but also enhanced his annual stipend].[94]

Appendix 5A.3

Amani: Slave-girl of a Mughal Princess[95]

Amani was her pen name, and she was an exclusive slave-girl (*kanīz-i khās*) of Zebun Nisa Makhfi. She had a house in Delhi, adjacent to Kalan Mahal.

It is narrated that once Makhfi was strolling in the flower garden, and all of a sudden the princess posed the question, 'Amani, why do the roses smile?' Amani replied thus: 'They smile at [the transitory nature of] their existence, and our ignorance.'

Appendix 5A.4

Jahan Khatun: Dejected Lover and the Poet[96]

Her name was Jahan Khatun, and she was the wife of Khwaja Qawamuddin Amin-ud Daulah who was the *wazir* of Abu Ishaq.[97] She was a contemporary of poets Salman and Ubaid. Ubaid Zakani[98] was charmed by her enthralling poetry and fell deeply in love with her. On the day of her betrothal (*nikāh*), he went up to her house and was informed that she had already married someone. Dejected, he sent her the following hemistich:

God's world is never bereft of opportunities.

When the well-mannered *wazir* came to know about the matter, he called him over, took him to a secluded room, and comforted him.

---

[94] *BN*, 98–99.
[95] *TN*, 72–73. Also see *BN*, 104.
[96] *TN*, 76–77. Also see *BN*, 126–27.
[97] The reference is to Abu Ishaq Inju (1343–57) who was then ruling over Shiraz and Isfahan.
[98] Ubaid Zakani (1369–71) was a Persian poet residing in Shiraz, then under Injuid control. His satires were quite famous, particularly his work *Mūsh-o Gurba* ('Mouse and Cat'), which attacks the ignorance and corruption among the religious classes. For details about his life and work, see A. A. Haidari, 'A Medieval Persian Satirist,' *Bulletin of the School of Oriental and African Studies* 49, no. 1 (February 1986): 117–27; and Thomas de Bruijn, 'Ubayd-i Zakani,' in *Encyclopedia of Islam*, ed. Kate Fleet, Gudrun Kramer, Denis Matringe, John Nawas, and Everett Rowson (Leiden: Brill, 2012).

It is believed that he also composed the following verse in her appreciation:

If the *ghazals* of Jahan were to reach Hindustan
The souls of Khusrau and Hasan would seek their author.

It is said that Khwaja Shamsuddin Hafiz Shiraz had met this poet and recited to her one of his *ghazals*. One of the distiches in that *ghazal* was:

Don't trust the ways of this world
The wheel of fortune has both its highs and lows.

Believing that this was a dig at her, Khatun wrote back the following verse in response:

Oh Hafiz! What kind of wine-worship (*mai' parasti*) is this?
That you are both fed up (*bezār*) and intoxicated (*mastān*) too.

Appendix 5A.5

Badshah Khatun: 'Remembered God from Dusk to Dawn'[99]

Badshah Khatun was her name. This princess was the daughter of Qutbuddin Muhammad Sultan, and during his reign she was indeed better than most of her contemporary poets. She was an accomplished scholar and a model of perfection in piety and devotion. She was a talented calligrapher and was so religious that she spent most of her time reciting the holy Koran. Wakefulness was a habit with her, and in remembrance of God, she prayed from dusk to dawn every day.

Badshah Khatun's Couplets

(1)
Within such a curtain of chastity resides my dwelling,
That even the visiting wind finds it impossible to pass through;
The coif covering my head protects me from the breeze reaching my hair,
The warp and woof [of the coif] protects my chastity.

Darūn-i parda-i 'asmat ki takiya gāh-i man ast
Musāfirān-i hawā rā guzar ba dushwār ast

---

[99] *BN*, 109–10; also see *TN*, 73.

Hamesha bād sar-i zan ba-zer miqna'a-i man
Ki tār-o- paud-i wai' az 'asmat neku kār ast.

Appendix 5A.6

Buzurgi: The Poet Who Had an Arab Lover[100]

Buzurgi was both her *takhallus* and her name. She was Kashmiri by origin.
In poetry, she was pleasantly creative, and adept in the arts (*ustād-i fan*). During
the reign of Jahangir, she had, turning her back on the profane world, settled for
a life of secluded contentment (*gosha-i qana'at*). Once, four poets dropped in at
her house to meet her, but she refused to give them audience, and the poets felt
bitter by her indifference. Just then, an Arab lad who was her lover (*'āshiq*) came
down, and was immediately called inside the house. The poets together sent her
the following quatrain:

> You imbibe both faith and sin in you,
> You have chosen the path of infinite sorrows;
> The signs of maturity show on your face,
> And yet, you have relations with [men who are] Arabs and non-Arabs (*'ajam*).

Buzurgi immediately retorted with the following verse:

> Since the moment I arrived in this world,
> I have lived in peace with both the Arabs and non-Arabs.

[Nadir's account has the same details but describes her as a prostitute (*kasbi*),
adding that 'during Jahangir's reign, she renounced her line of work (*pesha*), and
began to lead a contented life'].[101]

Appendix 5A.7

Bijah Munjimah: A Wealthy Poet with an Interest in Buildings[102]

Bijah Munjimah was an accomplished scholar of astrological sciences. She was
a poet with a refined sense of humour and was gifted with gnosis. She had an

---

[100] *BN*, 110–11.

[101] *TN*, 73–74.

[102] *TN*, 74.

abundance of worldly possessions and was generously patronized by the high nobles (*umara*) and rulers (*salātīn*). She had a witty relationship with Mulla Jami,[103] and there were amusing exchanges between them. It is said that Mulla Jami had built a public bath (*hamām*), madrasa, and mosque. She also built similar structures, and invited the elites in the city to come and offer prayers at her mosque. They welcomed her invite, but the Mulla refused to come and sent her a note saying:

> I will not offer my prayers in your mosque,
> Since its *mihrab*[104] is not pious enough.

> *Nā guzāram ba-masjid-i to namāz*
> *zān ki mihrāb-i ān namāz mī-nēst.*

His note incensed her, and she wrote back saying, 'What is the Mullaji saying? If he has built a mosque, so have I, and the qualities (*fazā'il*) that he has, I have too. If his mosque is a source of blessing, so is mine. Why then is he behaving with such arrogance?'

> *Mullājī kyā farmāte hain? Jo shay un-honē banwāyī' main ne bhī taiyār karwāī',*
> *jo fazāi'l un-men hain mujh men bhi hain. Phir unkō kis bāt par nāz hai'?*

Jami replied with the following note: 'I have something that she doesn't have' (*hum ek aīsī chīz rakhte hain jo uske pās nahin hai'.*)

She retorted by sending across to him the following note: 'I also have something which he doesn't have! He is actually at my mercy.' (*hamāre pās bhī aisi shai hai' ki woh nahin rakhte balke woh hamāre muhtāj hai'.*)

Jami was amused with her sense of humour and came down and visited the place [the mosque].

Appendix 5A.8

Jahanara: Shahjahan's Daughter and a Generous Patron[105]

Jahanara was the eldest daughter of Emperor Shahjahan. She was the sister of Aurangzeb, the ruler of Delhi. In 1681, she moved to her eternal abode.

---

[103] Abdur Rahman Jami (1414–92 CE) was a well-known Persian poet who lived in Herat in present-day Afghanistan.

[104] *Mihrab* is the chamber in the mosque from where the priest leads the congregational prayers.

[105] *BN*, 126; also see *TN*, 75–76.

Many poets benefitted from her generosity. She is buried in the mausoleum complex of Shaikh Nizamuddin Aulia. The following verse is engraved on her grave:

> Cover my grave with nothing but green foliage,
> The green grass is good enough to cover the grave of this abject person.

Appendix 5A.9

Hayat: Emperor Jahangir's Wife[106]

Hayat was her *takhallus*, and her name was Nawab Hayat-un Nisa Begum; she was the second wife of emperor Jahangir. This poetess was gifted with pleasant thoughts (*khush fikr*), aesthetic imagination (*nāzuk khyāl*), and sweetness in expression (*shīrīn maqāl*). She was an accomplished scholar of Persian and Arabic literature. In her disposition, she was graceful in her dealings, and, in addition, chaste and virtuous.

Hayat's Couplets

> When I circle around the tavern or the *ka'aba*, temple or the mosque,
> My heart venerates you [God] with my eyes collecting the dust every time;
> Come here, the virtuous devotee and drink wine with me,
> Don't head towards the *ka'aba*; there you get nothing to drink except your own blood.

> *Che sāzam tauf-i dair-o ka'ba wa but-khāna-o masjid*
> *Bagird-i chashm-i abruat dilam har bār mi-gardad*
> *Biyā zāhid ki jām-i bādah-i gilgun ba-nosham*
> *Marau dar ka'ba ki-anja nest juz khun-i jigar khurdan.*

Appendix 5A.10

Shirin: Begum Reziya Sultan[107]

Shirin was the *takhallus* of Sultan Reziya Begum, daughter of Sultan Altamash [Iltutmish]. After Altamash's death in 1236, Ruknuddin Firuz, following in the

---

[106] *BN*, 130–31; also see *TN*, 77.
[107] *TN*, 79.

footsteps of his tyrant mother, abandoned the affairs of the state and indulged in a life of vice and excess. He was deposed after seven months or so, and his sister, Reziya Begum, sat on the throne. She awarded the title of *Amir-ul-Umara* (Chief of the Nobles) to the superintendent of the stable (*darogha-i astabal*), an Abyssinian slave who was known to place her on the horse by lifting her with his hands under her arms. The high-ranking nobles of the Sultanate found this offensive, and in the ensuing conflict, both the Begum and her slave lost their lives. Her grave is located in the locality (*muhalla*) known as Qabr Bulbuli Khana in the city of Delhi; the *muhalla* lies in the Turkman Darwaza region.

Verses of Reziya

(1)

Be careful, Shirin, when you are traversing the path of love,
For nobody is interested in listening to the woes of Farhad.[108]

Bāz-ā shirin! munh dar rāh-i ulfat gām-i khwesh
Hān, wale na-shunida bāshi qissa-i farhād rā.

(2)

What is life, but wallowing in the light of the face of the beloved?
And so it is, I have been killed by the dagger of his looks;
From my side, what misdemeanour has this heart committed?
There was no reason to slay me with such indifference.

Ghaltīdan nūr-i rukh-i khurshid juz in-che?
Bismil shuda tegh-i nigāh-i ghazab mā-ast
Az mā-ast ki bar mā-ast che taqsīr-i dil-i zār
Ān kushta-i andāz-i gham be-sabab mā-ast.

[In addition to the biographical details about her accession and execution, Ranj lavishly praises her for her beauty, bravery, and literary skills. He says: 'This woman was delicate in constitution, and attractive and beautiful. Besides these qualities, nobody had seen or heard someone so brave and courageous. She snatched the crown from her brother with force, fought several tough battles, and

---

[108] Farhad is an iconic lover, and the story of his love for Shirin has been written and recited in numerous versions across the Persianate world.

ascended the throne. In addition, she was wise and talented as well. In poetry, no poet, however eloquent, could match her'.][109]

Appendix 5A.11

Makhfi: 'In the Field of Eloquence She Was Counted among the Men'[110]

Makhfi was her *takhallus*, and her name was Zebun Nisa Begum. She was the eldest daughter of Shah Alamgir [Aurangzeb]. She was chaste like no one else, and her intelligence reminded people of Khaqani. In her eloquence, she was the Sahban of her time (*Sahbān-i zamān*), and in poetic craftsmanship, she was exceptional the world over. She had a pleasant countenance, and her deportment impressed even the most respectable gentlemen. She was wholeheartedly devoted to literature, and the reach and grasp of her thoughts were insurmountable. Her temperament was chirpy (*tabiyat garmā garam*) and witty (*hāzir jawāb*); it is indeed true that in the field of eloquence she was counted among the men. In a poetic gathering, when she displayed her exceptional skill and witty temperament (*shōkhi zahn*), the poets turned pale [with embarrassment]. She was engrossed all the time thinking about poetry.

Anecdote 1

One day when she was strolling in the rose garden, the emperor joined her, and ordered her not to recite lyrics. Just then, a nightingale resting on the stem of a flower plant was chattering along; seeing her chatter, Makhfi spontaneously uttered the following couplet:

> Oh ignorant nightingale, be quiet and utter not a word,
> The sensitive emperor has no patience for conversation.

> *Ae 'andlīb-i nādān dam dar gulu girah-gīr*
> *Nāzuk mizāj shāhān tāb-i sukhan na-dārad.*

The emperor could not help smiling and permitted her to recite her poem.

---

[109] *BN*, 157–58.
[110] *BN*, 199–202.

Anecdote 2

Once the emperor was resting in a pavilion in a garden, and just then Zebun Nisa came down and joined him. She was delighted to see the river shore, the flowing streams, and the resplendent greenery all around. In her delight, she uttered the following couplet:

> What are the four things that captivate the heart?
> These are wine, greenery, flowing streams, and beautiful faces.

> *Chahār chīz ki dil mi-burd kudām chahār*
> *Sharāb-o sabza wa āb-i rawān rū-i nigār.*

Incensed by what he had heard, the emperor asked her to repeat what she had just said. She immediately changed the couplet, and repeated it thus:

> What are the four things that captivate the heart?
> These are prayers (*namāz*), fasting (*rozah*), rosary, and repentance.

> *Chahār chīz ki dil mi-burd kudām chahār*
> *Namāz-o rozah wa tasbih wa tobah istaghfār.*

Anecdote 3

Once a suppressed thought was troubling Zebun Nisa, and the following hemistich on her tongue reflected her state of mind:

> My lips refuse to leave the delights that come from the beloved.

> *Az hum nami shawad ze halālat judā labam.*

She reached out to other poets, asking for suggestions to complete the verse, but in vain. Nasir Ali was present at the time, and when he heard the hemistich, he suggested the following line to make it a complete verse:

> My lips, in other words, have reached the lips of Zebun Nisa.

> *Goyā rasīd bar-lab-i Zebun Nisa labam.*

Listening to this inimitable line, she was pleased but nonetheless resented this witty transgression and angrily wrote back to him the following verse:

Nasir Ali! Ali's name has saved you, indeed!
Otherwise, your head would have been severed with Ali's sword.

Nāsir Ali ba-nām-i Ali burda-i panāh
Warna ba-zulfiqār-i Ali sar barīd-ast.

Despite her youthfulness (*shabāb*), she was never interested in marriage and died a spinster in 1701. Her tomb is at Kabuli Darwaza in Delhi.

[In his entry on Makhfi, Nadir provides a detailed discussion about the debates concerning her alleged *diwān*. There were scholars who believed that the *diwān* that was attributed to her was actually authored by Makhfi Rashti who was the teacher (*ustād*) of Jami. There were *tazkira* writers who argued that Makhfi was not the *takhallus* of Zebun Nisa; her pen name was Khafi.][111]

Appendix 5A.12

Nur Jahan: 'The Scent of the Rose'[112]

Nur Jahan Begum was also known as Nur Mahal. This woman was extremely beautiful and attractive, and arguably there was none who could equal her. It is evident from the histories that her father, Khwaja Ayazuddin, belonged to a high-ranking household within the community of the Tartars. Owing to the adversities of destiny, they lost their fortune and turned bankrupt. Dejected, he left his homeland (*watan*), turned his back from his relations, and, accompanied with just his devoted wife, departed for Hindustan. His wife was pregnant at the time, and at some parched land in between Tatar and Hindustan, a girl was born to them. Both her parents were tired with their own existence and saw her birth as a curse. They thought that they were themselves so unsettled in their lives that they could not rear her up. With these thoughts in mind, they abandoned Nur Jahan at some deserted place, but just as they moved ahead, the motherly affection (*ulfat-i mādirī*) kicked in, and their feet refused to drag any further. The feeling of debilitating weakness and the sorrow of separation constantly forced their steps and dissuaded them from walking ahead. Ultimately, they returned to her and saw that around the body of this heavenly fairy was draped a snake; it had rested its mouth on her face, and was resting. When they saw this, they thought that she would, in a couple of moments, become the snake's morsel. When he [the father] reached

---

[111] *TN*, 83–87.
[112] *BN*, 223–26; also see *TN*, 92–96.

closer, however, the snake retreated towards its habitation, and when he picked up the child, he found that she was alive; he lifted her in his arms, hugged her, and brought her before his wife. With her daughter back in her arms, she was now happy and contented. Now, as they moved ahead, their dejection turned into joy; their good fortune favoured them and the evil forces (*balā*) disappeared. On their way, a caravan of travellers met them, and taking pity on their condition, provided them with provisions for their journey. They thanked God and travelling further ahead reached Lahore. Ayaz was a wise man, and quite gifted. Within a couple of days, he was appointed as the paymaster (*bakhshī*) at the court of Emperor Akbar. He then appointed several well-educated women for the education of her daughter.

When Prince Salim, who later became emperor Nuruddin Jahangir, heard about her enchanting beauty (*husn-i dil fareb*) and scholarship (*qābliyat*), he let go of his patience, and went about transacting (*saudā*) the wealth of his life in exchange for her captivating beauty. Finally, he succeeded in tying this priceless jewel, a precious pearl, in the string of his love. Since she was already engaged to Sher Afgan, the emperor Akbar, concerned with these developments, persuaded her father to immediately marry her off, and the marriage between them was solemnized at the court. The lovelorn prince was helpless in the face of the dictates of his father. Even so, when he later ascended the throne, in the desire to acquire the precious jewel, he relentlessly pursued Sher Afgan. A coward that he was, Sher Afgan eluded him for quite some time but eventually fell victim to his competitor in love (*raqīb*). Nur Jahan entered the imperial harem.

Anecdote 1

Once the Begum was playing *chausar*[113] with the emperor, and there was some repair work going on in the fort. Someone from the aristocratic family was hoping to catch a glimpse of the queen, and when his efforts failed, he changed his attire, and joined the labourers repairing the fort. Just when he was passing the quicklime to the artisan, he uttered the following line, in Nur Jahan's hearing range:

In your search, I have traversed the whole world.

[The emperor got suspicious but was put at ease by Nur Jahan. When he was suitably distracted, she thus retorted to her admirer's hemistich:]

If the others had heard you, your head would have been severed from your body.

---

[113] *Chausar* is a game that requires four players and is played with dice and cowries.

Anecdote 2

Once, on the eve of Eid, the emperor sighted the moon and, looking at Nur Jahan, recited the following line:

The moon announcing the Eid has come out with such distinction.

Nur Jahan replied with the following line:

The lost keys to the tavern have been found again.

Kalīd-i maikada gum gashta bud paida shud.[114]

Anecdote 3

One day, the emperor, trying to engage in a humorous conversation with Nur Jahan, recited the following line:

What does this delicate body conceal beneath the skirt?

Zer-i dāman-i tu pinhā chist ae nāzuk badan.

Nur Jahan responded with the following three lines:

There are traces of the hoof of the antelope on the petals of the jasmine,
If the whiff of breeze goes inside her body through her tightly closed mouth,
Drops of blood, as red as the roses in Badakshan, trickle down from her [wounds].

Naqsh-i sum-i āhu-i chain ast bar barg-i saman
Gar rawad pek-i saba andar dahān-i tang-i-ō
Qatra qatra mi-chakad l'al-i badakshān dar-in-man.

Nur Jahan's *Ghazal*

I am light and fire, and an orchard and the rose garden,
I am the temple and the idol, and the Brahman and his sacred thread (*zunnār*);
No! No! I am not whatever you have been hearing about me,
I am the scent of the rose, one that bears the disposition of the garden;

---

[114] *BN*, 225.

If I reveal my thread of love (*zunnār-i 'ishq*), the roses in the garden will burn with envy,
If I wail in loneliness, the candle in the gathering (*sham'a-i anjuman*) will burn in pain.

Nūram, nāram, hadiqa-'am, gulzāram
Dairam, sanamam, Brahmanam, zunnāram
Ne ne ghalatam har ānche guftaim ne-am
Bu-i gulam wa tabiyat gulzāram
Zunnār-i 'ishq gar zāhir kunam gul dar chaman sozad
Agar nālam bā-khilwat khāna sham'a-i anjuman sozad.

[Nadir raises the issue of authenticity, and believes that many of the verses that were popularly attributed to her were actually composed by someone else. As he says: 'The authors of poetic biographies have taken to extreme limits of fabrication in describing her, and have come up with the most ludicrous statements.' He is particularly irked by these authors attributing Rekhta verses to Nur Jahan when there is no evidence to suggest her familiarity with the language. One of the verses that he believes is a latter-day fabrication, but one that still sums up the popular perception about her, is the following:

Even as Nur Jahan is apparently a woman
In the ranks of men, she is the woman who can slay a lion (*sher afgan*).[115]

---

[115] *TN*, 92–96.

6

Secluded Poets in Literary Spaces

Memorializing Female Rulers, Consorts, and *Memsahibs*

In their biographical compendia, as mentioned earlier, Ranj and Nadir divide women poets into two broad categories: 'public women' and 'secluded women'. Seclusion was an important marker of difference but, within the literary space, they were both represented as contributing to the enrichment and diversification of art, aesthetics, and language. The *bāzārī 'aurat*, or 'the woman of the market', was defined by the absence of a household, and, of course, the word *bāzār* reflected her association with money – as someone who evoked the sensoria in exchange for an economic transaction. Definitions are elusive and reductionist; our *tazkiras* reveal these women as invested with a wide range of skills and linguistic abilities, leading an enriching life, and actively participating in the shaping of the social and cultural landscape. There was, as we have seen, a wide range of women who fell under this category, and there were considerable differences among them in terms of resources and patronage, caste and sub-caste affiliations, social location, profession, and place and type of performance. Furthermore, the boundaries that separated them from 'chaste women' were quite porous, and crossovers were not unknown.

Hindustani Poetry and Music in British Homes: English-speaking Women Composing Poems in Urdu

Described as *pardah nashīn*, or 'women who live in seclusion', these 'chaste women' were also marked by considerable diversity. There were some among them who belonged to the royal harem, but the harem was itself a diverse space; there were poets therein who had matrimonial relations with the rulers, and those who were their blood relations, and yet some others who served as concubines and slaves, but were still literate enough to compose poems. Our *tazkira*s refer to women poets who came from the homes of nobles, aristocrats, and, more interestingly, merchant houses as well. We also come across women poets who came from the home of an English official; the daughter of an English gentleman, Jami'at was a 'Hindustani' from her maternal side. Described by both Ranj and Nadir as a 'Christian woman' (*'īsayī 'aurat*), she was married to a high-ranking British army officer, Major R. Justin. 'Her lyrics were', says Nadir, 'on the lips of professional singers (*gawa'iyōn*) in the city of Agra'. She was also quite adept in the 'knowledge of music' (*'ilm-i musaqī*). She knew English well and composed poems in Braj, Persian, and Urdu.[1] Some of her lyrical compositions were deeply religious and reflected anxieties emerging from her encounter – embodied and affect-ridden – with God:

> In coming face-to-face with God, I feel over-burdened with shame (*nadāmat*),
> I feel so ashamed because I could do no virtuous deed [in my life].

> *Khudāke ru-baru jānā nadāmat mujh ko bhārī hai'*
> *Koī nēkī na ban āy'ī usī ki sharm sārī hai'.*[2]

Among her popular verses that were probably recited by professional women vocalists to entertain audiences were those that mentioned in lyrical intonations the pangs of the beloved's cruel indifference:

> Now that my beloved (*dilbar*) is annoyed with me these days,
> I live in a state of unceasing agony (*muztar*) these days;
> Is it because of my fate, or the kindness of my destiny?
> That my beloved is so annoyed with me these days.

> *Rūthā hai' hamārā woh dilbar kai' din sē*
> *Is wāstē rahtī hun main muztar kai' din sē*
> *Maqsūm ki khūbī hai' ya qismat ka hai' ihsān*
> *Rahtā hai' khafā mujh se jo dilbar kai' din sē*[3]

Interestingly, poets such as Jami'at underline the significance of women in social reproduction, for these women adopted the literary skills and aesthetic practices of

---

[1] *TN*, 138; *BN*, 124–25.
[2] *TN*, 138; *BN*, 125.
[3] *TN*, 138; *BN*, 125.

their mother. Her preferred language of expression, poetic tastes, and interest in music came from her maternal side, and in stressing this, our *tazkiras* re-situate the figure of the mother at the centre of the reproduction of culture. Jami'at's father and spouse were brought into the narrative not just to enrich her life story, but these figures metaphorically stood for, and represented, British colonialism – in particular, its inability to breech the realm of cultural norms and practices. British men who took Hindustani women could have daughters who could converse in English, or take their faith and accept Christianity, but in terms of their cultural choices, they still preferred to compose poems in Urdu and liked to play music on the sitar.[4]

Interestingly, our *tazkiras* also provide instances of British women learning Hindustani music, taking lessons in Persian and Urdu, and composing poems in these languages. Nadir refers to an English lady, Ainnie, who was married to the superintendent of police posted in Calcutta. She was expectedly proficient in English music and dance, but 'this exceptional lady was also an accomplished sitar player'. She learnt Urdu poetry from the well-known poet Maulana Nassakh, and composed poems under the poetic name Malika. Under the Maulana's influence, she renounced Christianity and converted to Islam.[5] Her verses abide by Persianate aesthetic norms; the following couplet, for instance, on longing and separation reflects the extent of her aesthetic rootedness within these norms:

The heart is restless because of separation (*hijr*),
And is constantly imploring, wailing, and mourning;
The eyes have turned into stone, and look pale,
Waiting to see the beloved [*but*: 'the idol'].[6]

Amidst this immense diversity in the social locations of women, we should be cautious when we refer to 'women's speech'. Clearly, the division of women poets into 'public' and 'secluded' categories and the subdivisions within each of them suggest that, in the prevailing literary culture, even as authors such as Ranj and Nadir were concerned with drawing attention to the contribution of women, gender was not the primary marker of difference. Women littérateurs spoke not exclusively as women, but brought in their compositions the entanglement of gender with class, caste, professions, and social location; they saw their identities

---

[4]   The sitar is a stringed musical instrument that was popular in courtly circles and music and
      dance gatherings at the salons of the courtesans.
[5]   *TN*, 224.
[6]   *TN*, 224.

as constituted in a multiplicity of contexts, and gender was only one source for identification and perception of selfhood. We should be careful when studying women's voices in early modern South Asian literary culture to not invest gender with a concrete identity, and be conscious of its fluid and malleable contours. Women certainly did 'speak' but not always as women. When they did speak as women, their gender was intertwined with the other markers of social difference and identification.

As we saw in the last chapter, both Ranj and Nadir invoked women from distant pasts – real and constructed – in seeking to concretize the fluid, changing, and indeed fast-diminishing memories of women littérateurs in cultural life. The social memories of women's presence in the literary spaces came from a wide range of temporal and spatial contexts, and included, on the one hand, women from the epic and Sanskrit traditions (for example, Sita, Parvati, and Shakuntala), and, on the other, women from Islamic history (such as Khadija and Fatima). And, if there were Mughal imperial women, there were aristocratic women from west and central Asia as well. Within this expanded and diffused commemorative space, the authors of *BN* and *TN* were also engaged in constructing and preserving the memories of contemporary women rulers, queens, and aristocrats with a view to highlighting their literary skills, but also the significance of their contribution to the reproduction and enrichment of cultural spaces.

Remembering the Awadh Kingdom: Poets and Performers in the *Nawab*'s Household

In the list of elite women mentioned by Ranj and Nadir, there are several that come from the deposed house of the Awadh *nawab*s. The Awadh state was known for its patronage to the arts, and once Delhi declined following the disintegration of the Mughal empire, Lucknow had become the centre for Persianate literary culture and elite norms of aesthetics and literature; well-known poets who had been enjoying Mughal state patronage for so long now shifted to the kingdom of Awadh in search of employment, audience, and appreciation.[7]

Of course, as has been shown by Carla Petievich, the differences between the Lucknow and Delhi 'schools' were more farcical than real in terms of the norms of literary aesthetics, but there were, for sure, contestations for cultural superiority. Awadh had increasingly in the nineteenth century come to be associated with

7 Abdul Halim Sharar, *Lucknow: The Last Phase of an Oriental Culture*, trans. E. S. Harcourt and Fakhir Hussain (New Delhi: Oxford University Press, 1994).

literary patronage and elite norms of connoisseurship and consumption.[8] Among
the literary critics, generally the credit for preserving and enriching the Indo-
Persian literary heritage has duly been given to the rulers and nobles of Awadh, but
the contribution of women in the field has largely been ignored. Our *tazkiras* seek
to correct the imbalance and point to the role of women in the *nawab*'s household
in the patronage and enrichment of literary culture.

It is in this context that the authors of our *tazkiras* mention the poet Jani, who
was 'among the begums of Awadh the most respected, and was honoured with the
title of Bahu Begum'.[9] Her wit and literary promptness were well known, and she
had the remarkable ability to compose verses in the spur of the moment. Once a
eunuch (*khwāja-sarā*) came to see her when she was unwell, and when asked, she
thus described her condition:

> Why do you ask about the condition of this frail body (*jism-i nā-tawān*), dear
> friend,
> Every vein is aching in pain, and there is no end to this conversation.

> *Kyā pūchtā hai hum-dam, is jism-i nā-tawān ki*
> *Rag, rag men neshi-i gham hai', kahiye kahān kahān ki.*[10]

It is hard to not notice that the memorialization of women from the Awadh
household was taking place merely a couple of decades after the deposition of the
Awadh rulers following the annexation of the kingdom by the expanding British
imperial power. It served to offer a succinct critique of British imperial aggression,
while reminding the readers of the rootedness of the dynasty with the rich
culture of the period. Repositioning the state's literary network into the hands of
imperial women, Ranj and Nadir also mention the queen consort (*khās mahal*)
of the last ruler of Awadh, Nawab Wajid Ali Shah (1847–56), Alam.[11] She was
one of the few women poets to have her own collection of poems (or *diwān*).[12]

---

[8] Carla Petievich, *Assembly of Rivals: Delhi, Lucknow and the Urdu Ghazal* (New Delhi:
     Manohar, 2020 [reprint]).

[9] *TN*, 137; also see *BN*, 121.

[10] *TN*, 137; *BN*, 121.

[11] Nawab Wajid Ali Shah was the last ruler of the Awadh dynasty before its annexation by the
     British in 1856; he was deposed and exiled to Calcutta, where he spent the rest of his life as a
     pensioner. He was known for his generous patronage to dance, music, and literature and was
     largely responsible for the revival of Kathak, a form of classical Hindustani dance. He was
     himself not without talent and was particularly skilled in music, poetry, and dance.

[12] *TN*, 177–78; *BN*, 174.

Interestingly, even as her *diwān* is about her compositions, she provides space within it for other women poets as well. It was while perusing her *diwān* that Nadir came to know about another woman poet by the name of Hijab.[13] Not only was Alam a talented poet, but she was also a skilled musician and could play the sitar quite well.[14]

Imperial Women's Patronage Networks: Commemorating the Begums of Bhopal in the Reproduction of Literary Culture

These powerful women were, above all, remembered for presiding over the networks of patronage for literary activities, providing stipends to poets, organizing poetic assemblies (*musha'ira*), inviting critics and scholars to compile biographical compendia, and subsidizing the publication of *diwān*s of poets living in straitened conditions. Written at a time when state patronage for literary activities was fast dwindling, the memorialization of women poets in these terms was a political act of some significance; it provided a succinct critique of the colonial state, in particular, its policy of withholding patronage to scholars and artists, and the centres for cultural activities. At the same time, these commemorative exercises sought to stress the contribution of women in the reproduction of sociocultural life in Hindustan. Referring to Askari Begum, who bore the poetic name Hijab and resided among the elites in Lucknow, both Nadir and Ranj inform us that she was a generous patron and, until her marriage, organized poetic assemblies at her house on a regular basis.[15] In this context, the contribution of the Begums of Bhopal was particularly significant.[16] They were known for their patronage to educational and literary institutions, and women's reforms were particularly close to their hearts. They were prolific writers, writing reformist tracts, travelogues, and memoirs;

---

[13] *TN*, 143.

[14] *TN*, 178; *TN*, 174.

[15] *TN*, 142; *BN*, 132–33.

[16] The princely state of Bhopal was exceptional in that it was ruled by four extraordinary women: Qudsia Begum (r. 1819–1837), Sikandar Begum (r. 1860–68), Shahjahan Begum (r. 1868–1901), and Sultan Jahan Begum (r. 1901–26). The Begums were littérateurs in their own right, but also patronized literary activities and bore a commitment to women's educational development. For more on the Begums, see Lambert-Hurley, *Muslim Women, Reform and Princely Patronage*; Shahryar M. Khan, *The Begums of Bhopal: A Dynasty of Women Rulers in Raj India* (London: I. B. Tauris, 2000). Also see Ian Copland, *The Princes of India in the Endgames of Empire, 1917–1947* (Cambridge: Cambridge University Press, 1997).

our *tazkira*s record their literary interventions, both as poets and patrons.[17]
Referring to the literary contributions of Shahjahan Begum (r. 1868–1901), Nadir
informs us that she was instrumental in the compilation of five *tazkira*s of poets
writing in Persian: *Shama'-i Anjuman* (The Candle in the Gathering),
Nigāristān-i Sukhan (An Arcade of Captivating Speech), *Subah-i Gulshan* (The
Dawn in the Garden), *Roz-i Roshan* (The Illuminated Days), and *Akhtar-i Tābān*
(The Shining Stars); interestingly, the last of these *tazkira*s was exclusively devoted
to women poets.[18] It was actually crucial for Nadir and he graciously admits,
'I have gone through it, and my own work could not have been completed
without it.'[19] There are several entries in his *tazkira* that are entirely derived
from the information found in *Akhtar-i Tābān*, but with a discerning eye, Nadir
is prompt to point out the inaccuracies as well. When he refers to Shahi, a poet
known for her bawdy compositions (*fuhsh kalām*), he admits that all his
information on her comes from *Akhtar-i Tābān*.[20] Even so, he believes that the
author of *Akhtar* was probably wrong in describing Sharam as a prostitute (*randī*)
of Lucknow; she was, as suggested in another biographical compendium, *Chaman
Andāz*, 'a chaste poet' (*pāk dāmina'*), and was 'the daughter of a respected
physician, Hakim Qamaruddin.[21]

An accomplished scholar, Shahjahan Begum composed verses in both Persian
and Urdu; when she wrote in Persian, she called herself Shahjahan, but when
composing poems in Urdu, her nom de plume was Shireen.[22] Ranj refers to her
charitable activities and applauds her for the peace and harmony that prevailed

---

[17] Along the lines of the reformist writings of Ashraf Ali Thanawi, Shahjahan Begum wrote
     a tract on women's reforms, entitled *Tahzibun Niswan wa Tasbiyatul Insan* (Women's
     Reforms and the Advancement of Humanity). Her daughter wrote several books and
     tracts on the instruction of children and women's issues, but also wrote a travelogue of her
     pilgrimage to Hijaz. The Begums were also prolific builders; among their many architectural
     wonders, their mosques in Bhopal were well known: Qudsia Begum's Jami Masjid (1833),
     Sikander Begum's Moti Masjid (1847), and Shahjahan Begum's Tajul Masjid built during
     the last quarter of the nineteenth century. For their scholarly and reform activities, see, in
     addition to the works cited earlier, Lambert-Hurley, 'Historicising Debates over Women's
     Status in Islam'; and Lambert-Hurley, 'Princes, Paramountcy and the Politics of Muslim
     Identity'; Siobhan Lambert-Hurley, 'Out of India: The Journeys of the Begam of Bhopal,
     1901–1930', *Women's Studies International Forum* 21, no. 3 (May–June 1998): 263–76.
     Also see Metcalf, *Perfecting Women*.
[18] *TN*, 109.
[19] *TN*, 109.
[20] *TN*, 110.
[21] *TN*, 110.
[22] *TN*, 110.

in her state.[23] Her daughter and successor, Sultan Jahan Begum (r. 1901–26), was also a well-known poet, and wrote poems under the pen name Makhfi.[24] Her poems are marked by an interesting blend of Persian and colloquial Hindustani terms; notice, for example, the combination of Persian words *khuftigān-i khāk* ('persons wallowing in dust') with the colloquial *ludhai'* ('spilling over') in the following verse:

Should the wretched (*khuftigān-i khāk*) hastily spill over (*ludhai'*) or drink wine?

I swear to God, the night watchman (*'asas*) has been accumulating a lot of goodness (*sawāb*) these days.

Ludhāi' mai' ki piyen khuftigān-i khāk
Qasam Khudā ki 'asas ko bada sawāb huā.[25]

The memorialization of the Begums as patrons of literature is not without some political significance. For one, it serves to emphasize women's multiple skills and, as against the dominant assumptions, their acumen and adroitness in managing the affairs of the state. In contrast to the British-ruled states, it is also an endorsement of the princely states in terms of their better rootedness in the cultural ethos of the region. Clearly, even as their primary concern is to recover women's voices, the authors of our *tazkiras*, in terms of their choices and language of representation, also make a sustained argument in favour of the deposed kingdom of Awadh, and the surviving princely state, Bhopal. In both cases, they demonstrate the significance of women's agency in sustaining patronage networks and reproducing cultural practices. These were, indeed, political activities of immense value, and in emphasizing the presence of women in these activities, these *tazkiras* draw attention to the significance of women's agency in the prevailing political dispensations.

Quotidian Practices and Women's Language: Persianate Allusions and Local Forms of Expression

Women spoke in the language of men. Of course, to be able to participate in poetic assemblies, publish their *diwāns*, and recite *ghazals* in the salons and public gatherings, they had to accept the constraints of language and the aesthetic standards prevalent in the Persianate world. Even so, their literary endeavours were not mimetic, nor were they bereft of freshness of expression and

---

[23] *BN*, 163.
[24] *BN*, 207; *TN*, 191–92.
[25] *TN*, 192; *BN*, 207.

literary innovations. In struggling to express themselves – to 'speak' as it were –
they made experiments with language, and learnt to combine Persian words
(and metaphors) with colloquial forms of expression that emerged from routine
encounters of daily lives often in spaces inhabited by women. Shireen Bega, a woman
poet in Lucknow, refers to her beloved's indifference as 'throwing the heart on the
stove' (*chūlhe men jāī' dil*).[26] In much the same vein, she describes her beloved's
flowing hair and seductive eyebrows as 'snakes and scorpions' (*sānp bichu*):

> I have fallen for the hair and the eyebrows of my beloved,
> Loving snakes and scorpions was written in my destiny.

> *Hui' hai' hamen zulf wa abru ki ulfat*
> *Muqaddar men thi sānp, bichu ki ulfat.*[27]

In much the same way, in one of her verses, Jafri, who lived in the imperial harem
during the reign of Akbar II (1806–37), uses a familiar expression borrowed from
day-to-day life, 'the house of the aunt' (*khāla ka ghar*), to refer to a welcoming
space; love, she says, required fortitude, for it was not the aunt's house:

> In the fort of love, only the daring lovers reside,
> It is not the aunt's house where everyone is openly welcome.

> *Muhabbat ke mahal men 'āshiq-i jān-bāz rahtā hai'*
> *Nahin khāla kā ghar is-men jo āye jis kā ji chāhe.*[28]

Indeed, the experiments with literary motifs and forms of expression were largely
inspired by the routine activities and daily rituals and practices surrounding the
lives of these women. In one of her homoerotic compositions, discussed earlier,
Rashk-i Mahal Begum, one of the wives of the deposed ruler of Awadh, Wajid Ali
Shah (1847–56), refers to her mate 'combing and braiding' (*kanghi choti*) her hair:

> You take care of my hair by combing and braiding them,
> My mate! I am indebted to you for doing so.

> *Merī kanghī chotī ki leti khabar tum*
> *Ye ihsān hai sar par do-gānā tumhārā.*[29]

---

[26] *TN*, 170.

[27] *TN*, 171.

[28] *TN*, 137–38. Ranj describes her thus: 'Virtuous and immaculate, she was an honorable and
      chaste woman' (*BN*, 122–23).

[29] *TN*, 132.

Commending her for her skills in *rekhti*, a form of erotic poetry centred on the desires and experiences of women, Ranj mentions her language of compositions as 'the language of the fort' (*qil'e kī zubān*).[30] It seems women's speech, commonly dubbed as 'the language of the *begums*', was not without distinctions and nuances that were specific to their routine experiences of life. The critics had certainly learnt to differentiate the speech of aristocratic women, in particular, those associated with courtly cultures, from those women poets who came from humbler sociocultural backgrounds. More interestingly perhaps, verses such as the one cited above indicate the extent to which women's poetry, across difference, centred on their everyday lives.

To take another instance, Habib, a 'chaste lady' based in Delhi, in a distich intended to tease her uncle's weakness for sweet dishes, mentions *sevaiyān*, a form of sweet dish that is served during the festival of Eid by Muslims in South Asia. Note how an ordinary event of the visit of the *chacha*, or paternal uncle, and the preparation of sweet vermicelli are used by Habib to compose the following verse:

We had placed on the table the fine textured *sevaiyān*,
Our uncle (*chacha*) came from Nabha[31] and devoured it all.

Rakhin hum ne bārik bat sivaiyān
Chachā āke Nabha se chat kar sivaiyān.[32]

Clearly, even as there were constraints on literary expression, women experimented with language to construct new norms of aesthetics, forms of expression, and emotions. The charge of mimesis is clearly mistaken, and women extended the range of significations by introducing words and phrases coming from quotidian practices into forms of aesthetic expression.

Conclusion: Women's Verse and the Tactile Apprehension of Truth

In our *tazkiras*, we also come across instances of elite women composing religious poetry, in particular, poems in praise of God (*hamd*) and Prophet Muhammad (*na't*). These devotional compositions are suffused with somatic possibilities, and the body is both the site and the instrument for the realization of

---

[30] *BN*, 113.
[31] Nabha is a town in the state of Punjab.
[32] *TN*, 141–42.

spiritual experiences. The relationship of the body to religion and its construction in the Persianate literary tradition is a complex issue, but within the Islamic tradition, the body was not antithetical to spiritual attainments, but a necessary device for 'feeling' God.[33] Shahjahan Begum, the Begum of Bhopal, who bore the poetic name Shireen, in one of her spiritual compositions, describes her body as 'the ritual attire' or *ihrām*.[34] In the same poem, reproduced below, she describes her different spiritual states as 'the restlessness in the heart' and the onset of 'the cold breeze', and then again 'the descent of the beloved in the rose garden':

Our Creator (*khāliq*) is the Lord of the dawn and the dusk,
He is the One who has given me this fame and respectability;
We are born in the community (*ummat*) of the beloved of God (*mahbūb-i khudā*) [Prophet Muhammad],
Why should not the status of [our faith] Islam be the most privileged?
The cold breeze has arrived, and the dark clouds have surrounded the skies,
Get someone to bring my pitcher, the wine, and the cup;
The restlessness in my heart should cause some stir in His heart as well,
This has been my message [to my heart] for so long now;
Oh! fresh breeze, take this broken body (*tan-i zār*) with you,
In the rose garden (*gulzār*) has arrived my beloved (*gulfām*);
I perform my hajj pilgrimage by visiting my beloved's place,
My body is the ritual dress (*jama-i ihrām*) I wear for the occasion.

Khāliq hai' khudā-i sahr-o shām hamārā
Mashhur usī ne kiyā nām hamārā
Paidā huē hum ummat-i mahbūb-i Khudā men

---

[33] Scott Kugle, *Sufis and Saints' Bodies: Mysticism, Corporeality and Sacred Power in Islam* (Chapel Hill: University of North Carolina Press, 2007); Shahzad Bashir, *Sufi Bodies: Religion and Society in Medieval Islam* (New York: Columbia University Press, 2013). For a study of corporeality in different religious traditions, including Islam, see Sarah Coakley (ed.), *Religion and the Body* (Cambridge: Cambridge University Press, 1997). For an analysis of these issues within European history, see Peter Brown, *The Body and Society: Men, Women, and Sexual Renunciation in Early Christianity* (New York: Columbia University Press, 1988); and Eve Kosofsky Sedgwick, *Epistemology of the Closet* (New York: Columbia University Press, 1990).

[34] *Ihrām* is the ritual attire that Muslims need to wear when entering into a sacred state before going on a hajj pilgrimage.

Bartar na-ho kyon rutba-i Islām hamārā
Ātī hai' hawā sard, ghatā uthti hai' ganghor
Mangwāo' surāhī, mai' wa jām hamārā
Betābi-i dil uske bhi to dil men asar kar
Muddat se yahī tujh se hai paighām hamārā
Ae' bād-i sabā tu-hi tan-i zār ko le chal
Gulzār men āyā hai' woh gulfām hamārā
Hum karte hain hajj kūcha-i dildār ka apne
Hai' chādar-i tan jāma-i ihrām hamārā.[35]

Marked by corporeal conceits, this poem represents devotion and desire as centred on the body; note, for example, the poet's equation of the *ihrām* with her body. The body is the site on which religious affect is experienced and stimulated, but it is also the means through which she realizes devotional desires in their ecstatic and heightened forms. In her influential study of penitential practices of female saints and mystics in late medieval Europe, Caroline Walker Bynum has highlighted the significance of their corporeal practices in religious expression. Far from the evidence of the abnegation of the body, her work reveals the significance of 'fleshiness' to their devotional pursuits. Physicality was never repudiated by spirituality; instead, the effort all along was 'the *experiencing* of body more than the *controlling* of it'.[36]

This was true not just for devotional compositions. Indeed, even in its profane manifestations, women's poetry, in its quest for love, was tied with embodiment, and it is within somatic, sensorial contexts that these women experienced and expressed the world of feelings and emotions. Embodiment was not exclusively based on gender identity, but was equally shaped and reproduced by other socio-economic and cultural markers of difference. Even so, the linkages between the body, emotions, and selfhood, and their articulation within the acceptable standards of Persianate aesthetic norms, constitute a shared, running thread to women's compositions across sociocultural differences.

---

[35] *TN*, 171–72.

[36] Caroline Walker Bynum, *Holy Feast and Holy Fast: The Religious Significance of Food to Medieval Women* (Berkeley: University of California Press, 1987), 245; also see Caroline Walker Bynum, *Fragmentation and Redemption: Essays on Gender and the Human Body* (New York: Zone Books, 1992). For a sympathetic critique of Bynum, see Richard Rambuss, *Closet Devotions* (Durham and London: Duke University Press, 1998), 2–3, 16–17.

Appendix 6A.1

Malika: An English Lady Who Played the Sitar and Wrote Urdu Verses [37]

Malika is her pen name (*takhallus*), and her family name is Ainnie Masihi. She is the spouse of Mister Blaker, the superintendent of police in Calcutta. It is no surprise that she is talented in British music and dance (*angrēzī 'ilm-i musaqī wa raqqāsī*), but this exceptional lady is also accomplished in playing the sitar. Since she turned into a poet under the guidance of Maulana Nassakh, she has refused to stay silent and has even converted to Islam.

Malika's Couplets

The heart is restless because of separation (*hijr*),
And is constantly imploring, wailing, and mourning;
The eyes have been tuned into stone, and look pale,
Waiting to see the beloved [*but*: 'the idol'].

Hijr men dil ko be-qarārī hai'
Josh-i faryād wa āh-o zāri hai'
Ānkhen pathra ke ho gayin safed
Kisi but ki jo intizārī hai'.

Appendix 6A.2

Dulhan: A Secluded Poet with 'A Manly Disposition' [38]

Dulhan was her poetic name, and her real name was Dulhan Begum, but she was better known as 'the Nawab's daughter-in-law' (*Bahu Begum*). She was the daughter of Nawab Intizam-ud-Daula and the spouse of the late Nawab Asaf-ud-Daula, the ruler of Awadh (*wali-i Awadh*) [1775–97]. At the time of the compilation of *Sarāpā Sukhan*,[39] she was living in Faizabad (near Lucknow). She had a pious temperament and a manly disposition (*mardāna tabi'at*).

---

[37]   *TN*, 224.
[38]   *TN*, 149–50; also see *BN*, 141.
[39]   A *tazkira* written in the latter half of the nineteenth century by Saiyad Mohsin Ali. Saiyad Mohsin Ali Musavi, *Sarāpā Sukhan* (Lucknow: Nawal Kishore, 1861).

Dulhan's Verses

(1)
Don't trouble yourself worrying about the buildings below the skies,
Repair instead, the broken heart that lies fallen on the ground.

Mat karo fikr 'imārat ki koī' zer-i falak
Khāna-i dil jo girā ho, use t'amīr karō.

(2)
Looking at the river, my heart is hit by a wave [of thought],
How sad it is that the ship of my existence (*kashtī-i 'umr*) sails along without
purpose.

Dekh daryā ko mere dil pe yeh lahr āti hai'
Kashtī-i 'umr ye afsōs, bahī jātī hai'.

Appendix 6A.3

Begum: The Daughter of a Celebrated Poet[40]

Begum is both her name and *takhallus*. She is the virtuous daughter of the deceased
Mir Muhammad Taqi; she is quite accomplished in the art of literary composition.
She resides in the city of Lucknow.

Quatrain Composed by Begum

For years you kept me entrapped in the curls of your hair,
You speak [of releasing me] now when you have already secured my death;
I committed no transgressions during the night of our meeting,
But I did admittedly place my cheek on his cheeks.

Barson sar-i gēsu men giraftār to rakhā
Ab kahte ho kyā tum nē hamen mār to rakhā[41]
Kuch be-adabī aur shab-i wasl nahin kī[42]
Hān yār ke rukhsār pe rukhsār to rakhā.

---

[40] *BN*, 112–13; also see *TN*, 131–32.

[41] In *TN*, '*Ab*' is replaced with '*Lo*' (*TN*, 131).

[42] In *TN*, this line is written slightly different: '*Kuch be-adabī hum ne na-kī yār se shab bhar*'
      (*TN*, 131).

7
Conclusion

Reading the biographical compendia of women poets written in the nineteenth century, we cannot but appreciate the impressive presence of women in the literary field. However, this impression fades away when we look at the more popular literary biographies, anthologies, critical literature, and instruction manuals; in the dominant literary strands, indeed women poets are scarce, if not totally absent. The nineteenth century was the period in which the figure of a woman poet evoked moral anxieties, resulting from the reformist zeal to keep women away from *eros* and love, and other emotions associated with Persianate poetry. Elite women should, for sure, be educated but only in the subjects that helped them efficiently manage their domestic spaces; there were, as we see in several reformist texts, detailed discussions on what women should and should not read, and among the books that they were instructed to shun were romantic tales and works of poetry. Commendably, the women's *tazkira*s contest these assumptions, and make available to the interested readers an archive of women's voices, and draw our attention to the ever-present but barely recognized contribution of women poets to the shaping of the literary culture in early modern Hindustan.

It is not without basis to argue that women's lyrical compositions represented a marginalized and incongruent literary culture, but doing so would be banal and simplistic and, above all, quite ahistorical. Women poets were present in poetic assemblies (*mushā'ira*) organized by aristocrats and rich patrons; and in the salons of the courtesans, young men learnt the niceties of language, and men of letters experimented with new forms of thought and expression. In our study of women littérateurs here, we have seen that their lyrics, despite their creative depths and fresh signifying practices, were firmly obedient to the literary *adāb*, or the norms of aesthetics and expression. Their interventions in the literary field served to enrich and deepen the field, even as they continually challenged and contested its dominant assumptions. It is for this reason that I described their compositions, in one of the earlier chapters, as situated within the realm of what Foucault terms as 'subjugated knowledges', reflecting a cultural practice that was 'masked' by the power-language ensemble of relations but still conversed with the dominant literary and aesthetic norms and values in an aporetic relationship where women's speech both reinforced and challenged them.

Of course, the potential antinomies in women's lyrics were largely managed through their polysemic and plural texture. Bereft of a fixed meaning, they traversed multiple emotions, experiences, truth-claims, and norms of aesthetics. Their poems, like the 'text' in the formulations of Roland Barthes, were not passively consumed by the reader/audience, but, through participatory and collaborative exercises, opened up spaces for ever new meanings and significations – a process that Barthes describes as 'playing with the text' or 'the engendering of the perpetual signifier'. The pleasure that the reader, more often the listener, derived from a woman's poem did not come from its passive 'consumption' but its 'delectation', that is, 'pleasure without separation'.[1]

'Delectation' is the key term here. Women's lyrical compositions were exercises in the constitution of selfhood, and, like any self-narrative, invited the readers and audience to experience pleasure from the aural, visual, and tactile exposure of the artist, in particular, her deep interior self. However, the pleasure they derived from their verses came not from their intended meanings, but the contingent meanings that emerged from the associations and connections that these texts produced with the reader/listener. Of course, the deep interior self, the core of self-identity, was constructed in language, but in the spaces of the interaction of the artist with the audience, women's literary exercises became the means for the constitution of selfhood, not just for the poet, but for her readers and listeners as well.

Unlike some other forms of life stories, women's poetry relied on emotions as central to the constitution of selfhood, and it is for this reason that the central motifs in their poems revolved around themes of love and beauty, and loss and separation. The relations of language to emotions and of emotions to self-identity are central to Persianate literature, but these linkages were particularly intense and purposeful in the case of women's poetry in the early modern period. The mutual constitution of the self for both the poet and her audience occurred within what Barbara Rosenwein terms as an 'emotional community',[2] but this

---

[1]   Roland Barthes, *The Rustle of Language*, trans. Richard Howard (New York: Hill and Wang, 1986); also see the following books by him: *The Pleasure of the Text*, trans. Richard Miller (New York: Hill and Wang, 1975); and *Image, Music, Text*, trans. Stephen Heath (London: Fontana Press, 1977).

[2]   Rosenwein, *Emotional Communities*.

was a community that was brought into existence in the activity of reading and performing the women's lyrics.

Gender was expectedly not absent in women's compositions, but it was articulated in diverse and plural textures. Given the wide differences in the social background of the remembered poets, this was, of course, not unusual, but in lending this ambiguity to the representations of gender, the heterogeneity in the community of readers/listeners also had its role to play. In their autobiographical reflections, our poets therefore articulated intersectional perspectives, combining their gender with their class, caste, and community identifications. Gender was not an isolate, but subsisted through networks of relations with other markers of distinction and difference. Even so, a unifying thread that runs across the women's lyrics was the primacy of the body to the articulation of emotions. The somatic representation of the emotions of love and loss required a tactile apprehension of words, in terms of their conversations with dance and music, and this is where our analysis appears so inadequate and limited, particularly in reading the verses of the poets described in our biographical compendia as 'the women of the market' (*bāzārī 'aurat*).

The poetic compositions of the courtesans and the ritually inferior dancers and singers entertaining audience in the markets and streets were not read, but performed; they derived their results from the accompanying music and the vocal intonations of the artists. Space was also important, and the spatial settings and the odours of perfumes and scents, gelling with the aroma of food and beverages, combined to create contingent meanings and states of mind from the speech-act of the poet. Indicative of the level of exchanges between the respectable households and the female entertainers, 'secluded women' also composed poems for the dancers, vocalists, and musicians that achieved their unintended, if still deep and meaningful, results from the accompanying music and the spaces of performance.

Women's compositions were read and performed; they conveyed meanings, but also caused effects. When we read them today, and wrestle with their meanings, we are surely, even with the best of our efforts, quite a distance from how these texts were apprehended and appreciated by the audience. Preserved in the women's biographical compendia, women's lyrics, in their process of memorialization, lost, in the language of Walter Benjamin, their 'here and now', or their 'aura'[3] that emerged from the interaction of words with music, dance, and space. The meanings of their songs were suggested, staged, and replaced by

---

[3]   Walter Benjamin, 'The Work of Art in the Age of its Mechanical Reproduction', in *Walter Benjamin: Selected Writings, vol. 4, 1938–1940*, ed. Howard Eiland and Michael W. Jennings, 251–83 (Cambridge, MA: Harvard University Press, 2006), 270–71.

the amalgamation of the visual, auditory, olfactory, and tactile modes of meaning apprehension.[4] It was the total experience that a person with 'taste' (*zauq*) aspired to; described in the literature of the period as *shauq*, this was a mode of engagement in which the 'text' was experienced in sensuous and visceral forms through the collusion of the verbal with non-verbal means of communication. *Shauq* only roughly translates as 'pleasure', for along with a sense of delight, it also imbibed transgressive and disruptive possibilities.

Of course, with the relocation of women's lyrics from their sites of performance to the spaces of literacy, they were invested with a new range of meanings. Preserved in the biographical compendia, they were no more free-floating signifiers, and their semantic range was in no small measure controlled by the literary devices that were inserted to apprehend their meanings. Clearly, the insertion of a biographical note before the presentation of a poet's work served to direct the reader to predetermined forms of meanings. In a kind of identification of the person with her work, details about her life were carefully chosen to set a frame within which a poet's verse was to be read and understood. While the work of the courtesans and public entertainers is duly appreciated, we noticed an effort to convey a picture of dependent agency, in which the poets and their tutors are jointly represented as sharing the credit for their literary skills and achievements. In the case of royal and aristocratic women, stories about their wit and banter abound, but these have significant political considerations. They intended to highlight the significance of women's political agency, and draw linkages between the household and the imperial courts.

One of the important consequences of the re-inscription of women's voice in these biographical compendia was that it came to be appropriated in the register of modern reforms, for the project of women's education. In the memorialization of women poets, our *tazkiras* also made fervent appeals for women's education, but unlike the other reformers who looked towards the modern west for inspiration, they pointed to the history of Hindustani women's active participation in literary

---

[4] Following the influential work of William Reddy, historians of emotions have generally looked at emotions as insularly constituted by language and have ignored the other media of communication (Reddy, *The Navigation of Feeling*). For a critique of this position, and the necessity to explore sensory modes of meaning apprehension in the context of the history of South Asia, see Margrit Pernau, *Emotions and Modernity in Colonial India: From Balance to Fervor* (New Delhi: Oxford University Press, 2019); Rajamani, Pernau, and Schofield, *Monsoon Feelings*; and Francesca Orsini and Katherine Butler Schofield (eds.), *Tellings and Texts: Music, Literature and Performance in North India* (Cambridge: Open Book Publishers, 2015); also see Pernau and Rajamani, 'Emotional Translations'.

activities instead. Their acts of memorialization had a political thrust in that they contested the assumption of innate European superiority and the progressivist model of modern reforms where the only route for the progress of British subjects in India was seen to lie in the imitation of their political masters. These biographical compendia presented the cultural history of Hindustan as inclusive and plural, but also one in which educated women were conspicuously present, lending a life of remarkable richness and creativity. It was by following them that the people in India would find freedom from the shackles of ignorance and falsehood.

Female entertainers make the bulk of the entries in both *BN* and *TN*, and these included the courtesans, prostitutes, street performers, cloth printers, and women of mixed parentage. For them, the street was an important space of experience, and so were the *kotha*s and *dera*s that were maintained by their patrons and clients. Their lyrical compositions were placed in the interstitial spaces between literacy, orality, and performance, and it is for this reason, perhaps, that in their biographical snippets we find notices about their musical and vocal skills, and, more importantly, their physical looks as well, including details about their age, bodily frame, facial features, and colour. There was a certain sense of identification of the poet with her work, and the reception of meanings emerged from the play of both the words and the bodies, or rather in their reciprocal engagements. Perusing the life stories in literary *tazkira*s, Carla Petievich has argued that these notes served to underplay their literary significance. She notices a certain 'ambivalence', for the compilers of these *tazkira*s expected that the 'poetesses should enter the historical register, but perhaps not in the same line as male poets'.[5] There is some truth in the point she is making, but I still believe that the thick description, occasionally bordering on the concupiscent, was a literary device that was intended to suggest the entanglement of the tactile with the textual, and of the body of the artist, in all its somatic and erotic dimensions, with the lyrical compositions in the reception and reproduction of meanings.

In the case of the 'secluded' poets, the texture of life stories expectedly changes, and while physical descriptions are absent, these stories are introduced to represent them as ideal women who imbibed in their biographies the Persianate norms of civility and appropriate behaviour. Introduced as models of emulation, these women came from the royal households and aristocratic families, and commanded respect not just for their literary skills but also their familial background.

---

[5]   Carla Petievich, 'Feminine Authorship and Urdu Poetic Tradition: *Bahāristān-i Nāz* vs. *Tazkira-i Rekhtī*', in *A Wilderness of Possibilities: Urdu Studies in Transnational Perspective*, ed. Kathryn Hansen and David Lelyveld, 223–50 (New Delhi: Oxford University Press, 2005).

Among them were queens, princesses, and women from aristocratic households. Women from the Mughal harem predominate, and this was not without some political significance. Memorializing them for their literary skills, patronage to artists, and wit and humour served to highlight the contribution of the Mughals in shaping the sociocultural life in Hindustan, and debunked the British colonial representations of the imperial harem as a degenerate and vice-laden site.

In the life stories of Mughal imperial women, we come across ample instances of their witty exchanges and banter with the reigning kings. In all these exchanges, women come out triumphant, and one of the objectives of the insertion of these episodes in the biographical notes was to emphasize their acuity and percipience; at the end of each of these verbal encounters, imperial women are shown to have demonstrated their superiority over their rulers. In their mutual relations, women constantly challenge the king, pushing the boundaries of his thought and intelligence. These anecdotes strive to present the rulers in a human form, vulnerable and inadequate; recorded from cultural memories circulating in spaces of social communication, they reflect popular perceptions of the Mughal state, but they can also be read as reflecting the ordinary people's discursive manoeuvres to render political authority fallible and imperfect.

In this context, stories about women's verbal duels with the rulers resemble the South Asian folk tales that describe the encounters between the court jester and the king. These stories abound in South Asian folk literature, but the ones that are probably most popular include Tenali Rama's witty and ironic conversations with the Vijayanagar king Krishnadevaraya (r. 1509–29), and Birbal's amusing anecdotes at the court of the Mughal emperor Akbar (r. 1556–1605).[6] In these stories, the jester represents the 'comic' mode of kingship[7] whose barbs and exchanges with the king unsettled the social universe and the sovereign's claim to a sublime and invincible position. Through their wit and comedy, the clown and the jester at the courts undermine the authority of the king and reverse the political order by relocating the boundaries between the rulers and the subjects. Anecdotes of banter between the Mughal king and the imperial women also lie within the

---

[6]   See David Dean Shulman, *The King and the Clown in South Indian Myth and Poetry* (Princeton: Princeton University Press, 1985), 152–213; and C. M. Naim, 'Popular Jokes and Political History: The Case of Akbar, Birbal and Mulla Do-Piyaza', in C.M. Naim, *Urdu Texts and Contexts: The Selected Essays of C. M. Naim*, 225–49 (New Delhi: Permanent Black, 2004).

[7]   Focusing on south India, David Shulman points out that kingship in South Asia was predominantly articulated in two different modes: the 'tragic' mode (*viraha*) and the 'comic' mode (*vilāiyatal*). Shulman, *The King and the Clown*, 152.

'comic' mode of kingship, and serve to emphasize the interconnections between the court and the household, and the significance of the agency of women in the reproduction of imperial sovereignty.

It is hard to miss the political context of the attachment and reverence with which the biographical compendia describe the literary contribution of the women of the deposed ruling dynasties, in particular, the women in the harem of the *nawab*s of Awadh. They are depicted not simply as accomplished scholars but also generous patrons of the arts, ever so keen to preserve and promote the cultural heritage of Hindustan. There is, in these appreciative details, an implicit indictment of British expansionist policy in India; written a couple of decades after the revolt of 1857, they share a concern for the multiple and diverse histories and cultural resources of Hindustan dying a slow death owing to the dwindling state patronage and lack of protection. The tenor of the biographical details about the Begums of Bhopal has the same objectives and concerns besides, of course, suggesting the impressive capabilities of women as rulers of a state.

The intellectual culture in Hindustan was marked by a constant circulation of scholars, ideas, books, and literature across the Persianate world, and so it is that these *tazkira*s take care to remember the contribution of women poets from such far-off regions as Khurasan, Samarqand, Herat, and Tabrez in shaping the literary culture in Hindustan. Circulating in the inter-regional Asian world, women's lyrics were a part of the shared cultural heritage that was not bound by the boundaries of the modern nation states. As has been argued by Muhamad Tavakoli-Targhi, with the emergence of nationalism and the nation, there was a stringent identification of texts with the nation, and a large number of texts that did not find a home and failed to be owned by any of the modern nations states were rendered 'homeless'.[8] The women's poems and the biographical compendia that preserved and memorialized them are clearly instances of such 'homeless texts'. These texts are 'homeless' for a variety of reasons. They are homeless because they spoke the voices of women in a literary culture that was largely homosocial and bore an aversion to women's speech and creative pursuits. They are homeless because they were written in a language that ironically had a home in Hindustan. Urdu was a product of Indian culture, and yet neither the language nor its speakers are identified with the nation today.

---

[8]   Mohamad Tavakoli-Targhi, *Refashioning Iran: Orientalism, Occidentalism and Historiography* (London: Palgrave, 2001).

Glossary

bāzārī 'aurat Literally translated as 'public women', the term refers to a wide range of women who were seen as entertaining and providing other services in public spaces. These included courtesans, prostitutes, dancing girls, and women singers and public performers.

bhāng A paste prepared from the leaves of marijuana and mixed with milk (or water) as a mildly intoxicating drink. It is also mixed with sweets and snacks and served on festive occasions.

diwān The compilation of the poems and verses of the poet.

ghazal A lyrical poem that has a fixed number of couplets, varying from five to fifteen. Each couplet stands on its own, but the ghazal is tied together by a shared cadence and rhyming pattern.

ghungru An ornament that women, particularly dancers, wear around their ankles, consisting of multiple metallic bells strung together.

hijāb A head covering worn by Muslim women to cover their hair and neck, and sometimes face.

ihrām A ritual attire that Muslims need to wear when entering the sacred state before going on a hajj pilgrimage.

kāyasth A person belonging to a literate-scribal caste group, traditionally associated with state service in subordinate capacities, such as account-keeping, drafting court documents, filing petitions, and revenue collection. They were hired by nobles, merchants, and aristocrats to maintain a record of their income and expenditure.

kotha	The place where the courtesans resided and entertained their clients, and shared their literary compositions and skills in music and dance with persons of aesthetic tastes and knowledge. This was also the place where the courtesans trained the untutored in the finer nuances of aesthetics and language, and norms of civility and deportment.
mehndi (or henna)	A paste made from the leaves of the henna plant, it was applied by women on their hands and feet to give them an alluring appearance. It turned the hands and feet endearingly red, and emitted a pleasant smell. Henna was also used by women and men to dye their hair.
pardah-nashīn 'aurat	A literal translation would be 'the secluded women', but the term has wider connotations. It refers to women who were considered pure and virtuous, and it is for this reason that I have understood it as referring to 'chaste women'.
pānzeb	A string of small bells that women wear around their ankles when dancing, or as a decorative ornament.
Rekhta	An early form of Urdu (and Hindi) language. A mixed dialect, Rekhta combined elements of Persian with Hindavi, and came to be known as Urdu later in the nineteenth century.
rekhti	A literary form derived from Rekhta in which the lover/narrator takes on a feminine voice.
shāhid-i bāzārī	See *bāzārī 'aurat*.
tazkira	A biographical compendium that served to memorialize saints, scholars, rulers, and nobility. Literary *tazkiras* usually included the verses and a biographical note, and not infrequently a comment on the poet's method and style.
tazkira-i zanāna	A biographical compendium of women scholars, in particular, poets.

Bibliography

Primary Sources

Ali, Mir Mohsin. 1861. *Sarāpā Sukhan*. Lucknow: Nawal Kishore.

Gardezi, Saiyad Fateh Ali Husaini. 1752–53 (reprint 1933). *Tazkira-i Rekhta Goyān*. New Delhi: Anjuman Taraqqi Board Urdu Academy (Hind).

Hai, Maulvi Abdul. 1882 (reprint 1891). *Tazkira-i Shamīm Sukhan*. Lucknow: Nawal Kishore.

Hashmi, Nasiruddin. 1940. *Khwatīn-i Dakkan ki Urdu Khidmāt*. Hyderabad: Razzaqi Press.

Mir, Mir Taqi. 1751–52 (reprint 1894). *Nikāt-ush Shu'arā*. Edited by Mahmud Ilahi. Lucknow: Uttar Pradesh Urdu Academy.

Mushafi, Ghulam Hamadani. 1816–17 (reprint 1933). *Tazkira-i Hindī*. Edited by Maulvi Abdul Haq. Delhi: Jamia Barqi Press.

Nadir, Durga Prashad. 1884. *Tazkirat-un-Nisā*. Delhi: Akmal-ul Mutabi'.

———. 1884 (reprint 2016). *Tazkirat-un-Nisā*. Edited by Mahmud Ilahi. Lahore: Sang-i Mil Publications, 2016.

Premchand, Munshi. 1920 (English trans. 2022). *Karbala*. Nishat Zaidi, ed. and trans. *Karbala: A Historical Play*. New Delhi: Oxford University Press.

Ranj, Hakim Fasihuddin. 1869 (second edition). *Bahāristān-i Nāz*. Meerut: Matba' Darul 'Ulum.

———. 1882, third edition (reprint 1965). *Bahāristān-i Nāz*. Lahore: Majlis-i Taraqqi-i Adab.

———. 1889. *Gulshan-i Na't*. Meerut: Fakhrul Mujtaba.

———. 1891. *Kulliyāt-i Ranj*. Edited by Hakim Muhammad Fakhruddin. Meerut: Matba' Hashmi.

Sauda, Mirza Muhammad Rafi. 1872 (reprint 1971). *Kulliyāt-i Saudā*. 2 vols. Allahabad: Ram Narayan Lal Publisher.

Sharar, Abdul Halim. 1926 (reprint 1971). *Guzashta Lakhnau: Mashriqī Tamaddun ka Ākhri Namūna*. Delhi: Maktaba Jamia Limited. (E. S. Harcourt and Fakhir

Hussain, trans. *Lucknow: The Last Phase of an Oriental Culture*. New Delhi: Oxford University Press, 1994).

Shaukat, Yar Muhammad Khan. 1871. *Farah Baksh*. Kanpur: Matba Nizami.

Shefta, Nawab Mustafa Khan. 1835 (reprint 1973). *Tazkira-i Gulshan-i Be-Khār*. Lahore, Pakistan: Majlis Taraqqi-e Adab.

Tharu, Susie, and K. Lalit (eds.). 1991. *Women Writing in India, Vol. 1: 600 B.C. to the Early Twentieth Century*. New York: Feminist Press.

——— (eds.). 1993. *Women Writing in India, Vol. 2: The Twentieth Century*. New York: Feminist Press.

Thanawi, Ashraf Ali. 1906. *Bihishti Zewar*. Lahore: Tauseef Publications, n.d. (Partially translated by Barbara D. Metcalf, *Perfecting Women: Maulana Ashraf Ali Thanawi's Bihishti Zewar*. Berkeley and Los Angeles: University of California Press, 1990).

Secondary Works

Abrar, Rahat. 1999. *Urdu Shā'irāt Ka Auwalīn Tazkira Nigar: Hakim Fasihuddin Ranj Meruthi*. Delhi: Bharat Offset Press.

———. 2010. *1857 Ke Inqilāb Ka 'Aini Shāhid: George Puech Shor*. Delhi: Educational Book House.

Alam, Asiya. 2021. *Women, Islam and Familial Intimacy in Colonial South Asia*. Leiden: Brill.

Algar, Hamid. 2013. *Jami*. Oxford: Oxford University Press.

Amer, Sahar. 2008. *Crossing Borders: Love between Women in Medieval French and Arabic Literatures*. Philadelphia: University of Pennsylvania Press.

Antrim, Zayde. 2012. *Routes and Realms: The Power of Place in the Early Islamic World*. Oxford: Oxford University Press.

Arberry. A. J. 1960. *Shiraz: Persian City of Saints and Poets*. Norman, Oklahoma: University of Oklahoma Press.

Arnold, David, and Stuart Blackburn (eds.). 2004. *Telling Lives in India: Biography, Autobiography, and Life History*. Bloomington, Indiana: Indiana University Press.

Arshi, Imtiaz Ali. 1943. *Makātib-i Ghālib*. Rampur: Matba Sarkari Riyasat.

Asif, Manan Ahmed. 2020. *The Loss of Hindustan: The Invention of India*. Cambridge, Massachusetts: Harvard University Press.

Azad, Muhammad Husain. 1980 (reprint). *Āb-i Hayāt*. Allahabad: Ram Narayan Lal Publisher.

Badran, Margot. 1992. 'Expressing Feminism and Nationalism in Autobiography: The Memoirs of an Egyptian Educator'. In *De/Colonizing the Subject: The Politics of Gender in Women's Autobiography*, edited by Sidonie Smith and Julia Watson, 270–93. Minneapolis: University of Minnesota Press.

———. 1996. *Feminists, Islam, and the Nation: Gender and the Making of Modern Egypt*. Princeton: Princeton University Press.

Badran, Margot, and Miriam Cooke (eds.). 2004. *Opening the Gates: An Anthology of Arab Writing*. Bloomington and Indianapolis: Indiana University Press.

Balabanlilar, Lisa. 2012. *Imperial Identity in the Mughal Empire: Memory and Dynastic Politics in Early Modern South and Central Asia*. London: I. B. Tauris.

Ballhatchet, Kenneth A. 1980. *Race, Sex and Class under the Raj: Imperial Attitudes and Policies and Their Critics, 1793–1905*. New York: St. Martin's Press.

Banerjee, Sumanta. 1998. *Dangerous Outcast: The Prostitute in Nineteenth Century Bengal*. Kolkata: Seagull Books.

Bannerji, Himani. 1991. 'Fashioning a Self: Educational Proposals for and by Women in Popular Magazines in Colonial Bengal'. *Economic and Political Weekly* 26 (43): WS50–WS62.

Bano, Shadab. 2013. 'Jahanara's Role in the Public Domain'. *Proceedings of the Indian History Congress*, 74th session, 245–50.

Benjamin, Walter. 2006. 'The Work of Art in the Age of Its Mechanical Reproduction'. In *Walter Benjamin: Selected Writings, vol. 4, 1938–40*, edited by Howard Eiland and Michael W. Jennings, 251–83. Cambridge, MA: Harvard University Press.

Barthes, Roland. 1975. *The Pleasure of the Text*. Translated by Richard Miller. New York: Hill and Wang.

———. 1977. *Image, Music, Text*. Translated by Stephen Heath. London: Fontana Press.

———. 1986. *The Rustle of Language*. Translated by Richard Howard. New York: Hill and Wang.

Bashir, Shahzad. 2013. *Sufi Bodies: Religion and Society in Medieval Islam*. New York: Columbia University Press.

Basseler, Michael, and Dorothee Birke. 2020. 'Mimesis of Remembering'. *Journal of Literary Theory* 16 (2): 213–38.

Basu, Aparna, and Malavika Karlekar (eds.). 2008. *In So Many Words: Women's Life Experiences from Western and Eastern India*. New Delhi: Routledge.

Bennett, Judith M. September 1989. 'Feminism and History'. *Gender and History* 1 (3): 251–72.

Bhattacharya, Malini, and Abhijet Sen (eds.). 2021. *Talking of Power: Early Writings of Bengali Women*. New Delhi: Sage Publications.

Bloom, Jonathan. 2001. *Paper before Print: The History and Impact of Paper in the Islamic World*. New Haven, CT: Yale University Press.

Bokhari, Afshan. 2009. 'Gendered Landscapes: Jahan Ara Begum's (1614–1681) Patronage, Piety, and Self-Representation in Seventeenth Century Mughal India'. Ph.D. dissertation, Universität Wien.

———. 2011. 'Imperial Transgressions and Spiritual Investitures: A Begum's "Ascension" in Seventeenth Century Mughal India'. *Journal of Persianate Studies* 4 (1): 86–108.

———. 2015. 'Masculine Modes of Female Subjectivity: The Case of Jahanara Begum'. In *Speaking of the Self: Gender, Performance, and Autobiography in South Asia*, edited by Anshu Malhotra and Siobhan Lambert-Hurley, 165–202. Durham and London: Duke University Press.

Booth, Marilyn. Summer 2013. 'Locating Women's Autobiographical Writing in Colonial Egypt'. *Journal of Women's History* 25 (2): 35–60.

Boucher, Geoff. 2021. *Habermas and Literature: The Public Sphere and the Social Imaginary*. London: Bloomsbury Academic.

Boydston, Jeanne. November 2008. 'Gender as a Question of Historical Analysis'. *Gender and History* 20 (3): 558–83.

Brown, Peter. 1988. *The Body and Society: Men, Women, and Sexual Renunciation in Early Christianity*. New York: Columbia University Press.

Bruijn, Thomas De, and Allison Busch (eds.). 2014. *Culture and Circulation: Literature in Motion in Early Modern India*. Leiden: Brill.

Bynum, Caroline Walker. 1987. *Holy Feast and Holy Fast: The Religious Significance of Food to Medieval Women*. Berkeley: University of California Press.

———. 1992. *Fragmentation and Redemption: Essays on Gender and the Human Body*. New York: Zone Books.

Carlson, Keith Thor, Kristina Fagan, and Natalia Khaneko-Friesen (eds.). 2011. *Orality and Literacy: Reflections across Disciplines*. Toronto: University of Toronto Press.

Chakrabarty, Dipesh. 2000. *Provincializing Europe: Postcolonial Thought and Historical Difference*. Princeton: Princeton University Press.

Chatterjee, Indrani (ed.). 2004. *Unfamiliar Relations: Family and History in South Asia*. New Brunswick, NJ: Rutgers University Press.

Chatterjee, Partha. 1990. 'The Nationalist Resolution of the Women's Question'. In *Recasting Women: Essays in Indian Colonial History*, edited by Kumkum Sangari and Sudesh Vaid, 233–53. New Brunswick, NJ: Rutgers University Press.

———. 2010. *Empire and Nation: Selected Essays*. New York: Columbia University Press.

Coakley, Sarah (ed.). 1997. *Religion and the Body*. Cambridge: Cambridge University Press.

Cole, Juan R. I. 1988. *Roots of North Indian Shi'ism in Iran and Iraq: Religion and State in Awadh, 1722–1859*. Berkeley: University of California Press.

Copland, Ian. 1997. *The Princes of India in the Endgames of Empire, 1917–1947*. Cambridge: Cambridge University Press.

Corbin, Alain. 1990. *Women for Hire: Prostitution and Sexuality in France after 1850*. Translated by Alan Sheridan. Cambridge, MA: Harvard University Press.

Dalrymple, William. 1993. *White Mughals: Love and Betrayal in Eighteenth Century India*. New Delhi: Viking.

De Bruijn. J. T. P. 2013. *Persian Sufi Poetry: An Introduction to the Mystical Use of Classical Poems*. London and New York: Routledge.

Dhawan, Nikita. 2012. 'Hegemonic Listening and Subversive Silences: Ethico-political Imperatives'. In *Destruction in the Performative*, edited by Alice Lagaay and Michael Lorber, 47–60. Amsterdam: Rodopi.

Erll, Astrid. 2011. *Memory in Translation*, trans. Sara B. Young. London: Palgrave Macmillan.

Erll, Astrid, and Ansgar Nunning (eds.). 2010. *Cultural Memory Studies: An International and Interdisciplinary Handbook*. Berlin and New York: De Gruyter.

Findly, Elison Banks. 1993. *Nur Jahan: Empress of Mughal India*. Oxford: Oxford University Press.

Forbes, Geraldine. 2015 (reprint). *Women in Modern India*. New Delhi: Cambridge University Press.

Foucault, Michel. 1980. *Power/Knowledge: Selected Interviews and Other Writings, 1972-1977*. Edited by Colin Gordon. Brighton: Harvester Press.

———. 1989. *The Archeology of Knowledge*. London: Routledge.

Gabbay, Alyssa. January 2011. 'In Reality a Man: Sultan Iltutmish, His Daughter, Raziya, and Gender Ambiguity in Thirteenth Century North India'. *Journal of Persianate Studies* 4 (1): 45–63.

Goody, Jack (ed.). 1975. *Literacy in Traditional Societies*. Cambridge: Cambridge University Press.

———. 1986. *The Logic of Writing and the Organization of Society*. Cambridge: Cambridge University Press.

Green, Nile. March 2010. 'The Uses of Books in a Late Mughal Takiyya: Persianate Knowledge Between Person and Paper'. *Modern Asian Studies* 44 (2): 241–65.

———. 2012. *Making Space: Sufis and Settlers in Early Modern India*. New Delhi: Oxford University Press.

Gupta, Charu. 2000. *Sexuality, Obscenity, Community: Women, Muslims, and the Hindu Public in Colonial India*. New Delhi: Permanent Black.

——— (ed.). 2012. *Gendering Colonial India: Reforms, Print and Communalism*. New Delhi: Orient Blackswan.

Habermas, Jurgen. 1989. *The Structural Transformation of the Public Sphere: An Enquiry into a Category of Bourgeois Society*. Translated by Thomas Burger and Fredrick Lawrence. Cambridge, MA: MIT Press.

Hakala, Walter N. 2016. *Negotiating Languages: Urdu, Hindi, and the Definition of Modern South Asia*. New York: Columbia University Press.

Haldar, Epsita. 2023. *Reclaiming Karbala: Nation, Islam and Literature of the Bengali Muslims*. London and New York: Routledge.

Harris, Rachel, and Martin Stokes (eds.). 2017. *Theory and Practice in the Music of the Islamic World: Essays in Honour of Owen Wright*. London and New York: Routledge.

Hasan, Farhat. 2021. *Paper, Performance, and the State: Social Change and Political Culture in Mughal India*. New Delhi: Cambridge University Press.

Hermansen, Marcia K., and Bruce B. Lawrence. 2002. 'Indo-Persian *Tazkiras* as Memorative Communication'. In *Beyond Turk and Hindu: Religious Identities in Islamicate South Asia*, edited by David Gilmartin and Bruce Lawrence, 149–75. New Delhi: India Research Papers.

Hirsch, Marianne. 2012. *The Generation of Postmemory: Writing and Visual Culture after the Holocaust*. New York: Columbia University Press.

Hoff, Joan. 1994. 'Gender as a Postmodern Category of Paralysis'. *Women's History Review* 3 (2): 149–68.

Hyder, Syed Akbar. 2006. *Reliving Karbala: Martyrdom in South Asian History*. New York: Oxford University Press.

Islam, Khurshidul. 1964. *Kalām-i Sauda*. Aligarh: Anjuman-i Taraqqi-i Urdu (Hind).

Islam, Khurshidul, and Ralph Russell. 2006 (reprint). *Three Mughal Poets: Mir, Sauda, Mir Hasan*. New Delhi: Oxford University Press.

Jackson, Peter. 1998. 'Sultan Radiyya bint Iltutmish'. In *Women in the Islamic World: Power, Patronage, Piety*, edited by R. G. Hambly, 81–97. New York: Palgrave.

———. 1999. *The Delhi Sultanate: A Political and Military History*. Cambridge: Cambridge University Press.

Jha, Shweta Sachdeva. 2015. 'Tawai'if as a Poet: Rethinking Women's Self-Representation'. In *Speaking of the Self: Gender, Performance, and Autobiography in South Asia*, edited by Anshu Malhotra and Siobhan Lambert-Hurley, 141–64. Durham and London: Duke University Press.

Jones, Kenneth W. 1989 (reprint). *Socio-Religious Movements in British India*. Cambridge: Cambridge University Press.

Karlekar, Malavika. 1993. *Voices from Within: Early Personal Narratives of Bengali Women*. New Delhi: Oxford University Press.

Kattago, Siobhan (ed.). 2016. *The Ashgate Research Companion to Memory Studies*. London and New York: Routledge.

Keay, Julia. 2014. *The Woman Who Saved an Empire*. London: I. B. Tauris.

Keshavmurthy, Prashant. 2016. *Persian Authorship and Canonicity in Late Mughal Delhi: Building an Arch*. London: Routledge.

Khan, Shahryar M. 2000. *The Begums of Bhopal: A Dynasty of Women Rulers in Raj India*. London: I. B. Tauris.

Kia, Mana. 2014. '*Adab* as Literary Form and Social Conduct: Reading the *Gulistan* in Late Mughal India'. In *No Tapping Around Philology: A Festschrift in Celebration and Honor of Wheeler McIntosh Thackston Jr.'s 70th Birthday*, edited by Alireza Korangy and Daniel J. Sheffield, 281–308. Wiesbaden: Harrassowitz Verlag.

———. 2020. *Persianate Selves: Memories of Place and Origin Before Nationalism.* Stanford: Stanford University Press.

Kugle, Scott. 2007. *Sufis and Saints' Bodies: Mysticism, Corporeality and Sacred Power in Islam.* Chapel Hill: University of North Carolina Press.

———. 2020. 'Mah Laqa Bai and Gender: The Language, Poetry and Performance of a Courtesan in Lucknow in Hyderabad'. *Comparative Studies of South Asia, Africa and the Middle East* 30 (3): 365–85.

Lal, Ruby. October 2004. 'Historicizing the Harem: The Challenge of a Princess's Memoir'. *Feminist Studies* 30 (3): 590–616.

———. 2005. *Domesticity and Power in the Early Mughal World.* Cambridge: Cambridge University Press.

———. 2018. *Empress: The Astonishing Reign of Nur Jahan.* Gurgaon: Penguin Random.

Lambert-Hurley, Siobhan. May–June 1998. 'Out of India: The Journeys of the Begam of Bhopal, 1901–1930'. *Women's Studies International Forum* 21 (3): 263–76.

———. 2003. 'Princes, Paramountcy, and the Politics of Muslim Identity: The Begums of Bhopal on the Indian National Stage, 1901–1926'. *South Asia* 26 (2): 169–95.

———. 2007. 'Historicising Debates over Women's Status in Islam: The Case of Nawab Sultan Jahan of Bhopal'. In *India's Princely States: People, Princes and Colonialism*, edited by Waltraud Ernst and Biswamoy Pati, 139–56. London: Routledge.

———. 2007. *Muslim Women, Reform and Princely Patronage: Nawab Sultan Jahan Begum of Bhopal.* London: Routledge.

———. 2018. *Elusive Lives: Gender, Autobiography, and the Self in Muslim South Asia.* Stanford: Stanford University Press.

Leonard, Karen. October 2013. 'Political Players: Courtesans of Hyderabad'. *Indian Economic and Social History Review* 50 (4): 423–48.

———. 2013. *Hyderabad and Hyderabadis.* New Delhi: Manohar.

Lefevre, Corinne. 2014. 'The Court of 'Abd-ur-Rahim Khan-i-Kahanan as a Bridge between Iranian and Indian Cultural Traditions'. In *Culture and Circulation: Literature in Motion in Early Modern India*, edited by Thomas De Bruijn and Allison Busch, 75–106. Leiden: Brill.

Lewisohn, Leonard. 2010. *Hafiz and the Religion of Love in Classical Persian Poetry.* New York: I. B. Tauris.

Loewen, Arley. December 2009. 'Proper Conduct (*Adab*) Is Everything: The *Futuwwat- namah-i Sultani* of Husayn Va'iz-i Kashifi'. *Iranian Studies* 36 (4): 543–70.

Losensky, Paul E. 1998. *Welcoming Fighani: Imitation and Individuality in the Safavid-Mughal Ghazal*. Costa Mesa, California: Mazda Publishers.

Maitland, Sarah. 2017. *What Is Cultural Translation*. London and New York: Bloomsbury Publishing.

Majumdar, Rochona. 2009. *Marriage and Modernity: Family Values in Colonial Bengal*. Durham, NC: Duke University Press.

Maldonado-Terres, Nelson. 2008. *Against War: Views from the Underside of Modernity*. Durham and London: Duke University Press.

Malhotra, Anshu. 2017. *Piro and the Gulabdasis: Gender, Sect, and Society in Punjab*. New Delhi: Oxford University Press.

Malhotra, Anshu, and Siobhan Lambert-Hurley (eds.). 2015. *Speaking of the Self: Gender, Performance, and Autobiography in South Asia*. Durham and London: Duke University Press.

Marlow, Louise. 2011. *The Rhetoric of Biography: Narrating Lives in Persianate Societies*. Boston: MA Ilex Foundation (distributed by Harvard University Press).

McKittick, Katherine (ed.). *Sylvia Wynter: On Being Human as Praxis*. Durham: Duke University Press.

Mernissi, Fatima. 1997 (reprint). *The Forgotten Queens of Islam*. Minneapolis: University of Minnesota Press.

Messick, Brinkley. 1993. *The Calligraphic State: Textual Domination and History in a Muslim Society*. Berkeley: University of California Press.

———. 2018. *Shari'a Scripts: A Historical Anthology*. New York: Columbia University Press.

Metcalf, Barbara D. (ed.). 1984. *Moral Conduct and Authority; The Place of Adab in South Asia*. Berkeley and Los Angeles: University of California Press.

Micallef, Roberta. Summer 2013. 'Identities in Motion: Reading Two Ottoman Travel Narratives as Life Writing'. *Journal of Women's History* 25 (2): 85–110.

Milani, Farzaneh. 2011. *Words, Not Swords: Iranian Women Writers and the Freedom of Movement*. Syracuse, NY: Syracuse University Press.

———. Summer 2013. 'Iranian Women's Life Narratives'. *Journal of Women's History* 25 (2): 130–52.

Milevski, Urania, and Lena Wetenkamp. 2020. 'Introduction: Relations between Literary Theory and Memory Studies'. *Journal of Literary Theory* 16 (2): 197–212.

Minault, Gail. 1998. *Secluded Scholars: Women's Education and Muslim Social Reform in Colonial India*. New Delhi: Oxford University Press.

———. 2009. *Gender, Language and Learning: Essays on Indo-Muslim Cultural History*. New Delhi: Permanent Black.

Misra, Rekha. 1967. *Women in Mughal India (1526–1749)*. New Delhi: Munshiram Manoharlal.

Mitra, Durba. 2020. *Indian Sex Life: Sexuality and the Colonial Origins of Modern Social Thought*. Princeton: Princeton University Press.

Morris, Rosalind C. (ed.). 2010. *Can the Subaltern Speak? Reflections on the History of an Idea*. New York: Columbia University Press.

Mozaffari, Ali. 2014. *Forming National Identity in Iran: The Idea of Homeland Derived from Ancient Persian and Islamic Imaginations of Place*. London: I. B. Tauris.

Muhlbacher, Manuel. 2020. 'Plotting Memory: What Are We Made to Remember When We Read Narrative Texts'. *Journal of Literary Theory* 16 (2): 239–63.

Naim, C. M. 2004. *Urdu Texts and Contexts: The Selected Essays of C. M. Naim*. New Delhi: Permanent Black.

———. 2004. 'Popular Jokes and Political History: The Case of Birbal and Mulla Do-Piyaza'. In *Urdu Texts and Contexts: The Selected Essays of C. M. Naim*, 225–49. New Delhi: Permanent Black.

Najmabadi, Afsaneh. 2005. *Women with Mustaches and Men without Beards: Gender and Sexual Anxieties of Iranian Modernity*. Berkeley: University of California Press.

———.2006. 'Beyond the Americas: Are Gender and Sexuality Useful Categories of Historical Analysis'. *Journal of Women's History* 18 (1): 11–21.

Nooshin, Laudan. 2015. *Iranian Classical Music: The Discourses and Practice of Creativity*. Ashgate: Farnham and Burlington.

Nora, Pierre, and Lawrence D. Kritzman (eds.). 1996. *Realms of Memory: The Construction of the French Past, vol. 1: Conflicts and Divisions*. Translated by Arthur Goldhammer. New York: Columbia University Press.

Oldenburg, Veena Talwar. 1984. *The Making of Colonial Lucknow, 1856–1877*. Princeton, NJ: Princeton University Press.

———. Summer 1990. 'Lifestyle as Resistance: The Case of the Courtesans of Lucknow, India'. *Feminist Studies* 16 (2): 259–87.

Olick, Jeffrey K. 2013. *The Politics of Regret: On Collective Memory and Historical Responsibility*. London and New York: Routledge.

Olick, Jeffrey K., Vered Vinitzky-Seroussi, and Daniel Levy (eds.). 2011. *The Collective Memory Reader*. New York: Oxford University Press.

Ong, Walter J. 2002 (reprint). *Orality and Literacy: The Technologizing of the Word*. London and New York: Routledge.

Orsini, Francesca. October 1999. 'Domesticity and Beyond: Hindi Women's Journals in the Early Twentieth Century'. *South Asia Research* 19 (2): 137–60.

———. 2000. *The Hindi Public Sphere, 1920–1940: Language and Literature in the Age of Nationalism*. New Delhi: Oxford University Press.

———. 2011. *Before the Divide: Hindi and Urdu Literary Culture*. New Delhi: Orient Blackswan.

Orsini, Francesca, and Katherine Butler Schofield (eds.). 2015. *Tellings and Texts: Music, Literature and Performance in North India*. Cambridge: Open Book Publishers.

Pauwells, Heidi. 2021. 'Cultivating Emotions and the Rise of the Vernaculars: The Role of Affect in "Early Hindi–Urdu" Song'. *South Asian History and Culture* 12 (2–3): 146–65.

Pernau, Margrit (ed.). 2006. *The Delhi College: Traditional Elites, the Colonial State, and Education Before 1857*. New Delhi: Oxford University Press.

———. 2017. 'Feeling Communities: Introduction'. *Indian Economic and Social History Review* 54 (1): 1–20.

———. 2019. *Emotions and Modernity in Colonial India: From Balance to Fervor*. New Delhi: Oxford University Press.

———. 2021. 'Studying Emotions in South Asia.' *South Asian History and Culture* 12 (3): 111–28.

Pernau, Margrit, and Imke Rajamani. February 2016. 'Emotional Translations: Conceptual History Beyond Language'. *History and Theory* 55 (1): 46–65.

Petievich, Carla. September 2001. 'Gender Politics and the Urdu Ghazal: Exploratory Observations on *Rekhta* versus *Rekhti*'. *Indian Economic and Social History Review* 38 (3): 223–48.

———. 2005. 'Feminine Authorship and Urdu Poetic Tradition: *Bahāristān-i Nāz* vs. *Tazkira-i Rekhti*'. In *A Wilderness of Possibilities: Urdu Studies in Transnational Perspective*, edited by Kathryn Hansen and David Lelyveld, 223–50. New Delhi: Oxford University Press.

———. 2007. *When Men Spoke as Women: Vocal Masquerade in Indo-Muslim Poetry*. New Delhi: Oxford University Press.

———. 2020 (reprint). *Assembly of Rivals: Delhi, Lucknow and the Urdu Ghazal*. New Delhi: Manohar.

Pollock, Sheldon (ed.). 2016. *A Rasa Reader: Classical Indian Aesthetics*. New York: Columbia University Press.

Qadeer, Haris, and P. K. Yasser Arafath (eds.). 2022. *Sultana's Sisters: Genre, Gender, and Genealogy in South Asian Muslim Women's Fiction*. New Delhi: Routledge.

Radstone, Susannah. 2020. *Memory and Methodology*. London and New York: Routledge.

Rajamani, Imke, Margrit Pernau, and Katherine Butler Schofield (eds.). 2018. *Monsoon Feelings: A History of Emotions in the Rain*. New Delhi: Niyogi Books.

Ram, Malik. 1984. *Talāmiz-i Ghālib*. Delhi: Maktaba Jamia Limited.

Ramaswamy, Vijaya, and Yogesh Sharma (eds.). 2018. *Biography as History: Indian Perspectives*. New Delhi: Orient Blackswan.

Rambuss, Richard. 1998. *Closet Devotions*. Durham and London: Duke University Press.

Reddy, William M. 1999. 'Emotional Liberty: Politics and History in the Anthropology of Emotions'. *Cultural Anthropology* 14 (2): 256–88.

———. 2001. *The Navigation of Feeling: A Framework for the History of Emotions.* Cambridge: Cambridge University Press.

Robb, Megan Eaton. 2021. *Print and the Urdu Media: Muslims, Newspapers, and Urban Life in Colonial India.* Oxford: Oxford University Press.

Rosenwein, Barbara. 2007. *Emotional Communities in the Early Middle Ages.* Ithaca and London: Cornell University Press.

Rothberg, Michael. 2010. *Multidirectional Memory: Remembering the Holocaust in the Age of Decolonization.* Stanford: Stanford University Press.

Sadiq, Muhammad. 1964. *A History of Urdu Literature.* Oxford: Oxford University Press.

Sarkar, Sumit, and Tanika Sarkar (eds.). 2008. *Women and Social Reform in Modern India: A Reader.* Bloomington: Indiana University Press.

Sarkar, Tanika. 2001. *Hindu Wife, Hindu Nation: Community, Religion and Cultural Nationalism.* New Delhi: Permanent Black.

———. 2013. *Words to Win: The Making of Amar Jiban-A Modern Autobiography.* New Delhi: Zuban Books.

Saxena, Ram Babu. 1990. *A History of Urdu Literature.* New Delhi: Asian Educational Services.

Schofield, Katherine Butler. April 2012. 'The Courtesan Tale: Female Musicians and Dancers in Mughal Historical Chronicles, c. 1556–1748'. *Gender and History* 24 (1): 150–71.

———. 2015. 'Learning to Taste the Emotions: The Mughal *Rasika*'. In *Tellings and Texts: Music, Literature and Performance in North India*, edited by Francesca Orsini and Katherine Butler Schofield, 407–21. Cambridge: Open Book Publishers.

———. 2018. 'Music, Art and Power in 'Adil Shahi Bijapur, c. 1570–1630'. In *Scent upon a Southern Breeze: Synaesthesia and the Arts of the Deccan*, edited by Kavita Singh, 68–87. Mumbai: Marg.

———. 2021. 'Emotions in Indian Music History: Anxiety in Late Mughal Hindustan'. *South Asian History and Culture* 12 (2–3): 182–205.

Scott, Joan Wallach. December 1986. 'Gender: A Useful Category of Historical Analysis'. *American Historical Review* 91 (5): 1053–75.

———. 2018 (revised edition). *Gender and the Politics of History.* New York: Columbia University Press.

Sedgwick, Eve Kosofsky. 1990. *Epistemology of the Closet.* New York: Columbia University Press.

Seyed-Gohrab, Ali Asghar (ed.). 2012. *Metaphor and Imagery in Persian Poetry.* Leiden: Brill.

Sharma, Sunil. 2009. 'From 'A'isha to Nur Jahan: The Shaping of a Classical Poetic Canon of Women'. *Journal of Persianate Studies* 2 (2): 148–64.

———. 2017. *Mughal Arcadia: Persian Literature in an Indian Court*. Cambridge, MA: Harvard University Press.

Shulman, David Dean. 1985. *The King and the Clown in South Indian Myth and Poetry*. Princeton: Princeton University Press.

Spivak, Gayatri Chakravorty. 1994. 'Can the Subaltern Speak?' In *Colonial Discourse and Post-Colonial Theory: A Reader*, edited by Patrick Williams and Laura Chrisman, 66–111. New York: Columbia University Press.

———. 1999. *A Critique of Postcolonial Reason: Toward a History of the Vanishing Present*. Cambridge, MA: Harvard University Press.

Sreenivas, Mytheli. 2008. *Wives, Widows, and Concubines: The Conjugal Family Ideal in Colonial India*. Bloomington and Indianapolis: Indiana University Press.

Tandon, Shivangini. 2013. 'Mooring the Mughal Tazkiras: Explorations in the Politics of Representation', NMML Occasional Paper, History and Society (New Series), No. 40. Nehru Memorial Museum and Library Publications, New Delhi.

———. 2016. 'Remembering Lives in Mughal India: Political Culture and Social Life in Indo-Persian *Tazkiras*, 16th–18th Centuries'. Ph.D. dissertation, University of Delhi, New Delhi.

Tota, Anna Lisa, and Trever Hagen (eds.). 2016. *Routledge International Handbook of Memory Studies*. London and New York: Routledge.

Vanita, Ruth. 2002. *Queering India: Same-Sex Love and Eroticism in Indian Culture and Society*. New York: Routledge.

———. 2012. *Gender, Sex and the City: Urdu Rekhti Poetry in India, 1780–1870*. New Delhi: Orient Blackswan.

Vatuk, Sylvia. 2004. '*Hamara Daur-i Hayat*: An Indian Muslim Woman Writes Her Life'. In *Telling Lives in India: Biography, Autobiography, and Life Story*, edited by David Arnold and Stuart Blackburn, 144–74. Bloomington and Indianapolis: Indiana University Press.

Venuti, Lawrence. 2011. 'Introduction: Poetry and Translation'. *Translation Studies* 4 (2): 127–32.

Waheed, Sarah. 2014. 'Women of "Ill Repute": Ethics and Literature in Colonial India'. *Modern Asian Studies* 48 (4): 986–1023.

Walkowitz, Judith R. 1982. *Prostitution and Victorian Society: Women, Class, and the State*. Cambridge: Cambridge University Press.

———. 1992. *City of Dreadful Delight: Narratives of Sexual Danger in Late-Victorian London*. Chicago: University of Chicago Press.

Williams, Richard David. October 2017. 'Songs between Cities: Listening to Courtesans in Colonial North India'. *Journal of the Royal Asiatic Society* 27 (4): 591–610.

Wynter, Sylvia. 2022. *We Must Learn to Sit and Talk Together about a Little Culture: Decolonizing Essays, 1967–1984*. Leeds, UK: Peepal Tree Press Ltd.

Index